What People Ar[e Saying About]
Teen Ink

"I started writing when I was a teenager, but I'd be embarrassed to compare my work to this. So much talent on these pages! I wish *Teen Ink* was around when I was a teen!"

R. L. Stine
author, *Goosebumps*

"Nothing compares to the experience of reading a story that you can not only relate to, but makes you also feel as though you already know the writer. This is what I find in *Teen Ink*."

Will Sandwick, age 14

"No topic is too personal or controversial to write about: drugs, suicide, divorce, unwed motherhood. In addition to students' trials, the book records their triumphs, offering a wide-ranging portrait of adolescence that refutes stereotypes."

Marilyn Gardner
staff writer, *Christian Science Monitor*

"The stories in *Teen Ink* are like reading a reflection of myself. It's as if the authors were able to see inside my mind and write down what I was thinking."

Melissa Thompson, age 17

"Warning—*Teen Ink* will expose you to the thoughts and feelings of real teens who are good and sensitive and intelligent and brave and truthful. It is not for the faint of heart. Be prepared for reality literature from young writers that will make your heart sing."

Cathy Greenwood
English teacher

"This book is an adventure that takes you through the minds, hearts and souls of teens who are brave enough to share their beliefs and experiences."

Kelly Donithan, age 15

"What I read in these pages is lifesaving stuff. Not only is much of it astonishingly good from a craft point of view, but it gives teenagers *voice*. In a culture where adolescents are often ignored or treated as second-class citizens, *Teen Ink* gives them a place to say loud and clear who they are."

Chris Crutcher
author, *Staying Fat for Sarah Byrnes* and *Whale Talk*

"*Teen Ink* is amazing. Finally a place that lets teens share their stories with other teens. This book lets teens know that they are not alone and there are others who are out there feeling the same way. I really loved reading all the different stories. Some made me laugh, some made me sniffle, but all made me feel I was not alone through those painful years."

Elizabeth Miller
contributor, *Teen Ink: Our Voices, Our Visions*

"If you want truth, open up *Teen Ink* and let the teens speak for themselves. This book is an original, honest and refreshingly un-cheesy approach to 'keeping it real.' Teenagers are infinitely more savvy, insightful, sensitive and talented than given credit for. *Teen Ink* gives them a much-needed opportunity to set the record straight. Let's face it, the American teenager is nearly impossible to understand— unless, of course, you're an American teenager."

Sarah Brennan
writer, *TEENREADS.com*

"*Teen Ink* has done a remarkable job of publishing work by authentic teens. This is the kind of book to give every teenager you know who might be in need of hope, encouragement and a reminder that they're not alone in their struggles."

Heather Amundson, age 18

"An extraordinary collection of ideas, experiences, hopes and dreams from America's teens. Open its pages and see the heart of our future."

Andrew Shue
cofounder of "Do Something"

"Teen Ink is powerful, exhilarating and emotionally soothing for the soul. I can laugh, cry, be depressed or be overly happy while reading the same book. I love it!"

Desirée Swanson, age 15

"This book is the answer to anyone who complains that American teens don't express their ideas very well or that they don't have many ideas worth expressing. The essays, stories, poetry and art in these pages let us see things through fresh and unspoiled eyes. There is youthful insight here that the world seems to take from us as we grow up, and grow old."

Charles Osgood
radio commentator and host, *CBS Sunday Morning*

"No adult reader can remain untouched by the drama in teens' lives; their writings provoke our compassion and insight. Teens themselves will savor every word from compatriots who so eloquently tell the truth, leaving no young reader alone. All these short pieces are smooth and succinct; a few emerge as works of art."

Cathi Dunn MacRae
editor, *Voices of Youth Advocates*

"Teen Ink invites young authors to write down and share their ideas, beliefs, feelings and aspirations. At a time of technological upheaval, this seemingly traditional practice may constitute the most radical innovation."

Howard Gardner
author and professor, Harvard University
Graduate School of Education

"You don't need to be a teenager to benefit from the passion and intelligence flowing from the prose, poetry and artwork in this inspiring collection."

ParentingTeens.com

"Teens will read the book cover-to-cover at one sitting because they won't be able to put it down. I recommend it to parents and teachers as a mightily effective way to recapture a vision of the world from a teen perspective."

Sara Hoaglund Hunter
parent and author, *The Unbreakable Code*

"Finally a book that touches and inspires teens to write to their full potential. A great piece of work that no one should miss."

Jason Laird, age 14

"Much of the writing . . . hits readers in the gut with powerful prose."

Jeanne Albanese
columnist, *Syracuse Herald Journal*

"The writings in the book not only provide a way for teenagers to connect with one another, but are a real eye-opener for parents and other adults who care for kids."

Amy Barry
The Sound (Madison, CT)

"*Teen Ink* provides a unique look into the challenges and passions of teens. I am especially impressed when a book can fully engage my teenage son and compete so successfully with his beloved computer games."

Victoria Sutherland
publisher, *ForeWord*

Teen Ink™ 2

More Voices, More Visions

Edited by

Stephanie H. Meyer
John Meyer

Health Communications, Inc.
Deerfield Beach, Florida

www.hci-online.com
www.TeenInk.com

The following pieces were originally published by The Young Authors Foundation, Inc. (©1989-2001) in *The 21st Century/Teen Ink* magazine. We gratefully acknowledge the many individuals who granted us permission to reprint the cited material.

"Close-up of Tulip." Reprinted by permission of Elizabeth Kreischer. ©1998 Elizabeth Kreischer.

"Shoes by the Washer." Reprinted by permission of Aimee K. Poulin. ©1997 Aimee K. Poulin.

"Row of Shoes in Sunlight." Reprinted by permission of Caite Powers. ©2000 Caite Powers.

(continued on page 361)

Library of Congress Cataloging-in-Publication Data

Teen ink 2 : more voices, more visions / written by teens; edited by Stephanie H. Meyer and John Meyer.

    p.   cm.

    A collection of stories and poems by teenage writers, arranged under the categories "Family," "Friends," "Challenges," "Love," "Imagination," "School Days," "Fitting In," "Milestones," and "Memories."

    ISBN 1-55874-913-6 (trade paper)

    1. Adolescence—Literary collections. 2. Youths' writings, American. [1. Adolescence—Literary collections. 2. Youths' writings.] I. Meyer, Stephanie H., date. II. Meyer, John, date.

PZ5 .T2949 2001
810.8'09283—dc21

                      2001016681

Publisher: Health Communications, Inc.
          3201 S.W. 15th Street
          Deerfield Beach, FL 33442-8190

Cover illustration and design by Larissa Hise Henoch
Inside book formatting by Dawn Grove

"Every secret of a writer's soul, every experience of his life, every quality of his mind is written large in his works."

—Virginia Woolf, *Orlando*

To our children, Alison and Rob
For your love, support and insight

Contents

3. Challenges

4. Love

5. Imagination

6. School Days

7. Fitting In

Foreword

by Todd Strasser

As a writer for teens I am often asked: "How *(at your advanced age)* do you manage to get inside a teenager's head?"

Here's the answer: I'm a thief.

Seriously. I steal from teenagers. I steal their ideas, their mannerisms, their ways of speaking, of dressing, of acting. What's nice about this kind of theft is that I can't be arrested for it. The worst that can happen is a teenager I know may recognize some aspect of themselves in a character I've created.

But no one's thrown a rock through my window yet.

It isn't as easy as it might sound. Teens don't relate to guys with gray hair the same way they relate to guys in their twenties or even thirties. Even worse, I am no longer always physically capable of enduring certain everyday teenage rigors. I realized this several months ago when I chaperoned my teenage daughter to a Deep Banana Blackout show. As much as I enjoyed the music, I couldn't take the smoke, the decibel level or the hours of standing. My knees hurt too much.

Ten years ago this might have spelled the end of my career. But thanks to *Teen Ink 2*, the successor to the incredibly valuable first *Teen Ink* book, I'm still going strong. Now when I need to know what's *really* on the minds of teenagers, I don't have to eavesdrop or observe. I don't even have to leave my office.

I just read these books. All the "real stuff" is here. Want a glimpse of what it's like to be a teenage boy? Check out "Locks" by Paul Constant or "The Making of a Man" by Rob Dangel. Could I have gotten a teenager to reveal those kinds of feelings and insights? It's doubtful. Guys may think this stuff. But they don't talk this stuff.

That reminds me of another question I'm often asked. "How, as a man, do you write female characters?"

The answer can be found in "Face Paint" by Katherine S. Assef, "Prom Night" by Erica Doughty, and "Still Me Inside" by Mai Goda. Put these snapshots of young womanhood together and you can create character.

Finally, a confession. I don't usually bother with poetry. But I read "Obituary" by Kathleen McCarney and it sent a chill down the back of my neck. "Pink Elephants" by Lisa V. Atkins brought a knowing smile to my lips. Read it and you just may see yourself.

So this is good news, not just for someone like me who wants to write about teenagers, but for anyone who wants to understand them, or relate to them, or simply read something by people like themselves so that they don't feel so alone in the world. Bravo, *Teen Ink 2,* you've certainly made my life easier.

At this rate I may never get caught.

Todd Strasser is the author of many award-winning novels for teens, including Give a Boy a Gun *and* The Wave. *He is also the author of* How I Changed My Life.

Preface

by Timothy Cahill

houghts and memories take many forms. The smell of freshly cut grass on a brisk, autumn weekend, announcing soccer season. The crackling of a campfire, demanding blankets and 'smores.

But words. Words have a life of their own. Words that praise, words that comfort. Words that wound, words that sting. They linger—simmering, swirling, repeating themselves. *Would you like to dance?* Or perhaps, *Let's just be friends.* They might read like lines from a movie, nothing more than dull, trite clichés. Unless, of course, someone actually says them to you.

Words don't need to be original to have meaning. They don't need to be eloquent or poetic to capture something true. They don't even need to be real words. A teacher of mine frequently expressed distaste by exclaiming *Merf!* No one ever dared ask him what it meant. No one needed to. Did Dr. Seuss need a glossary to define *sneetch?*

For me, writing has always been a means to collect those words cluttering up my thoughts and memories. They may be words I never understood. They may be words I wish I'd said. They may be words that just grew on their own, into shapes, people, places and imaginative worlds. Whatever the words, writing lets them escape into the world. It gives them room to stretch, air to breathe and a chance to speak. And the one thing that words must do is *say something.*

The works you will find in this book are compiled from *Teen Ink* magazine, a forum that encouraged me to offer my words to others. Having a piece published is a wondrous experience, especially as a teenager, when it seems so often that your words are doomed to suffocate in the flood of relationships, activities and responsibilities that dominate day-to-day existence.

In this second *Teen Ink* volume, you will find many, *many* words. They are words that grew from different experiences; words that were collected by different minds. They have been assembled in poetry, short stories and nonfiction. Yet more fundamentally, these words have a common source. They all came from teenagers who had something to say—and who discovered that by writing and sharing these words, they had the means to say it.

The words you find here are something to be cherished. They are, in fact, original, eloquent and poetic. But that's just a bonus. These words are special because in them lies access to the worlds of those who created them.

Read them. Pore over them.

Let them speak to you.

Let them become your words, too.

Timothy Cahill, currently a sophomore in college, was published frequently in Teen Ink *magazine as a high-school student. One of his stories, "The Stranger," appears on page 160.*

Introduction

Call it *Teen Ink 2,* but do not call it a sequel. Sequels, for the most part, take a tried-and-true idea and repackage it. Scarier and more gruesome villains face good guys with bigger ideas and more attitude than the first time, but the setting and plot seem very much the same. *Teen Ink 2* is so much more than a sequel. It displays a brand-new world, a vivid landscape of teen expressions, as imaginative and diverse as the individuals who crafted these pieces.

The greatest part about the *Teen Ink* series is that a unique vision is created with every piece, each one brought to life by teen writers, artists and photographers who see their worlds in astonishing ways. As editors of *Teen Ink* magazine during the past decade, we have published 25,000 teens and read 300,000 of their submissions that have dispelled any notion that teens can be catalogued, grouped or labeled. There is no doubt that in the coming decade, more teen voices and visions, submitted by you, your children and even grandchildren, promise to be just as creative, emotional and insightful.

Although the voices are new in this volume, some of the ingredients remain the same. Just like the first, *Teen Ink 2* is written entirely by teens. After we selected our favorites, more than twenty-five hundred teens in schools across the country read sample chapters and told us which they liked best. And, of course, all royalties from these books are donated directly to the nonprofit Young Authors Foundation to offer more opportunities for teenagers to express themselves.

As you explore these writings, you will quickly discover the great candor, emotion and insight expressed by these teenagers. Some scream about the injustices they experience, while others sing eloquently of a special moment. Many describe the challenges of friendship, while still others delve into their relationships with family members. So, open up these pages and sample one or two of these amazing pieces, and you will be compelled to continue reading to discover more of the depth and sensibility of these teens.

As parents, editors and advocates for teenagers, we invite you to enjoy this next installment of the *Teen Ink* series, brought to you by the hundreds of thousands of teenagers who took a chance, and shared their experiences and creativity with us all.

Stephanie and John Meyer

Welcome

This is your book! All the words and images were created by teens and gathered from pieces that appeared in *Teen Ink* magazine during the last decade.

You can join these teenagers by sending us *your* voices and visions to be considered for the monthly *Teen Ink* magazine and future books in this series.

If you want to participate, see the submission guidelines on pages 321–322.

To learn more about the magazine and to obtain a free sample copy, see our Web site at *www.TeenInk.com.*

1 Family

Photo by Ellie Kreischer

Shoes by the Washer

by Aimee K. Poulin

My mother always knew when my sister had come home because her shoes were by the washing machine—until that one night. I was awoken by a knock on our front door. I laid there in bed as I heard my mother answer it. *What could someone want at 3:47 A.M.?* I wondered. Soon I found out.

My older sister had been in a car accident. I quickly said a prayer and pulled on jeans. I sloppily put my hair up into a ponytail and grabbed my shoes which were by the washer. I looked at my younger sister's teddy bear lying on the couch. *I should bring it,* I thought, so she can think of home. *Nah,* I thought, deciding against it. Mom called me, and we left for the hospital.

When we arrived, we were told to stay in the waiting room. The same officer who had come to our house asked to see my parents alone. I remember sitting and staring absently at the TV. My thoughts began to whirl. *What if she is in a coma? What if she has broken legs and needs a wheelchair?* I would gladly push her around, maybe knock her into some furniture while I'm at it.

I looked up as the officer came back into our room and asked my younger sister and me to follow him. We went to a room with a small sign: Family Room.

When we went in, the officer shut the door. My mother looked at me with her tear-stained face and said only two words I will never forget: "Becky died."

I sat down. I was in shock. I sat there for a long time. Then I began to cry.

It took us months to find out what had happened, and we're still not really sure. All we know is that Becky had been worried about coming home late and hadn't wanted to call for a ride, afraid my parents would be mad. So she found a ride with some friends. All seven packed into a small car and my sister had to sit on someone's lap. The driver was drunk and ran into a telephone pole. Becky died instantly.

To this day, I'm still confused and sad. I ask God why. Didn't she know that Becky was my best friend? Sometimes, I stare at the empty spot by the washer where my sister once put her sneakers and think sadly that her shoes will never sit there again. 回

Photo by Caite Powers

Still Handsome

by Julie White

"I hate my hair so much!" I complained to my mother. It had bothered me all my life, especially in the winter when the wicked wind had a way of turning my hair into a giant knot. That day when I reached over and turned on the heat full blast, I noticed my little brother, Jason, was shivering uncontrollably. I figured it was from the chilly temperature, but it seemed odd that a half hour later, he was still cold and complaining that his arm ached. Mom didn't seem fazed, but I realized he had been complaining a lot lately about his arm. The night before I had awakened to hear him crying. I'd crept to his door and listened as he sobbed in the dark, murmuring about his arm. When I told my parents the next morning, they explained he was just having trouble adjusting to kindergarten.

The next day Jay and I were playing in the driveway. We took out the new Power Wheels Jeep he had received for his birthday. When he rode over a bump and toppled out, he began to cry hysterically. As I scampered to him, he was screaming about his arm. The next thing I knew, he began to vomit. I scooped him up and ran inside the house. My mom and I immediately took him to the doctor, who sent us to the hospital. Jay cried the whole way; I had never seen him carry on like that.

At the hospital we waited for the X-ray results. The doctor spoke to my mother alone, telling her Jay needed a bone specialist. Later we found that Jason had broken his arm and had bone marrow cancer in that area. I tried not to cry, but I couldn't help it. I wondered why God would do this to my little brother.

If I told you how many times I went to the hospital, you wouldn't believe it. I told myself I had to be strong for Jay, that I couldn't let him see me upset. Our family had to be strong; we would get through this together. Once when we were playing Nintendo in his room, I started to cry and Jay did, too, because I was. He didn't understand what was going on. After that I vowed I would not cry again. There was nothing to cry about; Jay would win.

I had no idea what chemotherapy would be like. I didn't know I would spend Christmas day holding my six-year-old brother's hand as he threw up uncontrollably. I never would have guessed he would lose so much weight, that dark circles would form around the sockets that used to hold shining blue eyes. Or that the medication swabs he wiped in his mouth would make him gag and vomit. This little boy went through so much that many could not survive. He was so brave and so strong; it killed me to see other children running around while my brother was cooped up in a hospital room.

But, worst of all, he lost his hair. I recall sitting on the floor of his room playing the hilarious game Hungry Hungry Hippos. I lost miserably every time, which amused him. He'd toss his head back as he erupted in giggles, but when he shook his head, a clump of hair fell onto the red game board and our laughter ceased. We stared at the wispy hair.

"Why is my hair falling out?" he asked innocently. I gulped and replied it was only happening to make him better. He began to scratch his head and more fell out until the board was covered. I bit my lip so hard to keep from crying that it bled.

He looked up and smiled. "Do I still look handsome?"

"You look totally awesome," I choked out. "Just like Michael Jordan."

He started to giggle again. He took the hat my grandmother had bought and tossed it in the laundry bin. He said he was proud to look like Michael Jordan.

That night I cried myself to sleep. I was so worried Jay wouldn't make it. This little boy who had not even finished kindergarten yet had to struggle through each day just to make it to the next. I cried remembering how full of energy he had been only months before. And I cried harder because it just wasn't fair.

The doctor decided Jay needed surgery. We were so nervous, but he got through it perfectly. Finally Jay was on the road to recovery. It was tough. It's hard even to describe what he dealt with. His hair eventually grew back, and he gained weight, too. One day, as I was helping him with his arm brace, I remembered months before when he was diagnosed with cancer. It had been winter, a season I despised because it was always so cold and windy, messing my hair into knots. And I remembered complaining how much I hated my hair. Since then, I have never complained again. 🔲

I Grew Up at 14

by Jillian Balser

A friend once told me a little saying:

You start your life crying for your parents to hold you.
You make your way through childhood testing things out,
trusting that your parents are right behind you.
With adolescence, you begin by saying,
"Trust me, guys; I know what I am doing."
Then by the time you are a teenager, it's
"I wish they would leave me alone."
As thirty rolls around you begin to wonder,
"What would my parents think?"
And at seventy you say,
"I wish I COULD ask my parents."

Well, if this saying is true, I grew up at fourteen.

Growing up in any family has its difficulties: Siblings snore, parents fight, some members live too far away and others battle disease. As a kid, I felt above all that; my family was going to be one of the lucky ones that coasts through life without a problem. But something happened to change that, something I was forced to accept and live with for the rest of my life.

With my birth, my mom and dad swore off drugs and

alcohol, relapsing only a few times, but always trying their hardest. My mom got a good job and when I was young, it was always just me with my dad. When Mom went to sleep, I would tiptoe in to watch "Saturday Night Live" and eat crackers, cheese and pepperoni with Daddy. I wouldn't have my Froot Loops until he helped choose which color to eat first. We were best friends.

The next few years brought the arrival of two siblings to boss around, annoy and steal toys from—all things I figured big sisters were supposed to do. But when my parents, once high-school sweethearts, started fighting, my perfect family began to fall apart. When I was seven, the arguments were finally resolved with one decision: divorce. I began to build a wall around myself so that neither hurt nor love (which seemed to bring hurt) could enter.

Years later I remember coming home one day holding my arm in an awkward position. You see, I was a real baby when it came to having blood taken, even though I'd been through it many times. At five years old, I had gotten hepatitis from my dad. Drinking had worn away his liver until hepatitis became a part of his life—and mine. The day I came home with the little circle bandage on my arm, I wasn't expecting adjustment time to be over yet. I was thirteen and looking forward to starting high school as a freshman.

So, when I got home, I was suddenly frustrated to be there. Home meant swearing and fighting, but of course I thought it was everyone else's fault. My sister was cooking and gave me what I thought was a hostile look, and I took the opportunity to pounce. We were at each other's throats when she said something I will never forget.

"You are so stupid. You don't even know that Dad has AIDS! Bet you didn't know that he did heroin for two weeks."

"What are you talking about? And you're the stupid one! No one can get AIDS after trying a drug for two weeks!"

"Oh! I'm stupid. I guess you thought I was a liar, too?"

"You said it. . . ."

"Well, explain this!!" She ran into the other room and grabbed as many books as her eleven-year-old arms could carry. *AIDS Awareness, Surviving with AIDS.* "Explain that and the twenty others on the shelf."

"Stop! You don't know what you're talking about. I would have known first. I'm older!"

"No one wanted to tell you!"

She ran off crying, and I didn't know what to believe or do. I held onto my hope until it was crushed by my mother. Suddenly I could hardly breathe and the room was spinning.

Then I thought of the surgery from which my dad was having such a hard time recovering. He had had his spleen removed in an attempt to cure his thin blood from years of drinking. Suddenly everything was becoming clear.

Months went by and neither that day nor the virus was mentioned. It didn't need to be—it never left my mind. My dad was in and out of the hospital, and I was faced with the prospect that he wouldn't bounce back. I spent my days pretending everything was fine and my nights trying to figure out when it happened. I felt betrayed, not just because I was never told, but because my parents gambled away life and my happiness over a quick high.

Things began to seem hopeless. My dad was spending more time in the hospital than at home. I tried to help. I wanted my perfect life back. I got moodier, my grades were fluctuating and I often didn't care about anything. My mom tried to get me into counseling, but that only made me angrier.

When the pressure became too severe, I finally confided in friends. They were sympathetic, but no one could stop the pain. I was so scared of losing the one man I loved and after whom I modeled my every action. This man who had turned his life around and become someone any daughter could respect. It seemed impossible to me that he would die so young.

The last time I saw him, he was in the hospital and I was going to a school dance. If someone had told me that this visit would be our last, I would never have left him. My daddy died that November 29. At fourteen, I had lost my thirty-eight-year-old father. He was my life and without him I couldn't breathe. I'll never be able to eat another bowl of Froot Loops because no one will be there to tell me which color to eat first. I'll only be able to remember how soft his hair was or how much his five o'clock shadow tickled my cheek. I would trade almost anything just to hear him say that he loves me again.

It's been a few Christmases, hundreds of sunsets, and thousands of smiles and frowns since my daddy passed away, and I am living proof that life does go on. I have a wonderful boyfriend now who, although he never met one of the world's most wonderful men, has been there for me. With his help and a great group of friends, I am slowly relearning how to breathe. I try to guide my brother and sister the way my father would have. I visit schools and after-school programs trying to inspire a struggling generation to keep trying. It seems so hard for my rebellious generation to understand that drugs and alcohol don't equal a good time and there are always consequences.

My only advice for kids and parents is never to stay mad, never do anything that you'll regret and never give up on life or love. Both are precious and too easily forgotten. To those who have lost a loved one, hug a friend; that's what friends are there for. And to everyone else, grab everyone you love and tell them. 🔲

My Mom and Me

by Megan Hayes

I look out our kitchen window on a hot, sunny, summer morning. I drink my orange juice with ice cubes while I sit at our small kitchen table in my bathing suit and sandals. My mom sits across from me clipping coupons and sipping iced tea.

My mom looks young and pretty, and I often find myself hoping that I'll grow to look like her. Something about her is fresh and healthy. We're talking, as we often do, about what we normally talk about—friendships, pressures and love. She tells me for the millionth time that she hates the small silver hoop in the upper part of my right ear. That earring goes along with my small beaded necklace with my favorite symbol—the Christian fish that stands for the sea, love and peace. I sit with my daisy ring, my beaded anklet, my loose blonde hair tucked behind my ears; I wear a flowered bathing suit, with my tattered red backpack next to me, with my hand-drawn dancing bears. My backpack contains my clothes and CDs—The Grateful Dead, The Band, Chicago.

This is me, what I'm all about, and my mom knows it. She calls me her crazy little hippie and her nature girl, but I know she is laughing inside because she, too, was all this when she was young, and even now I see fragments of what she used to be.

My mom tucks her blonde, blonde hair behind her ears, with her bright green eyes, and her tall, willowy figure, and her tan face, not hidden by makeup. We talk together, freely. She says she trusts me; she tells me she loves me. And I think how I trust her and love her, too. We speak of love and broken hearts. She tells me it will get better, that the hurt will subside. We laugh at my friends and the things that they do, when silently we agree that nothing would be the same if they were not there. We talk of athletics; she tells me she's proud. She's proud of the way I push my body to its limits. She's proud that I am not afraid to sweat or get dirty.

As we talk, I ask my mom about her teenage years, the handsome boyfriend she had in high school. I ask her about Nettie, her best friend and soul mate who had long blonde hair and all the crazy things they did, and how she will never forget their friendship. She tells me that my best friend Ann-Marie reminds her so much of Nettie and I, too, realize the similarities, both physically and emotionally. She tells me of her summers on that island during college, where she used to "hang" with my dad until they eventually fell in love.

Every once in a while our opinions clash and tension grows, but then it eases and another subject is swiftly introduced. I sometimes wish that I could go back in time to meet her when she, too, was young, opinionated and wild. But it is here and now, and I realize how lucky I am to know her and have her as a mother. She smiles and laughs because I've zoned out. She says she knows me well. Perhaps she sees herself in me, and I hope she does. I get up to refill my glass, but on my way over to the fridge I stop to look at my mother, who sits in a bathing suit and sandals in some sort of a daze, looking out the kitchen window. ▣

Photo by Charlie Semine

The "Stupidity" Choice

by Robert Sickel

Y ou would probably guess—hearing that I live in a trailer park—that I'm supposed to be some slacker who enjoys smoking marijuana and drinking alcohol, and you would probably guess my sister would be, too, because she lives in the same lousy home I do. Well, you'd be right about her.

She didn't start out this way. At the beginning of the year she was in the advanced math class for eighth graders, a class I took as a freshman. But now she is an average student in an average class. I know she has the intelligence, but I also know she forgot how to use it. "They" helped her forget.

"They" are your trailer-park stereotypes, the ones you make fun of—and for good reason. To me, they all look the same: sagging, oversized pants, an emotionless frown, and a stench that reeks of tobacco, and sometimes alcohol and marijuana. I didn't really care what they did or how they lived their sad lives as long as it didn't involve me. But, it involved me when they started hanging around with my sister.

I saw major differences within a week. First, she was demoted to pre-algebra, and then school called saying she had skipped and received a three-day in-school suspension. I also noticed that she acted differently. We both used to enjoy jokes at the expense of the "real park kids," but now she was saying that whatever they did was their choice. She also would try to use force when she wanted something, which didn't work on me. Although I'm not much bigger than she is, I'm considerably stronger. Then, she started to smell like tobacco and alcohol, and her grades continued to slide. When I asked her if she had been smoking or drinking, she would say she hadn't. I couldn't argue, because I had no evidence. So I started looking.

My "pre"-park sister would have known better than to leave incriminating evidence in her backpack where anyone, especially a nosy older brother, could find it. There were a couple of letters bragging about her adventures skipping class, and some to a friend about a "cool" shelter in a nearby city that she was planning on asking Mom if she could move to. Most alarming, though, was one note in which she said she wanted to sleep with a particular boy, again. When I asked her about it, she denied everything, saying it was a note to her from a close friend. I'm a fairly smart kid; I didn't believe her for a second.

As any intelligent, immoral person in my situation would do, I tried to blackmail her. My goal was not monetary gain, just my sister's well-being. My terms were simple; I didn't want her hanging around with the park kids anymore. She agreed, and that pact worked for a couple of days.

Then one Monday night she told us she was staying out with her friend, Jane. When she didn't come back we didn't worry, since she often broke her curfew. Early Tuesday morning I started searching for her. The first place I tried was her friend's. I wasn't surprised when her mother answered the door and asked where *her* daughter was; however, when she showed me the letter Jane wrote proclaiming she was running away to live in a girls' home in the city, I was shocked. I knew my sister had gone with her.

I told my mother, and the next day both girls were taken into police custody and Jane's mother brought them back. My sister was ready to defend herself as soon as she walked in, saying she only went to support her friend, and it was my ridicule that had made her run away.

I know what made her run away. The park kids showed her an appealing way of life with no responsibility. Their philosophy (in my words) is: "If you want to mess yourself up, it's *your* choice." I don't ever remember learning that stupidity was a choice.

Now my sister is under their influence more than ever, and there is nothing I can do except state my obvious objections about her situation. I can't use force. I might be able to take some of them in a fight, but even if I won, they would avenge their loss by teaming up on me and I'd end up in the hospital.

Although there is little I can change, I can take pride in being their opposite, totally challenging their ideas. My sister can live her life the way she wants; however, this will not come without my persistent reminders that she is ruining her life. As for me, I'm going to live it the way I want to. I'm not going to opt for the "stupidity" choice. 回

Another Chance

by Crystal Lynn Evans

I stared out into the gray gloom of the pouring rain.
The winding road had turned into a body of
   black water.
I stared out past the sloppy swishing
Of the tired wipers.
I looked over at Mom
And I thought of the mother she never
Had a chance to know.
And now, never would.
The tears fled down her pale face
And into the crack between her rosy red lips.
The tires of our old brown truck sliced through
The water separating the mass of blackness for a
   single moment
Before it melted back together once we had passed.
And we drove farther and farther away from
   the memories.
I felt my heart sink into my stomach
And the glistening pools began to form in my
   own eyes.
I felt I was frozen in someone else's life.
I tried to think of something to say.
Finally, I shifted uneasily and I spoke.

All that came out was "I'm sorry"
And I just stared out the window
Hoping that maybe she didn't hear me.
She drew a deep breath.
The kind that seems to take all your strength.
"It's not your fault," she said.
She laced her weak fingers within mine
And it became uncertain
Which fingers belonged to me
And which belonged to her.
I had become this woman beside me.
And I felt ashamed of the fact that
Like my mother
I didn't know my own mother.
She didn't say anything more that night.
She just kept one hand on the wheel
And dried her tears with the back of the other.
Both eyes straight ahead into the gloom.
Trying to quiet the sobs coming from her
Mourning soul.
And I said a little prayer that night
Listening to the sloppy swishing.
And as I stared out into the black water
I asked God for another chance
And I prayed that this time we could stay afloat.

Locks

by Paul Constant

When are you going to cut your hair?" my father asks in his standoffish voice. We sit on the backyard porch, staring at each other.

I know what I want to say, "When I WANT to cut my hair," but instead I come out with "I don't know. . . ."

"You look like a slob." His mouth curls around the words; newfound disgust for the Son Who Could Formerly Do No Wrong.

"I like it this length," I argue quietly, touching the edges of my hair. It would scrape the top of my collar if I lifted my head a bit, hardly headbanger length but long enough for my father to get mad about. He has his hair cut every two weeks.

"But it doesn't even LOOK nice!"

I argue (within the safe confines of my mind) that I think it does look nice, that I am happy with my hair for the first time since . . . ever.

"It's disheveled! It's not neat!"

But, in my mind, I tell him that I wash it every day, I comb it . . . I like it.

"It embarrasses me!"

What right do you have, I cry out in my mind, visibly shaking in the real world, *to be embarrassed by anything*

I do? Embarrassed? How typical . . . how sadly typical. We only go skin deep, my dad and I, only as deep as the physical world. Nothing more. Stick with the superficial world, with "practical things," and we won't be disappointed.

Embarrassed? Shaking, my hands in my lap, my breath is ragged and soft.

"It's not you! It is just NOT YOU!" His voice is tired and upset.

My mind reacts; a flurry of vengeful comments, hateful, stupid actions held back, held in check by the self that says, *It's not worth it. Don't do something stupid because of hair.*

Oh, but I do think. He can't stop me from that. I wonder, *How do you know who I am?* You dismiss my every thought as a stupid eighteen-year-old flight of fancy. My dreams, my hopes, my needing to write are all just immature things that I have to get out of the way before my real life can begin. *How can you know me?* I scream in my mind. *How can you even look me in the eye and say that you know me? You've never tried!* Since I was four, I've wanted to write, but it's just not "practical." Not practical enough, like being an insurance salesman, to appease you. You don't know me. You never will. You have no idea how sad that makes me, how much that hurts me. I wish it didn't, but it does. It really hurts.

"But you know what makes me mad most of all?" he asks, not expecting a response from the undeserving thing that has usurped his son. "It's that I don't ask anything of you. I never ask anything of you, and I ask you to do one thing . . . ONE THING . . . and you ignore

me. You don't do it. Just one thing—that's what makes
me mad."

And my mind screams. *You don't ASK me anything.
You TELL me things.* I have gone to YOUR church every
single week since I was born, and hear people who
belong to YOUR church tell me what my morals should
be at Sunday school. It hasn't been MY life, MY morals.
It's been yours. You don't ask. You give me no choice.

But you know what? I ask in my mind. *I think I've
turned out pretty well.* I've never come home drunk or
high; I've never done the stupid things my friends have
asked me to do; I've been my own person. I've spent my
entire life from behind a window, watching my friends
do everything, not joining them. I've gotten fairly decent
grades (except some classes, but I've tried my best), and
I don't think I've complained too much. You never ask.
You expect. And the one time I don't go along with your
expectations, I'm a slob, and that hurts. It shouldn't, but
it does.

"You're being so childish! I don't understand."

And everything, every part of me, wants to fight that
statement—I'm being childish. This afternoon, in a
restaurant, you pulled my hair . . . YOU PULLED MY
HAIR! That's childish. That's abusive. It's humiliating to
have you pull my hair just to get me to realize that my
hair is long. You've told me that I couldn't go anywhere
with my friends until my hair is cut.

I realize my father is a bully, a childish, brutal bully
who will pout and complain and moan until he gets his
way. He'll bully anyone into his way of thinking. There
is no other viewpoint in a bully's frame of mind, only

his own. A bully will keep pushing, keep demeaning until finally you just roll over and let him control you. He will hurt you physically, mentally and spiritually until there's nothing strong left, only a child who can't defend himself.

And I am reminded of Samson, in the Bible, who lost all his strength when his hair was cut, but I realize that my strength is already gone. It's been sapped through years and years of bullying. I try to fight it this time, and he pulls the leash until I choke. Finally, I do speak, but I am surprised that my voice is weak, shivering more than my body. And I'm crying. He's won.

"But you never asked me," I say, looking away as though that would hide the tears. "You always told me. I wanted to be asked. I wanted a little respect."

His nostrils flare. I've gone too far. "No matter what I said, whether I've told you or I've asked you, the sentiment is the same. I want you to get a haircut." *And you'll bully me into it, won't you?*

He sits there, smug that his job is done. I'm desperately fighting the tears, and he's happy. He's won. He knows it. He's just waiting for an answer, a confirmation.

I nod, realizing that the battle was not even about locks of hair, but locks of another kind. ▣

Apple Orchard

by Natascha Batchelor

We searched endlessly for a tree with apples that were just right: big enough (the size of a fist), sweet enough, but a bit sour, and flawless (no abrasions or rotted parts). My attention was drawn to trees with dark red apples clinging to the branches in great clusters. Our hopes of finding McIntoshes deteriorated. After biting into one, I found these were red Delicious apples: yum. I began to gather these in my bag while Mother went off on her own search.

When my bag was half full, she reappeared holding out a McIntosh. I bit into it, exclaiming, "Where did you get it?"

She pointed to a tree near the swamp. My smile turned to a frown when I realized they were too high for my five-foot, two-inch body. There were apples scattered on the ground, but instead I grabbed one of the rotted carcasses, a big, round hurling object. The apples fell all around me. Each time I tried to catch the falling sweetness, my hands would gather about my head.

One apple even got stuck up high in the vee of the branch. My mother began to laugh even harder. I hadn't noticed, but as her tone increased, I knew she had been laughing the whole time. In fact, we both laughed. I threw a few more at the tree.

My mother helped me gather the harvest saying, "These are enough."

She was afraid I might get hurt. *Hurt, how silly. I play field hockey,* I thought proudly. I have hard objects hurling toward me all the time. I even felt the scare of a bloody nose once from one of those field-hockey sticks. A little apple couldn't hurt me.

Ouch, well not that much. I grabbed one final apple, enjoying the fruits of my labor, literally. We headed back through the grove, the overgrown, pressed-down, tangled grass, and I looked over my shoulder at the swamp. The water was green on the surface from algae. The trees were gray, with broken bark forming incomplete puzzles. It was flooded with light from the sun, yet the scene appeared full. I smiled at the landscape as the lackluster apples donated a tinge of red to the picture. The swamp's beauty remained with me even though it was not bright.

I turned, walking quickly with a hop just large enough to catch up to my already-departing mother. She pointed out trees containing possible on-the-run candidates. I gathered more red Delicious apples for my father. I thought how happy he would be at our having thought of him. He was the one who really loved them. We began to walk up slight slants in the land to each new line of trees, toward the store where we'd pay.

I had been noticing the grass with its strands faded green, weathered by the rain and frost. Once again I had fallen behind my mother; her pace was constant as opposed to my curious stopping feet. As I approached her, I could hear a panting, wheezing sound.

I've always known she had a lung disease, but at that moment the reality thrust itself closer, hitting my consciousness like a bullet shot from a rifle. She had to stop, catching her breath, her chest heaving, gasping for air. The remainder of our walk passed step by step. Each pace passed, beating irregularly against the ground, in tune with her breathing, but without real rhythm. I thought of the altitude. *Step.* The cold air. *Step.* The day I found out she had the illness. *Pause.*

She was talking to my father. Something about "with my lungs the way they are." I became afraid. *Step.* Not knowing what it was all about. Some disease . . . no cure. *Step.* I did a report on it once as an excuse to look into the foreign words. It was so rare, "sarcoidosis." *Step.* So little research had been done. *Step.*

She didn't want to take the drugs because of the side effects. "Mind over matter is all I need." She knew what would happen if she took the treatments again. In pictures she looked obese. The steroids had made her body swell. *Step.* She didn't want to go through that again. *Pause.*

Her X rays are illegible because of damage done by the disease. *Step.* She could even have lung cancer and they wouldn't be able to tell. *Step.* The doctors wouldn't take a CAT scan of her lungs to see if there was anything else wrong besides the sarcoidosis. Too much money. *Step.* What is money compared to the life of a mother, wife, sister, friend?

She is dying. *Step.* The doctors are amazed that she's

made it this far without steroids. She's fifty. How much longer will she stay here with me? *Step.* I thought that my only option was to make her final months, years, as pleasant as possible. No, that wouldn't do. *Step.*

What makes our mother-daughter relationship so close is our differences. Those little disagreements when each walks away a little wiser, a little bit more understanding. We see eye-to-eye, singly in each conversation, and together as a whole. Love binds us. *Step.* I know she has little time left with me. She is dying, dying faster than she should. A little bit quicker each day. *Step.* Our apple groves make her immortal, though. I will always remember. ◫

Photo by Jonathan Roper

The Gift in Disguise
by Mallie Allison Owsley

Rolling into our lives like a gentle breeze tickling our cheeks, she made our lives more worthwhile since that day she was born.

Lauren Glenn Allison was born in Oklahoma City late one night in July. Her family was on their way to visit her grandmother's house when Aunt Lenore went into labor. Since she was not due for three months, Uncle Jeff, scared to death, drove her to the nearest hospital, where she gave birth. Weighing only three pounds, Lauren could easily fit into his hand. She was born with a problem. Lauren had cerebral palsy.

I remember Nana and Papa rushing to Oklahoma to be with them all. They were distraught beyond belief. Aunt Lenore was a healthy woman, in her second pregnancy, taking proper precautions. How could this have happened? Lauren was paralyzed from the waist down.

I remember going to the hospital and seeing her small body lying in that tiny bed. She was surrounded by blinking machines. She was so small, smaller than anything I had ever seen. I remember Aunt Lenore with huge bags under her eyes and Uncle Jeff's failure to be funny. He usually greeted me with a noogie (where he puts my head under his armpit and rubs his knuckles across the top of my head—hard). This time he just said hello.

A year later, I spent Christmas at their home. Lauren was still hooked up to machines, and I could hear her crying at night. She was so uncomfortable and couldn't do a thing for herself. I felt awful for her family; they didn't deserve this.

Then all those feelings changed. Now Lauren is the axis of our world. She happens to be one of the smartest kids I know. Lauren can remember things from years ago. Right now she probably speaks more Spanish than I do, and I'm graduating from high school soon! Lauren began in a wheelchair that someone had to push. But she progressed and now can operate her own motorized wheelchair. We call her a terror on wheels. She can flat move that thing!

There is something about Lauren that simply captivates you and keeps you transfixed. She can take something terrible and make it great. Lauren seems happy even though she has so many restrictions. She can take your worst day and make it into your best, just by being her happy self.

I spent a week with her family one summer. It was fun and a learning experience. I discovered how hard it is to live with someone with a disability; it's a full-time job. But I also saw the bond Aunt Lenore and Lauren have, and how happy she makes my uncle. She is a remarkable girl with a lot of love to share. Instead of being bitter, Lauren makes the most of her abilities. She has shown others hope.

This small child has undergone many operations and yet she still wears a smile. Her thin frame is covered with scars, though she feels little pain. Her heart is one of a champion. She took one small, rural school that was not keen about her attending, and has completely changed their minds—and their outlook on the disabled. Even though she is still a child, she has touched many hearts and lives.

Lauren Glenn was our gift from God, wrapped in the most glorious eye-catching paper you have ever seen. Every day she pulls a small gift out from inside herself and teaches a lesson—whether she realizes it or not. ▣

We Go Together

by Amy Danielle Piedalue

As we pull up to that ivy-covered brick building, I spot a figure waving from a first-story window. By the time my mother turns off the engine, I'm already standing on the steps of the university, ferociously hugging my sister. My mouth launches into hyper-speed as I attempt to bring Alicia up-to-date on the last two months of my life. "You'll never believe what happened at school on Tuesday. . . ."

Alicia's dorm room has a distinct smell. The aroma of detergent and fabric softener floats up from the laundry room below and mixes with her perfume, creating an intimate, snug atmosphere. At 10:00 P.M., we sit on the floor with an empty pizza box between us and *The Breakfast Club* playing on the television. I tell a joke only Alicia would think funny, and our laughter fills the tiny room. As I'm about to recommend Judd Nelson for a "makeover," Alicia blurts out, "Judd Nelson would be so much cuter in khakis and a haircut."

"Quit having my thoughts," I say for the third time that night.

Two hours later, I lay blissfully in my sleeping bag, gazing at the glowing solar system on her ceiling. I had wondered if two months apart would change our relationship. That night, three years ago, I realized that separation did not weaken our kinship, and I still appreciate the unwavering intensity of our bond.

Forrest Gump might say we are "like peas and carrots." Just as peas and carrots are connected by their vegetable family, so my sister and I are united by common upbringing. The compatibility of peas and carrots stems from their complementary tastes, not from their classification as vegetables. After spending that evening with her, away from our family, I recognized that our relationship's strength does not rely entirely on our blood connection.

I glance around my sister's dorm room, past her tiny refrigerator to the metallic door beads marking the closet, her twelve-cup coffee pot, her neatly made bed and her desk in the corner. I admire Alicia's autonomy. Since birth, my sister has been in charge of her life. Like a carrot, she grows independently; I develop within my cozy, little pod, depending on my fellow peas.

The next evening, Alicia takes me to meet her friends. The music blares, and the air vibrates with energy and excitement. Knots form in my stomach as I see dozens of students talking in large circles and dancing to Bob Marley. Alicia sticks by my side, introducing me around. Everyone has a different opinion of us, alternating between "You two look and act exactly alike" and "Are you sure you're sisters?" A few people remark on our similarity, while pointing out that our kinship is obvious when we are together, but harder to see when we are apart. Our different tastes only serve to enhance the delicious quality of our combination.

As I watch Alicia visit with her pals, she seems to take

on an orangish hue. Carrots develop underground, hidden from view. These shy vegetables are, at first, crisp and hard. If one takes the time to cook them, however, carrots warm up and become softer. I conclude that while my sister is hard to get to know, I hide very little about myself. I sit and talk with strangers as if I've known them for years. An image of a pea flashes into my mind, and I see myself with a faint outer covering that breaks easily, revealing a sweet and soft interior. My unrestrained expression of thoughts and emotions mirrors the growth of peas, which occurs above ground where these bold vegetables are easily observed. Although Alicia and I have very different manners, in a warm environment our textures are almost identical.

Alicia and I roll out of bed the same time Sunday morning. At 10:00 A.M., we are standing on the stone steps. Once again we hug. Alicia pulls away, smiling. "I love you," she says. As my mother and I drive home, I remember my sister's farewell. I realize that while we have always been close, my sister and I never said "I love you" until Alicia lived three hundred miles away. Somehow, those three words are more significant knowing we only started using them when we truly understood their meaning. ▣

I Love You, Uncle Kurt

by Lucy Coulthard

I stood silently staring out the row of windows lining the bedroom wall. My knees were pressed against the bed, keeping me steady. I gazed out at the overgrown field of grass and the tops of cars as they sped by. One after the other. A red one, then a black. People with different lives and different problems. Everything in the room sat undisturbed. The puzzle was still there, half-finished, pieces strewn across the small card table. The old oak desk was silently collecting dust. The glass paperweight and small porcelain figures stood untouched. The baby-blue alarm clock rested quietly on the nightstand. The hands were motionless at three o'clock.

I took a breath, allowing the stale air to fill my nostrils. How odd it seemed that the room was still perfumed with his scent. Bed perfectly made. The cat was sleeping lazily at the foot, as always. I could smell him as if he had been here that morning. I stared out the window as I had many times as a child. But instead of idle thoughts of butterflies and candy, unmistakable dark words raced in my mind. *He's gone. He's gone.*

I ran my fingertips over the flowered bedspread. I closed my eyes and tried to conjure an image of him in my mind's eye. Through all the chaos and pain, I tried to remember him. Before the cancer. Before the morphine and swollen feet. Before the balding head and shrunken stomach. Back before the days when IV bags sat in the refrigerator next to the milk and orange juice. He was a large man with jet black hair. He loved to eat. How ironic that the cancer hit his esophagus first. An honest man with a heart of gold who cared for me more than the world itself. He was a second father.

My body began to sway as my knees started to buckle. I lay on the bed, sending a cloud of dust and cat hair into the air. I waited patiently for a sneeze. Why did I feel so much pain? Why did the pain run so deep I could almost feel it in the depths of my soul? My only consolation was he no longer was in pain. His three years of treatments and operations had ended in death. An untimely death that I despised.

Looking out the window again, the events following his death flashed through my mind. Every moment would stay with me forever. The funeral parlor. Family. The sight of his lifeless body lying awkwardly in the casket did not cause me to break down. It was my grandparents saying good-bye to the son they had outlived. It was the sight of my father with his face contorted in pain, his eyes showing sorrow I had never seen before. My aunt sitting silently, strongly, eyes fixed on the casket, bidding farewell to a husband she stood by until the end.

I sat alone on a stiff pink loveseat in the room next to the casket. The sliding doors connecting the rooms were open, so that I could see the top of his head and his pale hands folded lightly on his chest. I felt him sitting next to me. Every emotion in my body seemed to blend as one, creating a feeling I had never had before and haven't had since. I saw nothing. Did I think I would see him as a younger man, smiling back at me with the same silly grin? Everything will be okay. I saw nothing, but felt everything. And in that moment I knew there was only one thing left to say, "I love you, Uncle Kurt." The emotions and my uncle slipped away. ◙

Photo by Louise Turner

My Inspiration

by Luis Steven Miranda

My mom has been through immense suffering, but she has persevered. My mom never had a chance to have a prestigious career, and during my childhood she always had more than one job. In fact, I almost never saw her. She would be home long enough to ask if we had behaved that day, then she would leave for another grueling shift. All the work she did, hour after hour, year after year, was to earn a few extra dollars. She could have used this money to buy things for herself, but she never did. She only bought herself the bare essentials to make sure her children had food on the table at every meal.

My mom moved us from one of the worst neighborhoods in Los Angeles to a nice home in a nearby community. Who helped her? No one. She did it on her own. She alone made the down payment and pays the mortgage every month. My mother's education was limited; she did not even finish grade school. In her country, where she lived until her twenties, she had to start working at a young age so her family could survive. School was not an option.

My mom rose above poverty and made something of herself. Despite her lack of formal education, she became a successful life-insurance professional who has won many awards from her company.

People used to say she was living off the government because she received welfare. My mother showed those critics she could better her situation. They no longer look down on her; she proved she could overcome anything. Only recently has she slowed down, but not by choice. She had many back operations that have improved her chances of living pain-free. Doctors believed she might never walk again, but just days after she was released from the hospital, she was on her feet watering her garden.

Her accomplishments are many, although not world-renowned. They are amazing because she achieved them in spite of the distrust people showed her. She defied the stereotype: People thought a single mother on welfare living in the worst part of Los Angeles could never make it out. She did. My strength comes from hers. She is my inspiration. All I want in life is to make her as proud of me as I am of her. I will always remember what she has taught me and who she is. ◙

Somebody's Child

by Jennifer A. Eisenberg

To me, adoption is a beautiful thing. Sixteen years ago I was adopted. Although I know some things about my past, the question of who I am is puzzling to me. Here is my story.

I was born Carmen Julia to a couple who lived in Chihuahua, Mexico. I don't even know their last name. My birthparents were poverty-stricken. When I see those commercials on television showing poor people who live in third-world countries, I tend to believe that is who my birthparents are, and who I once was. I was their ninth child. I don't even know if I was born in a hospital or a cardboard box they called home. I was born on the twenty-seventh of May, and for three months, Chihuahua was my home. I only lived there briefly because they had no money to feed me. To top that, I was sick. They needed to get me out of there, which they did. At that moment, I was nobody's child.

At that same time, in New York, a young couple who had been married for eight years was desperately seeking a child. When they heard about my situation, they knew that there was hope. On August thirteenth, I was renamed Jennifer Anne and adopted. The adoption united that young couple and me. We were now no longer a world apart, but a family. The prayers of four people had been answered, and my life was renewed.

As I grow today, like so many other kids, I still wonder about what happened so many years ago. I wonder about my past, my heritage and my family in Mexico. When I was younger, my parents explained why Daddy has strawberry-blond hair and I do not. Or why Mommy has a light complexion, while mine is dark. Yet, those are only surface details to me. The answer to my real question is hard. I want to know why I am the way I am. It is my struggle for identity. I understand why my birth-parents could not keep me or my siblings. I want to know what my siblings look like. Do they have brown hair like me? Is my heritage based on Aztec beliefs? Do I act like my birthfather or mother? I want to know these answers. I want to see them, even if only for one second.

I love my adoptive parents. They are my one and only parents. They have given me a life no one else could have. They are my world. But somewhere out there is my blood line. My ancestors are the ones I want to blame for my stubbornness and want to thank for my talents. No one else feels exactly the way I do. I know I have an interesting history, and yet I know nothing about it. It is hard to look in the mirror and not know from whom I inherited my features. It is difficult, but I am hopeful. One day I will find the answers. ▣

Grandma's Gift

by Andrew Briggs

"You've never been here before!" my mom said with a sharp, new edge to her voice. Even though these words were directed at my grandmother sitting next to me in the back seat, my head snapped up at the tone. In the instant that I met my mother's eyes, I remembered the talk we had when I was nine and found out that my grandmother had Alzheimer's disease.

Back then it was a mysterious disease that had no effect on my life since I rarely saw my grandmother. Even though I knew there was something wrong when my parents sat me down and had a serious talk about her illness, the information went in one ear and out the other. It did not seem real, and, therefore, I considered my grandma's ailment as just another bit of news to be shoved back into the compartment of my mind where I kept imaginary things. But my mother's voice and the look in her eyes suddenly illuminated that compartment. Reality now upset my imagination.

Here we were, four years later, traveling along Route 91 on our way back from the beach house my parents had rented for a week, perhaps the last vacation my grandmother would be well enough to spend with us.

Since my grandma was the smallest one in the car, she sat between my friend Ross and me. Every now and then she would look over at me, and I would give her a wink and a smile, which she returned.

Ross was a little nervous around Grandma because she kept asking the same questions again and again. Although he smiled, it looked more like a nervous grimace. Everyone should have been in a laid-back, let's-take-a-break-from-everyday-life mode, but it was like we were traveling with a new exchange student, someone who no longer spoke our language. The best way to communicate with her was through the eyes and through laughter. Actually, I was enjoying her new "don't sweat the details" way of looking at life. She had a funny laugh and was behaving like a mischievous little brother.

When Grandma saw the sailboats in the harbor, her wrinkled face relaxed and she looked like the schoolgirl she must have once been. Overcome with glee, she exclaimed, "I remember when I was here before." This was the comment that evoked the sharp response from my mother. I immediately flushed with anger at my mother's voice, but when I looked in her eyes I saw more than anger; I saw her frustration at seeing her mother, the woman she looked up to her whole life, losing ground, and the fear of all that would be faced in the future. Even though my mother only paused momentarily before taking charge in her lawyer-like fashion, I saw in that silence a need I could fill. I could build a bridge and in so doing cross into adulthood, as I allowed my grandmother to ease back into innocence. The process would help us all.

Realizing my mother and grandmother had reached uncharted water, I threw them a line. I asked Grandma what her favorite seafood was. Once again, her eyes brightened, and she licked her lips with new appetite. She asked me if we could stop somewhere to eat lobster. I nodded enthusiastically, and any discomfort Grandma felt from her verbal exchange with Mom was completely erased as easily as erasing chalk off a blackboard. I quickly filled the blank board with new facts and equations, ignoring the fact that these, too, would be gone from Grandma's memory, possibly forever.

My grandmother died two years later, but she left me a valuable gift. For the first time, I had faced a difficult situation on equal footing with my parents, and Grandma's smile and wit encouraged me to take the lead. 🔲

2 Friends

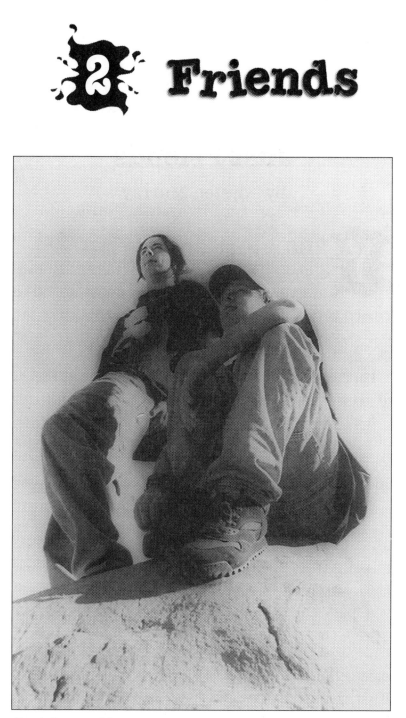

Photo by Teresa Bendokas

Just Friends

by Kirsten Murray

You're one of those guys that all the girls talk about. Whenever you do something bad, everyone in school knows about it. You've broken two of my friends' hearts. Yet you're one of the coolest guys, and we're friends. I stick up for you. You're like the big brother I always needed.

I'm the kind of girl guys like in a sisterly way. I seem to get along with guys better than girls.

It all started when I was five. I was friends with some of your friends. We ended up being around each other a lot. You were there when I needed you, and you cared about my feelings.

Once we got to high school, everything was different. To be "just friends" with a guy is basically impossible without people thinking things. Yet somehow we're still friends. I've watched you go with girls, break hearts and have your heart broken. I want to help; I want to call you, but I can't.

Everyone thinks it's weird that you're friends with me. I'm not that popular. I'm not really pretty, or funny, or outrageous. But this makes me respect you even more. If you look close, we're a lot alike. Neither one of us talks a lot, and we're both unpredictable. We're both lost and scared inside, and we don't show our feelings.

People ask me about you, since you're so popular. They ask me what you're like and if the rumors are true. I tell them that you're nice, thoughtful. Then they say, "Isn't he strange?" and I reply, "Yeah, he's strange. Everybody's strange."

You've done some pretty bad stuff I don't approve of, and yet I'll always be there for you. With all the problems you've had, it's amazing that you've made it this far. But you're strong on the inside as well as the outside. You give me strength, and somehow you get me back on track when I get in trouble. There are certain people who are just plain comforting to see every day, and you're one of them. It's hard not seeing you even for a couple of days.

I'm scared because you graduate soon, and I won't get to see you for a long time. I should probably tell you all this, but I'm not that brave. You need someone to believe in you and teach you to listen to yourself. Before your game or the big test you always say to me, "Do you think I'm ready?" I reassure you that you're fine, you'll do great. "You gotta believe it though," I tell you. And you do. You make me proud.

Right now, I just want to say thank you for our friendship. I love being with you. I love having those deep conversations. I love the way you push me around, and I love the feeling I get when your arms are around me. I love your deep, questioning eyes and your messy hair. When it comes right down to it, I guess I just love you . . . and I need you. And all I can do is dream that you might feel this way about me. ▣

Her Unforgettable Smile

by Lee Ann Sechovicz

Susan was one of my favorite camp counselors. She was always energetic and fun. Her beautiful face was perfect. It would always be shining down on you, making you laugh. But not now. Not anymore.

Early one morning, after two weeks at camp, we were called to gather at the ball field. I was annoyed and wanted to know why we were having an assembly so early. "Oh great, we're not going to go to the beach today," I said angrily. But afterwards, I was sorry those words had left my mouth.

It wasn't until we were all seated on the carpet of green grass that I noticed how solemn all of the counselors looked. It scared me.

The next few minutes were a huge blur of words that got jumbled up in my mind and didn't make sense. My mind had become a maze for words with no end. I tried to listen, but it was as though my ears had flown away. I just barely managed to catch a few of the words:

". . . There was a car accident . . ."

". . . Nine counselors were in the car . . ."

". . . Some counselors were hurt; others are just in shock . . ."

Terrifying scenes ran through my mind. I felt dizzy and sick.

No, this isn't happening! It is only a dream! I thought horridly. The walls in my mind were caving in on me. My whole life was falling apart. The most shocking news in my whole short life was yet to come . . .

". . . Susan Samuels did not survive the crash . . ."

I felt a sharp chill shoot up and down my spine as the hideous words echoed rapidly through my mind. *What? This is impossible! No! This can't be true. Everything is fine.* I tried desperately to persuade myself I was just having a nightmare. But I knew in my heart that it was real.

I felt hot tears pouring down my cheeks and splashing onto my T-shirt as I ran toward my bunk. When I arrived, I found two of my friends already crammed into the bottoms of their sleeping bags. I threw off my shoes, shot into my sleeping bag and buried my face in my pillow. We cried for a long time. Although I didn't know why, I couldn't accept Susan's death. My friend Anne suggested we share some of our good memories of Susan. Even though we had known her for only two weeks, she had already become a part of us.

"She always made me smile," I added to the conversation. After a bit, we just sat and thought to ourselves, remembering our times with Susan.

I know she is gone, and I will never again hear her cheerful voice, but I still have not really accepted what happened. This, I know, will take time. Whenever I think of her, I think of an exciting person always smiling down on me with her perfect face. And that smile lands on my face. ▣

Angel

Fiction by Lindsay Starr Muscato

It is summer. The sun slips gold over everything, polishing it with heat, yet Lydia wears a long-sleeved NYU sweatshirt. This puzzles me.

"Aren't you hot?" I ask. "It's, like, eighty degrees." The weight of my own clothing is killing me, and I'm in shorts and a T-shirt.

"No," she replies, looking down. She examines her knuckles, and I try to think of something else to say. We sit awkwardly on my porch swing and feel the silence four years of separation has created.

"So, what kind of music do you like?" This is a lame, lame guy-attempt at conversation. Lydia has endured so many tragedies, I can't think of anything else to say. I am an idiot. Certifiable.

"Chopin," she replies simply, and I nod, not sure where to go from here. I don't know much about Chopin. "What about you, Kevin?" she asks as an afterthought.

"Um, I like lotsa stuff. Metallica, Nine Inch Nails, Nirvana." But none of these names seem to register with her.

"Oh," she says. We used to be best friends, I remind myself. Find some common ground.

"So, do you remember Miss Whiting?" Miss Whiting

was our homeroom teacher in eighth grade, the only class we had together that year. That was the year Lydia's mom died, and she and her dad moved up to New York.

"Yeah, she's the one who told me my mom died. She pulled me aside that day and told me about the accident." Her striking white-blonde hair tumbles in front of her pale face as she looks down at her fingers again. I am stupid, stupid, stupid. *Way to hit a nerve,* I tell myself.

"I'm sorry . . . to bring that up again," I say.

"It's okay," she says, shrugging. "I'm used to missing my mother. It was much harder when my dad first moved us to the city, but it's better now."

"Why did you guys move way up there?"

"My dad was an artist. There are more galleries and stuff in the city."

"Did he ever get to be, I don't know, famous or anything?" My lack of knowledge, both about her and the art world, is becoming embarrassing. Lydia half-smiles.

"Famous? No. We lived on what he made doing tattoos, actually. My dad was crazy." I'm not sure whether she means clinically insane or just eccentric.

"How did . . ." and I catch myself. I am not supposed to be asking her about this stuff. A red warning light flashes in my brain: new topic, new topic.

"Do you want to know how he died? Did your parents tell you?"

"No, they didn't tell me much," I say. "Just that you were coming home to live with your grandmother."

"He—wait, you mean you didn't read about it? He killed himself. He was crazy. An absolute mental case. He pretty much lost it after my mom's accident." *Gosh, she's beautiful,* I find myself thinking. Stop it, stop it, you're not here to kiss her.

"Wow."

"Yeah. Why do you think my grandmother's sending me to therapy as soon as I'm unpacked? These last four years were insanity."

"I'm sorry."

She stands up, never meeting my eyes, and carefully steps off the porch.

"He thought I was an angel."

"You are," I say without thinking.

"No, a real one." I stand up and follow her as she picks her way through the landscaping into the backyard.

"Huh?"

"Never mind." Suddenly I remember that I used to write to her, and I hesitate.

"Did you ever get my letters?"

"You mean the ones proclaiming your 'undying love'?"

I flush red; I can feel it. "I was only thirteen. What did I know about being subtle?"

"Enough not to be," she says, surprising me. "You were the only one who wrote to me after we moved. I used to hide under the bed and read them over and over late at night with my Fisher-Price flashlight. I pretended you really loved me." She doesn't look at me, which leads me to think she's embarrassed or something.

"I did, Lydia. We were best friends. You lived right next door, remember? I had a crush on you for, like, three years."

"Nobody really loved me ever, in my whole life. Not even you."

"Why would you say something like that?"

She selects a swing, and I take the one next to her. "Because. Because I'm not really an angel. My father thought I was an angel, but I'm not."

"You're an angel to me," I say, toeing the sand under the swing. She's confusing me.

"No, a real angel. He thought I was a real angel." Tears tinge her voice.

"Calm down, calm down. What's wrong?" I put a hand on her shoulder, feeling only a sharp bone, but she shrugs it away.

"Nothing. I'm fine." She looks up fiercely, swiping at the tears tumbling down her cheeks.

"I missed you," I say, finally—saying what I've been wanting to say. "Why didn't you write back?"

"Because I couldn't get out of the house. I never left. Don't you understand? He never once let me out. Never. In four years, Kevin. Four years. And when you stopped writing, I was all by myself."

"Lydia, come on. I mean, why didn't you do something? Couldn't you call someone? Didn't you have other relatives?"

"When Mom died, it was just the two of us. There was my mom's mother, but she didn't want anything to do with my dad. She was still upset. Plus we didn't have a phone, or anything. I mean, for one thing, it cost money. For another, my dad didn't want any distractions when he was working. He did his stupid body art or whatever in the living room and painted and sculpted in his bedroom. He was always busy."

"So, what did you do? How did you live?" My jaw slackens so I can hardly speak.

"I lived in the apartment, and that's all. My dad worked at home, so it's not like I ever had the chance to get out. Even when he left the house to get food or something, he locked all the doors from the outside."

"Didn't you go to school?" My mind is spinning too fast to grasp what I want to say.

"He brought books home from the library, and there was always plenty of music around—records and stuff. He was a huge fan of classical music. We had a piano, and I taught myself to play."

Finally, I ask the question my mind has been stumbling over. "Why? Why didn't he let you out?"

"He thought I would fly away." She says it so softly I can barely hear her, but her words ripple through my head like an earthquake.

"Lydia? Are you serious?" Of course I know she is serious. She is sobbing at this point, soaking the ends of her hair. I find her hand and hold it. I don't know what to do. It's not as though I've had any experience with this type of situation. I can't help but think how beautiful she is. So this is why I adored her so much back then. I know I'm an idiot for thinking this at such a time.

"Do you want proof, Kevin? Do you?" Angrily, she looks me square in the eye, blinking back tears. She isn't angry at me, but she is certainly angry about something. I stammer a word or two, but she interrupts me.

"Remember when we used to sit in your basement?" she says suddenly.

"Yeah," I say.

"Can we go down there again?"

"Yeah, sure," I tell her, completely bewildered. I am

still holding her hand, so I lead her in through the garage and down the steps, never letting go. Memories wash over me—that was where we first kissed. Or, actually, it was our only kiss, the night before she moved away. But I have to stop thinking about this stuff.

"Remember the last time we were down here?" she whispers, sitting on the couch as though it is somehow fragile—or maybe as though she is fragile. She *is* fragile.

"Of course, I do," I reply as I sit next to her.

"Kevin, why did you stop writing to me?"

"I thought you didn't want to hear from me anymore."

"He wouldn't let me leave. . . ." With fresh sobs, she collapses on my shoulder. I am wearing my Nirvana T-shirt, and I can feel her tears soak through after a few seconds. I can't think of a single thing to say, as usual.

"Do you want to see them?" she whispers, her voice muffled by my shoulder. I can't imagine what she means.

"What?"

"I love you," she says.

"I love you, too," I manage to utter in shock. She turns around so her back is facing me.

"Promise not to tell," she says, her voice weak from crying. "Go ahead. Look. Look what he did."

"Where?" My confusion is embarrassingly thick. She grasps the bottom of her heavy sweatshirt, lifts it up past her shoulder blades, and I inhale sharply.

There, in deep blue ink, is a pair of wings, beautifully tattooed, spreading across her entire milky-white back, and at last I realize what she's been saying:

"Angel wings." ▣

Photo by Jennifer Tepe

No Mountain Too High

by Joanne Wang

Amid the lessons on fractions and spelling, I learned something else in elementary school: Every girl needs a best friend. There must be that special girl who hands out cupcakes on your birthday and always chooses you first for kickball. As a pig-tailed eight-year-old, I agonized over this prerequisite to girlhood happiness. I needed a best friend.

I decided on Stephanie, a girl I had known since my days in diapers. Actually, she was my second choice. My first choice already had a best friend, so I settled for Stephanie. She lived far away (a half-hour, but to a third-grader, that seemed like another country), and didn't attend my school. But, she loved to play with Barbies, our parents were friends, our brothers were friends and we were friends. She was a fine candidate.

We did the best-friend things: buying best-friend necklaces and rings, planning matching outfits and saving the best goody bags for each other. When other girls asked me The Question, I happily responded, "Stephanie is my best friend."

Lucky for me, Stephanie turned out to be more than a nominal friend. She was my sidekick. We flooded the church grounds, and created mud pies; we collected the largest leaves for handmade brooms; we pretended to be princesses and moms; we climbed the highest trees, sang the loudest songs and teased the peskiest boys.

But, the time came when mud pies and silly songs were set aside for homework and sports teams. The pesky boys transformed into potential boyfriends for whose attention we competed. Though we promised to let nothing ruin our best friendship, we hardly saw each other.

Skiing came to our rescue since our families continued annual trips to Vermont. Over the years, with Stephanie by my side, I had conquered my first bunny slope, lost my first pink mitten and experienced chair-lift trauma when my hair froze to the bar.

And then there was one trip just a couple years ago when, having graduated from Snowflake Ski School without broken bones, we felt ready for the mountain's toughest challenge—the black diamond trails. Even though I was still more comfortable skiing blue square trails, I would never admit that to our boastful brothers. If they were going to ski the black diamonds, Stephanie and I would be right behind them. Our first test was a steep trail covered with bumpy moguls, aptly named Needle's Eye.

"We can do this," cheered Stephanie. Every part of my still-intact body said otherwise, but I gave in to her pleading. I was adjusting my skis and looking for the easiest way down when I realized I was alone at the top of the slope. I looked ahead and thought I would faint, but started down. My half-parallel, half-pizza-pie maneuver failed, and I fell ten feet from my starting place.

Stephanie made it a bit farther, but she was on the ground, too. We looked at each other from across the dreadful moguls and giggled.

"This is a disaster," Stephanie yelled.

"Whose idea was this?" I smiled back.

Pushing off with my poles, I rose and ventured farther. I traveled a decent distance, but my speed caught up with me. Unable to control myself, I flew off a mogul, lost my skis, took a few rolls and returned to the ground on my behind.

The only positive was that I rolled farther down the hill. One big disadvantage: My skis were behind me. Uphill. I was aching, tired and cold. Scanning the mountain for our brothers, I saw them at the bottom, waving their arms and urging us to hustle. I was doubtful I could make it down alive. I wasn't even sure I could make it to my skis. I made my decision: I would wait until the ski patrol came to rescue me.

"Jo! Jo, get up," Stephanie yelled, tugging on my jacket. "We have to get your skis." She took one look at me, gave me up for defeated and turned around to retrieve my skis herself. Up the mountain she went, inching her way. By the time she made it to the closest ski, a man had brought the other one down to me.

Well, I couldn't complain. I had two skis and a best friend. What could stop us now? Moguls were just bumps in the snow. Ice? No problem, I just laughed in the face of ice! Ha ha! Poles in hand, I set off once more.

Fifteen seconds later, I was back in the snow.

"Joanne, can you ski this?" Stephanie asked. I shook my head no. I was angry with myself, angry with the boys and angry at the ski resort for making the trail, but not angry at her. Stephanie didn't say a word. Holding her skis, she pushed off with her legs, and down she went on her behind. As I watched this lump of neon yellow attempt to slide down the mountain, I laughed so hard I cried.

I sat down, held my own skis in my arms and also pushed off with my legs. Down I went after my friend. It was difficult to keep up the momentum, but eventually I worked out a technique. Stephanie and I were going to get off this mountain. Snow hit our faces, and water seeped through our snow pants, but down we went.

There we were, fifteen-year-old girls, sliding down a black diamond trail, crying and laughing. Up, down, up, down, across the moguls. As we got closer to the bottom, we could hear our brothers exclaiming, "You girls are insane!"

When people ask me what love means, I always picture Stephanie sliding down that mountain. She didn't profess her undying devotion to me, rather she expressed it in her noble, crazy actions. That day, Stephanie not only calmed my nerves, but brought a huge smile to my frozen face. Because of her, I conquered that mountain. And, I continue to overcome my own moguls, knowing there's no such thing as the wrong way when I have a best friend beside me. ▣

Lies and November Nights

by Rebecca Danielle Onie

Behind me, a circle of friends huddles together, and from their intense talk, an occasional word drifts through the air to my ears. Just minutes before, as we had walked to the corner, past houses shrouded with the night and street lights hunched over, I asked Sara not to get into her boyfriend's car. Now, as I stand shivering in the November night, waiting for Sara, the piercing air singes my fingers and burns my cheeks. She stands three steps in front of me. In the maroon car, a shadow sways uneasily, black against the blue darkness of night. The hushed drone of his deep voice from the car is punctuated by Sara's higher tones, and through all the talk, the radio permeates the air with music.

Although he said he hadn't been drinking, I was sure he was lying. If I was right, he might turn a corner too suddenly, not see the telephone pole as he rounded the bend, or miscalculate the size of a driveway. Into the night I poured out my fears to Sara, and she promised that she would not get into the car. Looking at me with her pure blue eyes, holding my cold hand in hers, with her awkward half-smile, she swore to me. "Rebecca, I will walk home. He can follow in his car." I turned to her, and we exchanged a quiet smile, for we were the best of friends. Her word was as good as gold. She was so honest and sincere.

Now, as she leans against the car and the minutes drag on, everything is very clear in my eyes. The trees stand out, with their bent limbs reaching like gnarled hands, for the few remaining leaves. The stars burn like pinpoints of fire. Sara and the figure talk on. Our friends move around impatiently behind me; rustling their winter jackets, they urge me to start walking back with them. They tell me Sara will follow. They tell me she will come home soon. And so, I step to her side and whisper to her. I strain to see the guy buried in the black interior of the car, but to no avail.

"You're walking, right, Sara?" I ask one more time. She nods, and I move off. But, looking back from the end of the street, I see her get into the car and the shape inside swallow her up. As I turn back to my friends, the night dissolves into a sea of tears.

Countless times she had spoken my thoughts, dreamt my dreams and read my mind. Why then does she refuse to accept my logic? Why does she coldly ignore my suggestions? Why are my fears so alien to her? Desperately, I try to create answers to the questions that flood my shattered mind.

I search wildly for an excuse for her actions but despite my panic, reason forces itself into my thoughts. I know, even in my disbelief, that this is the bitter reality I must face. All the little lies from the past year worm their way into my head. All excuses for her duplicity fall apart under this concrete proof that her word is nothing.

My words that I thought made such a difference had fallen on deaf ears. Now her total disregard for all I had said shocks and hurts me. The shadowy figure has taken her in with sugary words that I know meant nothing. As the car passes us, the red taillights glow like bloodshot eyes, mocking me. Finally, they disappear with the shadow and Sara, leaving me betrayed and lost in the November night. ▣

Photo by Dan Baldwin

Mirror Image

by Meghan Heckman

I have known her only a short while, but somehow I know she is my friend. It is not the kind of friendship I've had before—built on habit or fueled by fear and insecurity. No, this is a friendship that, although new, feels as comfortable as a pair of old, leather boots. Around her I am not afraid to be myself, but rather I am unguarded. I tell her everything, but it seems as if she already knows. She knows because it is also about her. She can truly understand what is going on inside of me—she understands my life, because she is going through it, too. Both of us are venturing away from what may be considered normal, comfortable and familiar, and are venturing toward the unknowns of adulthood and independence. But with this new staunch independence we are glad we have each other to hold onto.

It is strange for me, though, to have this new support because I am so used to going forward alone. It has always seemed that no matter how close I got to another person, they never really understood how I felt. I knew this because none of my old friends shared my interests, and none were willing to try what I enjoyed. I always ended up conforming to their needs and standards because I felt what I did was unimportant—until I met her.

When I look at her I see myself looking back. Though her eyes are a different color, they see the world as mine do. The mouth may be a different shape, but it smiles at the same things mine does. Her ears are not the same, but they still delight in the same music. Her voice differs in pitch and intonation, but says the things I cannot put into words. When my hands reach out looking for something to cling to, her hands catch mine and cling back, just as hard. She is my friend, my other self, my mirror image with a different face.

When I peer into the mirror, however, I do not see a carbon copy of myself. Her hands paint and draw, while mine write stories and essays. Her lips sing and play the harmonica, while mine just speak incessantly.

She wants to live beneath the ocean with the dolphins and orcas, but I want to spend my life among the stars in the sky. Still, together we make a solid image. It is as if with the strokes of her paintbrushes, she fills in all the holes my words leave behind. Then she sets my words to music, writing the most expressive songs.

I am apprehensive about having a friend like her, though, because a friendship like this involves opening up, exposing my heart and mind and soul. Doing this means trusting the person and with trust comes risk—risk of losing, of being rejected, of getting hurt. I know what it's like to be hurt, betrayed and abandoned by a friend. But I think she is different. Of course, I have been wrong before. I have been sure that I've found a lifelong friend, a soul mate, only to discover that my heart had huge blinders on, and the "friend" actually was a foe. No matter how much I pretend I don't care, I am afraid of getting hurt again.

Above all, I don't want to be reduced to hiding behind a vacant smile, so as not to offend anyone. I don't want to have to pretend I'm someone I'm not just to make people happy. I hate the awful, closed-in feeling I get when I can't be myself. But I am myself with her, and she seems to like it. Still, out of habit probably, I sometimes catch myself guarding my words or actions around her. I know I can't do that if I want this to be a real friendship. But what if I'm wrong? What if she doesn't feel the same way? What if she's only putting up with me so as not to hurt my feelings? I've had these doubts before and have discovered they were well-founded.

Still, this time might be different. I must have faith in that. If I want this to work, I must open up; I must lay out my heart, mind and ego, and truly believe that she won't stomp all over them. I must believe that somewhere, someone is watching me and guiding me along. This must be true, because somehow in this great big universe of ours, somewhere between her sea and my sky, we found each other. ◙

Final Curtain

by Kristi Gentile

Alone in the dark dressing room
Yet surrounded by dozens of chattering,
  porcelain-faced girls
Lingered two precious ballerinas
No more than the age of ten
Awaiting their cue to perform their act
Their blue and white costumes shimmered
  in the glossy light
And the buns in their hair pulled their soft faces
  into bright smiles
Their stomachs twisted like the knot in the
  center of a pretzel
But their feelings smoothed like the waves
  crashing gently into the sand
Because they knew they always had each other

The curtain spread open like the wings of an eagle
And the two girls slowly pranced out to the beat
  of the soothing music
The usually rock-hard wooden stage seemed
  to soften beneath their petite feet
As if they were dancing among the fluffy clouds
  of the open sky

Then as fast as a tornado clears away the earth
One of the dancers twirled right off the stage
Leaving the other stranded like a kitten on the
    highest branch of a tree
To continue the dance all alone
She'll never return to dance by my side
Yet deep in my heart I can still feel the beat
Of her delicate little-girl steps
As she spins her way along, into God's open arms

Dedicated to Julie Dawson
March 23, 1982 – January 17, 1998

Photo by Megan Galipeau

Cleaning the Closet

Fiction by Jessica Tenaglia

I am cleaning out my closet when I find a crumpled piece of green paper. I can barely make out what it says. Then I realize how long it has been since I have seen that handwriting. The note was from her:

Hi—

Where are you? Your mom says that you are at another lesson. My mother is such a freak! You won't believe what she did. Once again she mortified me in front of my friends. Be happy that you missed it. She punished me for not informing her and my father of my every move in life. This is the third time this month that I have not been able to go out on a weekend. I am sorry, but that means that we won't be able to go to the movies tomorrow. If you get around to it, give me a ring, okay? I want to discuss the mall guy. Love, Robin

P.S. Call before the beast (a.k.a. Mom) comes home from work. The phone is off-limits, too.

Now I remember: She was grounded for going out with someone her parents did not know.

"I think that I am going to go and ask that guy for his phone number. What do you think?"

"Robin, I think that you are nuts."

"I am going to do it anyway."

"What are your parents going to say?"

"Parents shmarents. How will they find out?"

So, she went right up to him and asked for his phone number, and he gave it to her! I would never do such a thing.

When Robin and I first met, we disagreed on everything. We were the two most opposite people in the world.

"No, Robin, the name of the book is not *Peace and War,* it is *War and Peace.*"

"Who cares? Does it really matter in the long run? Peace and war are practically interchangeable."

"Sure . . . just do what you want. You will anyway."

I cry when I get a B. Robin does not know what crying is.

"Why do you let a little letter ruin your life?"

"I don't know, Robin."

"Exactly."

I have never been sheltered. My parents are so liberal that they sometimes forget that their last name is not "Kennedy." Robin's parents have not been able to keep her leash short enough. I blame them for Robin's problems. If she had been able to express her feelings to them, she would not have gotten mixed up in a really bad crowd.

"Robin, what possessed you to start smoking?"

"One word: Mommy."

"What?"

"I do it just to bug her."

"You are ruining your life."

"No, she is ruining mine."

I know that she wanted to get into trouble. She loved attention from her parents—whether good or bad. I can't blame her parents now. It is time to forgive them.

And that brings up another difference between us. She is strong and stubborn, while I am forgiving. I hope that she can forgive me. It has been so long since the last time we spoke. I really should visit her. I hope she is happy.

Robin has been my best friend since kindergarten. We met on the town playground, and since then we have been kindred spirits.

"Hey, wouldn't it be fun to make a friendship pact with our blood?"

"You are so crazy, Robin. I'll do it, but let's use catsup instead."

"Sounds good to me."

We thought that by rubbing the catsup we would have a lock of friendship by blood. I think that our friendship runs deeper than blood, though.

I really should go and visit her. I'll bring my new magazine. Her mother never lets her buy them. She says they are "trashy." If it were up to her mother, Robin would be reading the encyclopedia for fun. What the "beast" does not know won't hurt her.

I begin to remember the last time we saw each other. Robin was going out with this guy she barely knew. He was such a sleaze.

"Robin, what are you doing hanging around with

him? He is just using you. Can't you see that?"

"Chris is a great guy. You are just jealous that you can't have him."

"Ha, Ha, Ha . . . you are so NOT funny. All that I'm saying is, watch your back with him."

If she had only listened. . . . No, she never listened to my advice—or anyone's, for that matter.

"I can make my own mistakes without anyone's help. It is the best way to learn."

I think that for the first time in her life she was wrong. It is time to face up to her.

I hate cleaning out my closet because I always find stuff that I should throw away but don't, and so the whole process becomes pointless. Her note lands in my pile of memorabilia. It falls next to a pair of concert tickets, folded notes we had written each other in school, birthday cards, a picture of us at an amusement park, and a playbill from a musical that she was in. It's really just a pile of junk, but to me it's all a piece of the friendship between Robin and me—a friendship that will never die.

Suddenly I forget about my closet and grab my sneakers and parka. I don't bother asking my brother for a ride because it will turn into twenty questions. Instead, I grab my bicycle and start pedaling. Sweat pours off my face, or is it tears? My face turns red and my body shakes with chills. The sun is out, but the air creates an icy barrier around my body. It is tears that wet my face. I hate myself for not coming sooner.

I stop at Smith's farm and pick up a box of Russell Stover candies. I will bring them as a peace offering. Robin loves them and can finish them in one sitting. I hold the box in my hand as I hop on the bicycle again. I am almost there now. I am so close that I can almost hear her voice singing along with the radio. I reach the lawn and start walking toward her. She is happy to see me.

Only it is not her; it is just a piece of marble. Engraved it says: *Robin—our beloved daughter and friend 1983–1999*. I dust off her tombstone, sit on the wet grass.

"Hi, Robin. I hope you like the chocolates. I picked out all of the coconut, since you are allergic to them. I still remember the day that you ate one, and practically choked to death. . . ."

My throat is so tight that I am struggling to breathe. The memories are overwhelming. My tears fog my eyes, and my head is spinning. I wonder why I came here. Remembering just hurts; it never helps.

"I found a note you left me. I remembered that I had not seen you in a while. I have not forgotten you and never will. You will always be my best friend. I would do anything for just one more day together . . . wonder what you would tell me if you were here right now."

Why do you always resort to the mushy stuff? You are such a crybaby. You are still a classy friend, though. I guess I can forgive you—since you brought the chocolates and all. Now open up that magazine and tell me what's been going on in Hollywood.

"Okay . . ." I brush away my tears. "Robin, guess who's on the cover. . . . You will not believe what he says about his new movie—you know the one I mean. The one with the girl . . ." ▣

Across the Miles

by Laura Oberg

Have you ever had a best friend move away? Someone you confided in, cared about and shared everything with? Jen and I were friends through middle school; for years we were inseparable. People referred to us as "twins" because we looked and thought alike.

One day she asked me to come over because she had something important to tell me. We decided to walk to Dairy Queen, and it was there my friend hit me with the heartbreaking news. She was leaving to start a whole new life. Her dad had been promoted and had to move. I figured they were just going to a nearby town, but when she said Texas, I began to realize just how different my life was going to be. From then until Jen left, we spent every possible moment together.

The day she walked out my door for the last time is one of the saddest I can remember. Both of us were sobbing. We embraced one last time, and then my best friend was gone. I cried that night and many others.

I heard from Jen that weekend. She hated Texas; it was nothing like home, but it *was* home, her new home. We made a pact that we would talk every Saturday at 1:00 P.M. And, every Saturday at 1:00 P.M. I hear Jen's voice. I think we've only missed our Saturday conversations five times in two years.

No one thought we could maintain our friendship. Our parents thought we'd lose touch after a couple of months, but we knew in our hearts we wouldn't. All the moments and secrets we shared were too precious to let slip away just because we were a few states apart. Our friendship hasn't changed that much. Jen is one of the only people who knows everything about me. She "knows" all my friends, even though they've never met.

People think that when a friend moves, the friendship ends; they're wrong. It's not good-bye forever.

A friendship as close as ours doesn't come along often. When you find your soul mate, you have to hold on, no matter what. We work harder each week to keep our friendship close. The best feeling in the world is knowing that I didn't lose my best friend. Jen and I will always be best friends, no matter how many miles separate us. ◙

Photo by Lara Chard

What's in a Name?

by Carrie Meathrell

I had watched you
for six small months
wondering
who you were by yourself at night
who you were when you woke up in the morning
who you would be if you were my friend

Then, one tiny Monday
for one brief half hour of hope
I was with you
you were on my left
sitting easy, smiling brazenly

I was an infant
who could not walk or speak
my legs tangled and rebelled
like defiant children
my tongue forgot all words except "cool"
my self-confidence fled
laughing at my sudden and violent unease

your initials scrawled on my shoe
flew in front of my eyes

seeming six feet tall
how could you miss them?
I tried to rearrange my anatomy
so my feet would disappear

I wondered—
where had my ego gone?
where was my quick and eager wit?
my poise?
my crash and caffeine rush
personality?
I wanted to shout to you
Here I am! Exceptional Person!
but I was silent
and you were vibrant and sparkling and loud

Then,
the sweet syllables
twisted and fumed and tasted
you finally said my name.

Taunting Todd

Fiction by Kristi Ceccarossi

Give it back!"

I desperately tried to retrieve my backpack from Todd. I've come to terms with the fact that for my entire high-school career I would never live to see a single day of peace. Every day, Todd had some novel and ridiculous action to express his annoyance with my presence.

A million fantasies rushed through my mind of different ways to hospitalize Todd. I stared up at his grin. He wasn't much bigger than I was, even though he had acquired more muscle power with all his wrestling practices.

"Fine, keep the thing."

I couldn't take much more. Perhaps if I hadn't been in such a crowded area where so many kids watched Todd drain every ounce of dignity out of me, I wouldn't have given in. No, what am I saying? That wouldn't have mattered. But I had gotten an unwarranted scolding from my English teacher, so I wasn't in the best mood.

"Hee, hee, hee." His stupid giggle indicated he was pleased. Cleverly, as always, Todd tossed my bag at me as I walked away. He had achieved his goal; I was officially intimidated.

When I was a freshman, I thought that it was natural to be tormented. I had heard enough about Judy Blume books. My theories about sophomore year had proved false. I anticipated starting a new year, free of pointless conflicts, but Todd wouldn't let up. He was a year ahead of me; I thought juniors had more important things to do.

Lately, however, Todd has been more than gracious with his teasing. Last week, I made the mistake of wearing elastic-waist shorts. I reached my fifth-period class. Spanish. Great. I spent the entire class thinking of the day when I would stand up to Todd. But I'm a wimp, the perfect target. Ahhh, I was thankful the cafeteria wasn't serving *hot* soup. Otherwise it might have been really painful when Todd decided to dump it in my lap. Luckily, I had my gym shorts in my locker. Looking down at my mismatched clothing on the bus ride home, I got more upset.

"Why don't you just fight him?" my friend Paula asked from the seat across from me.

"Paula, you know I can't. It's just . . . not my nature."

When I got off the bus that day, I knew something had to change. I was determined to come up with a plan, even if I had to resort to physical confrontation. I almost backed down—until I pulled my wet shorts out of my bag. I knew what I had to do. This was something, however, that would require careful planning and perhaps several attempts to execute.

Two days later, I entered school, ready. Todd. Oh, Todd. Oh misguided, wayward youth who hath dampened my days and left a permanent scar upon my high-school memories and self-esteem—thou shalt soon know mine own fury. I know I sounded too excited about this. Perhaps those of you who have been a victim will understand my anxiety. I had my Wheaties and a nice tall glass of juice. I came close to swallowing a raw egg yolk.

I knew that when that bell rang to file to second-period class, I would have to see Todd in the hall. I took a deep breath.

"Hee, hee, hee." A simple shove into the lockers doubled with a snicker. Okay, I reviewed my plans.

"Uh, freak, you want to . . . like . . . talk to me?" What can I say? This guy put Shakespeare to shame.

"No, not really." Ha! I prepared myself.

"Okay. Then maybe you want to, like, start something with me?" Another scholarly statement.

"Hm . . ." I was almost ready.

"All right. Now this is fun. Come on, Markie."

I looked right at him. I honestly think the intensity of my stare shocked him. I was concentrating all my strength in my right fist and thinking of nothing but slamming it into Todd's left ear.

I was standing there, silently getting a good look at my target. And that's when I did it. I started laughing hysterically. I had never realized how large Todd's ears were. I'm talking large potato chips, open car doors. Enormous. I can't believe it had never occurred to me how foolish he looked. It was great! I was dying of laughter and he was befuddled, to say the least.

"Yeah, real funny, Freak. What are you laughing at? Whatever." He motioned to his buddies that it was time to exit. I was close to tears and still laughing; partly in amusement, but mostly in relief. And then it hit me. All these months I'd withstood such merciless treatment from Todd and what was he? If he fell so easily, as I had just witnessed, there couldn't be so much difference in our characters and confidence. And I understood there must be some other, perhaps surprising, cause behind the whole concept of Todd. Maybe he just wanted to fit in. Like me. I considered this idea and almost started to feel sorry for him. As far as I know he never actually fought anyone in school. I guess he never looked too happy, either. I decided that it wasn't worth it to carry out this contest any further, as I had initially planned, seeing that I now had a chance at winning.

Wow. All that work staring at ear diagrams and all that practice making a fist. All for nothing. A simple laugh was all it took to hush the beast forever. I was afraid of someone who was just as weak. I guess we both want the same things; we just go about getting them in different ways. I feel I know him and his aim so well that I don't have to care about his threatening glances anymore. ▣

3 Challenges

Photo by Emily Evans

The Verdict

by Michelle E. Watsky

Six years ago, I stepped into a courtroom. The guilty verdict we'd all prayed for filled the room. The charge: sexual abuse of a minor. But the sentence? Two years of house arrest. The price my family paid to get this man behind bars: everything. My father lost his job and his wife. My mother's boyfriend was the assailant. What bothers me most is that all he got was two years of house arrest. Want to know something worse? I was not the only one. He had a whole street of kids. Now, tell me, does he deserve only this as his punishment? I lost my self-esteem. I don't trust guys. I still feel trapped. I'm a walking nightmare.

What deranged person would put a five-year-old girl through this? Two years of house arrest? That's the going rate for a lost soul, a child's happiness, a child's memories?

Every six minutes, a child is sexually abused. Why do parents think these children are too young to remember? They do remember. I remember. Five years old, six years old, seven, eight, nine, ten—does it matter how old? It doesn't slip a child's mind. Every day these chilling memories return, affecting school, relationships and dreams. It eats away at me. I am not good enough for my expectations. The nightmares come like a song playing in my head that I want to forget, but can't. It won't stop, like a clock that ticks and ticks and ticks, waiting to explode. What if one day the ticking stops? What happens? All of a sudden, you'll hear a sharp pain, like the screeching of a fingernail on a chalkboard. You are in a trance, and then you snap. One day you realize you have been stalking your molester for days. Staking out his house, leaving obscene messages on his answering machine. You feel alone in the world.

Many sexually abused teens—and adults—fight this constant battle. They struggle to fit in with friends. They want to be normal, but this uncontrollable force convinces them they are not. They usually end up spewing their stories to therapists. All that it can do is help you try to forgive and forget. Therapists try to make you feel "special." Why? Because some man had intimate thoughts about you?

I know the feeling of being dirty, worthless and abnormal. I would not wish these feelings on anyone. It feels like when you want to take a deep breath, but can't. The breath of fresh air will never come, just like feelings of being safe. Therapy helps you feel better about yourself. But until you can forget you were molested, you won't feel relief. I know. I have been there. If you don't tell someone, anyone, you are making your life even more miserable. You are the only one who can make it stop. Help yourself. Tell someone. ▣

Mirror Mirror

by Lia Kristyn Underwood

*"I'll never be like my mom, never do that to my kids,
family, the man I'm with. Most of all, I will never
drink."*

Broken promises.

*I had lied to myself, fooled myself. What I would
    give to rewind time.*
*I looked in the mirror at a serious reflection. After
    staring hard into these lost eyes for some time, I
    realized all I had become but felt lost. I couldn't
    find myself. I quietly whispered to the reflection
    as I glared deep into those fearful eyes,*

"Who are you?"

*I stepped closer to the mirror, enough to see the
    shades of brown in the iris of my eye.*
*Squinting, my eyebrows pointing to the top of my
    nose, I tried again,*

"Lia—This—Is—You."

I couldn't believe who I was.
I couldn't admit it.

My fright was upsetting.

"What have you become?"

I was now speaking to a stranger across from me.
A stranger.
I don't know who I am.

Or do I?

But I hate it. I hate who I am.

My eyebrows raised and I watched my tears
  gather in bloodshot eyes.
Ashamed.

The fat black tears ran down my face.

"Just like your mother," I scolded myself.

She would always let the mascara run down her
  face and would look like a crazed fool.
And then Me.
More drops poured down my puzzled, despicable,
  guilty face.

I know who I am.

The alcoholic idiot.
The repulsive liar.
The selfish . . . oh, I slipped right under without
*   even knowing. I was blind! I didn't open my eyes!*
I am her. Just like her!

Nervous anxiety invaded my stomach. This is the
*   feeling we always drank away. We drowned*
*   ourselves. We tried to escape reality. All those*
*   who need us, those who care, those who may*
*   not always be there.*

Each other.

The pain . . . Oh, the pain through my veins.

My stomach is inside-out.
My heart is shattered.
My fingers are bitten raw
craving,
*   waiting,*
for just that first sip.

Mom doesn't have nails.

I sat on the hard, cold bathroom floor.
"Remember?" I questioned myself.
All and everything you wanted to be,
*   what Mom brought to the family and me.*
I promised myself I wouldn't be like her.

*All those terrible memories of childhood I wish
    would disappear.*
I start to bite my nails.
Shaky . . .
    Craving . . .
        Nervous . . .

*I ran to the kitchen, opened the refrigerator,
    rushing through fruit and shoving the milk aside.*

*"Where is it!" I slammed the fridge shut and
    climbed on the counter. Tore open the cabinets,
    reaching far back, searching. "Please, come on,
    come on," I murmured knocking a mug off the
    shelf. Glass shattered on the hardwood floor. I
    didn't look back at it. I crawled over to the
    next cabinet shelf and unscrewed the Vodka.*

"I need this," I convinced myself.

Photo by Cerys Wilson

Control

by Gulielma L. Fager

My head starts to spin and my eyes begin to hurt as I stand up. Looking briefly at what I ate for dinner before I flush gives me a sense of control. I have been doing this for more than a year now, and I have never felt better—or worse.

I feel better because I now feel more in control of my body; like I'm deciding what food does to me, not the other way around. I know my trigger foods, and I know what I can eat without feeling guilty. There are few of these. I eat breakfast so I don't get migraines and at lunch (if I eat anything) it's a plate of tomatoes with salt and pepper or macaroni and cheese, which doesn't stay in my stomach long. Cake at dinner is a staple, as is bread and rice and whatever else I feel like eating, mixed with a lot of milk to help it come up. One of the stalls at school has a thick door that locks and a window so that during the day I can see without having to turn on the light and the fan, which would make me unable to hear someone coming in. It's harder to do it at night, but I have learned which times are easiest.

I know that there are others like me, even though we don't talk, especially about food. We are not friends. Whoever said "It takes one to know one" wasn't kidding.

You can recognize the white spots on their teeth and the redness in their eyes, and you know you're looking at your own reflection. Often these girls are the best—at school, sports, music, dance, whatever—and always appear very strong, a useful facade for keeping a secret.

Before I quit, I had told only one person, a best friend. When she asked how I stayed so skinny, I didn't want to say something obnoxious like "I can eat whatever I want and not gain an ounce." So I told her. She didn't judge me. She wasn't eating much either, so she understood.

I had a few close calls. A roommate (whose sister was like me) confronted me after noticing my body wither during swim practice, but I told her that swimming two hours a day would make anyone thin. She knew I was lying, but we left it at that. Another roommate walked in on me once, and I just told her I was sick. She didn't think twice. Once we were at Denny's and I guess I had been gone a long time because, when I got back to the table, everyone was joking about how I had been puking in the bathroom. I just laughed along.

It's hard to do it. First of all, it hurts. And you have to distance yourself from others for it to work. You can't let anyone come to the bathroom with you, which is contrary to female instinct, and you can't talk about anything serious since you don't want to slip and tell. You let a few people get close and that's it. Restaurants are easy because they have single bathrooms with doors that lock and loud fans. I used to go to a restaurant with my dad and get turkey, mashed potatoes, macaroni and cheese, cornbread and root beer and have a great time. He had no idea, mostly because I am so "strong" and so "independent." I guess that's why everyone was so shocked when I told them. My then-boyfriend freaked out, believing it was his fault, and thought it wasn't cool to have a girlfriend with a "problem."

My friends and my mother were totally shocked when I told them. My mother was half the reason I did it. She had gone to the same school, but was thinner than I was. She often reminded me, saying, "When I was your age, I was a lot thinner than you are" or "You're not skinny, you know" or "Have you put on some weight?" when I hadn't. I think she was jealous of my strength and intelligence, two qualities she did not have at my age. Maybe she tried to make me feel bad that I lacked her strong points: her physique and her social nature.

It also gives you a bad feeling when your friends are skinnier than you. You always size people up, girls more than boys, because you constantly need to know where you stand in relation to them. If they look better, you have no control over the unconscious hate that invades your consciousness.

I had to tell the school administration so I could stay home for the time I needed in order to quit. I hated them knowing and talking about me at faculty meeting as the girl with the "eating issues." I didn't like them knowing anything about me, my body or my real life. I had to go through counseling with this woman whom I grew to like. Another student was seeing her, too, since she specialized in our problem. That girl and I had a silent understanding even though we didn't speak and weren't friends.

It's funny (well, maybe not funny, exactly, but interesting) to look back at what I put myself through. I have a picture of a supermodel on my wall that says in big black marker "YOU ARE NOT MY IDOL," but that was a lie. I shouldn't want to be her or look like her, but you can't help but know that she symbolizes what I am supposed to be. This impossible standard of slenderness makes many things challenging. It's hard to concentrate on school work, hard to love, hard to let people love you, because you think all the time, *How could that person love me? I'm so fat and heinous and disgusting and stupid. How could anyone want me?*

Even though I haven't *done* it in three months, there isn't one day I don't *think* about doing it. I have come close many times, but have resisted. Sort of. I don't look at it as a success. The hardest thing to say is, "I know I'm beautiful even in this short skirt, and everyone knows it, including me."

Even now, with my incredibly wonderful, supportive boyfriend, I feel gross sometimes. He really does love me the way I am. I believe him, and he has helped me a lot. I'm moving, slowly. I work out, and I eat the best I can, treating myself to potato chips or jelly beans or nachos once in a while. It seems the less I care about what I eat, the less it can do to me. Maybe someday the fist ruling my world will be not one of iron, but one of my own. 回

Right on My Street

by Mike Friedman

Life is so fragile and death so final. These truths were demonstrated early in my childhood. My experience was pretty traumatic, and I'm sure it has affected me in ways I cannot even imagine.

I'd like to say it was a dark, gray, heavily overcast day with large rain clouds hanging low over our aging two-story suburban house. But that would be untrue and a bit too wordy. It was actually a fairly clear day, totally devoid of any meteorological foreshadowing. Mother Nature is not melodramatic.

I was out on the street, talking to some neighborhood friends. I was just about to take them to see a fort I had discovered. We were standing across from the Wilkson residence, a bright yellow house with a nicely cared-for lawn full of healthy grass. Mrs. Wilkson was placing a broken blue bicycle by the curb to be picked up by the town.

All of a sudden, a black car with red plush seats pulled up, and an old man wearing a suit got out. He had a shotgun. The old man's hair was white and sparse, barely covering his head. He got out of his car and started to shoot at Mrs. Wilkson while slowly advancing toward her across the beautiful lawn. The sound of the shotgun firing was not loud; it seemed like nothing more than a slight puff in the suddenly still air. Mrs. Wilkson screamed. She raised her hands to her head and started shaking violently. She made a mad dash for her garage while the old man sent bullets chasing after her.

My friends and I stood watching, struck dumb. Finally, one of us started running. The rest followed. I ran, but kept my eyes on the old man who was screaming and holding his shotgun. He stood on their beautiful lawn and raised the shotgun to his chest. He pulled the trigger and fell backwards with a horrible scream, the sounds filling the deathly quiet street. His scream was not manly and deep, but the high-pitched wail of a man in utter desperation.

I did not see him hit the ground. I turned my head and ran as fast as I could, putting all my energy into getting away from the old man with the shotgun.

The police came and went, taking the old man's body with them. But they could do nothing to take away the fear and awful memories that haunt us still. Fortunately, Mrs. Wilkson made it to her garage unscathed. Surprisingly little was said about the incident afterwards. And the next school day, our carpool drove right up their driveway and took the two Wilkson children to school. I looked out of the car window at their well-cared-for lawn and could see the impression in the grass where the old man had lain and the reddish-black stain of his blood clinging to the beautiful stalks of dark grass. ▣

Life of a Teen Mom

by Kerri Erskine

Motherhood is not as easy as people think. It is hard having a baby when you're young and trying to stay in school at the same time. You want to do your best and show your parents that you still can get good grades even with a baby.

I got pregnant when I was fourteen. I didn't know how to tell my parents because I was scared about what they would say, and because my boyfriend was older. I didn't want to ruin their holidays with this news, so I waited until January.

When I had Corey, he was the sweetest little baby. I was sure I wouldn't have any problems because he was too cute to be sick. Well, I was wrong. He never slept through the night and when he started getting ear infections at three months, he never slept. So I never slept since I had to take care of him. He also had eczema, a dry skin condition that needed care. Medication for his skin and his ears? That is where money became a big problem.

So, every time I brought him to the doctor, he had an ear infection. It got very expensive. Then I had to go to the dermatologist because he was a very itchy boy. That doctor gave me four prescriptions for his skin. Now you figure nine dollars a prescription, and I had to get him four a month, if not more. That is thirty-six dollars. How many people have thirty-six dollars a month for medication? It may not seem like much, but when you do not have it, it is a lot.

That is where my parents came into the picture. I lived at home with them, and they bought Corey clothes and food when I needed help. When babies are little, food doesn't cost that much. My boyfriend was not making much money, but he would buy the formula, diapers, food, juice, etc. He also had an apartment to pay for, which was not cheap, let me tell you.

I still to this day do not know how to thank my parents for how much they helped me. I love them a lot and, without them, I don't know what I would have done. I tried to get federal assistance, but I wasn't eligible.

Having a baby is not a joke. It is hard, stressful and very tiring. A lot of people want a baby because they are so cute. I didn't plan to have a baby so young, but it happened and it could happen to any girl out there.

Live your teenage years the way you want to; don't push it and grow up too fast. Think about it: Do you like to go out and have fun with your friends? With a baby, you can't. You have to stay home. It is not all fun! I do not regret having him; he is the love of my life. Also, don't think your parents will watch your baby so you can go out and have fun. They already raised their kids. They don't want to be stuck home raising your child. You had that baby, so it is your responsibility to raise him or her.

So, take it from a teen mother: wait. WAIT is all I can say. ▣

Art by Andrea Denise Starkey

The Night Is Back

by Brandy Belanger

I sit on my bed, my arms wrapped around my knees rocking back and forth, tears pouring down my face. This happened last night, yet I can remember and feel every detail because that night has been repeated so many times. The feelings are so strong that I rock back and forth faster and harder, maybe hoping that the rocking will make the tears go away.

I reach for the phone, desperately needing to hear a friend's voice tell me I'll be okay. I pick up the phone, trembling, and stop to think. There is no one to call. I throw it across the room and look for something sharp to put into my skin, then decide against it. It would hurt my mother too much.

I jump out of bed and throw myself against the wall. But it doesn't help. I am still here. My feelings are still here. It doesn't help. I throw myself onto the bed again, desperately clutching my pillow. I feel as if my body is going to burst because I am crying so hard. Too hard to stop. I start to write, but I can't see the page. I can't see the words.

I look into the mirror and see someone. Is it me? Yes, I am there. I recognize this face. It's been there too many times not to be me. I start to think about running away, but I'm not sure how I would do it. So, I decide to ask Tara in the morning since she will know and understand. Slowly the tears die down. I am too tired to hurt myself, too tired to sit up anymore.

I start falling asleep. I do. Very easily as if nothing had happened. But it has. It was real. I can feel the puffiness of my eyes. I can't breathe through my nose, and my face is tight with dried tears. It was real. I fall into a sleep. A deep sleep with too many dreams. I can't keep track of them all.

In the morning, I wake up. I wake up late, not wanting to get up. I do, and drag myself to volleyball practice where I see tired, but happy people. How could this be? Slowly, I feel parts of happiness come into me. It slowly rises and settles. It never completely takes over. There's still that lump in my body left from last night, and the many nights before.

Slowly the day continues, and I realize it would not stop just for me. Only I could stop it for me. The day goes on, and the feelings are still with me. Sometimes I feel really great and—then boom—it hits me. Sometimes so hard and strong.

Days go by. Weeks. Months. I slowly feel life come back into me. I feel my old self. All I can think is, *I'm here! I'm back again! It's me.* My counselor thinks so; everybody thinks so. I begin each day and make it through. Life isn't the best, but it's better.

Then slowly it again slips from me. Maybe I wasn't holding on tightly enough, or maybe I was just fooling myself. I can sense the same feelings as before. They are back. I try so hard to push them away with my tears. They are back. I sit on my bed with my arms wrapped around my knees, rocking back and forth. I pick up the phone, but I already know the answer. The night is back. ▣

Photo by Andrea Jalbert

Behind Bars

by Jennifer Wood

Can I have the name of the person you're here to see?"

"Ronnie Wood."

"Are you on the visitor's list?"

"Yes, I'm his sister."

"Can I see identification?"

I handed over my license.

"Go down the hill, third building on the left. The guard will take you from there. Before you go, I'll need to check your bags."

This was the first time I had visited my brother without my mother. I noticed that the grounds resembled a college campus. The grass was well kept, and the buildings had ivy growing up the sides. If there hadn't been bars on every window and a security fence around the area, I'd have felt like I was visiting my little brother at school.

The second I walked through the heavy steel doors, I felt a chill run up my spine. What am I doing here? As much as I missed my brother, I never wanted to go visit him. The place made me feel sick. The bag of fast food I had brought for him was checked before I walked through the metal detector.

"Go to the end of the corridor and ring the bell. The

guard will show you where you can see him." The door knob was very cold, the long hallway empty. Even through the thick door, I could hear the familiar sound of the guard's keys as he walked toward the door. "I'm here to see Ronnie Wood."

"Wait in here. I'll get him." So this was where Ronnie eats his meals. I was waiting in a small room, not even the size of a classroom. There were three aluminum tables fastened to the floor with stool-like seats. The metal was extremely cold. The seating chart for the lunch shifts was posted on the wall. I was sitting in my brother's seat. Next to the chart hung a list of rules:

1. *No talking in the dining area.*
2. *If there is a problem, raise your hand and wait for one of the guards to address your question.*
3. *If "group" is requested of you more than two times in one week, you will be dismissed from meal time for a week.*
4. *If you are caught trading food or stealing others' food, you will be removed from the dining area and sent back to your cell.*

Finally he came in. "Ronnie," I said, "Mommy couldn't come today; she had to work."

"What did you bring me to eat? I skipped lunch today hoping you or Mom were coming. I almost thought you weren't gonna show." His face was thin and full of scraggly facial hair and a trace of acne. His hair looked like it hadn't been washed in a month, and was past his chin. He looked like hell. I wanted to take him out of there and take care of him. The one-piece blue jumper and worn-out slippers were not Ronnie's usual attire. I couldn't stand to look at him.

"What do you do in here all day?" Read and work out were his answers. I didn't know what else to say. "Has anybody, you know, tried anything on you?" It was a legitimate question. Ronnie got that disgusted look on his face: "Not over my dead body." I prayed he was telling the truth.

A girl about my age came into the room with a woman who looked like her mother. The girl was wearing the same dirty blue jumper. Hers fit her a little differently—she was seven months pregnant. The ratio of girls to boys in the facility was about 1 to 10. What was a young, pretty girl doing in jail? What was my little brother doing in jail?

He had gotten himself in trouble with the police many times since he was twelve; he just didn't know when to keep his mouth shut or his hands to himself. He had just turned fifteen—in jail. Drinking and smoking pot didn't help his temper. After being placed in rehab instead of jail, he broke out and stole a car. "I just wanted to come home," he had said.

I wanted to hug him and tell him I loved him. But if the guards saw us getting close, they would do a full body search. I couldn't help it; I had to hug my brother.

The guard allowed Ronnie to walk to the first doorway. We passed his cell on the way. I peeked in the window. The room was no larger than your average school bathroom. There was a small cot bolted to the floor, with a mirror-like piece of metal bolted to the wall, and a sink with a toothbrush and a tube of toothpaste. No window, no fresh air. The average stay, and Ronnie's sentence, was eighteen months.

"This is where you sleep?"

"This is where I live."

The ride home was the longest hour of my life. There was no getting used to visiting my brother in jail. ▣

Photo by Doug Mahegan

No One Told

by Melody Shaw

I don't know why I was hit. I guess in the coils of time that detail of my beatings has escaped me. I was frequently "whipped," as my family called it, like something out of Huck Finn, with a broad leather belt and its silver buckle with three eagles.

Sobbing, I tried in vain to protect my backside and legs from the striking lash that retreated and returned again and again. His anger was plain as he shoved me into my room, unbuckling the thick belt with jerky motions, rage hanging about his body like a bleeding hurricane. I remember being slammed into the wall, my mind frozen with fear. I struggled, my face rammed into the cold, eggshell-white wall; my cheek pushed so that my eye was forced shut.

One arm brutally kept me from running away while the other jerked the belt back and unleashed hatred.

I screamed, crying out apologies, anything. I wanted mercy and for the blows to stop, for it to end. Pain! Pain . . . I was a terrified animal trapped in a cage.

It ended, tears tumbling down my cheeks as I leapt away from him, stumbling, retreating . . . my chest heaving, choking on tears and my own breath . . . across the room, away from danger.

Hate. Fear. Pain. Confusion.

I couldn't sleep; it hurt so much. I couldn't sit; the bruises wouldn't allow it. At school I teetered nervously, scared, in pain. No one asked. No one cared, it seemed. Wasn't it obvious? Didn't I wince?

I knew it was wrong, what my father did. I knew. But I was scared; I didn't know what to do. I didn't know how to help myself. A light flickered in my mind; I wanted to tell someone. Anyone. I wanted them to know. To pity me. To save me. To help me.

I shared my secret with friends. "Don't tell anyone," I said, hoping they would. I feared rejection and misunderstanding, but I was crying for help; I needed them to betray my trust.

"I knew you were going to say something like that!" Jenny said when I told them what was happening. Fear was on their faces. I made them swear not to tell.

No one told. How much they should have. How much I needed them to. How much more I would suffer. ▣

Three Millimeters

by Sally Schonfeld

At the end of my sophomore year, I thought I was on a perfect track for my life. I had a 4.0 grade point average, held the school record in the 800-meter run, was a two-time champion in track, had been all-conference in cross-country for two years, and was involved in just about every club and organization at school. My life revolved around my activities. But, as I defined my life by these accomplishments, I had been overlooking the obvious.

Two weeks into that summer, something three millimeters in diameter slammed me off my track into a granite wall, spit the obvious in my face, and changed my life. My mom had an unexpected brain aneurysm. Neurosurgeons presented every option, every risk of death, and looked me in the face and said, "You are lucky your mom is still alive."

I will never forget the fear I felt, the fear I saw in my dad's eyes, a doctor himself, who could no longer reassure me. It was a fear I hope I never experience again, but one that taught me more than any class, organization or race. Suddenly, I did not care about any accomplishment or even school; they seemed trivial and insignificant. I wanted my mom. For the first time in my life all I could do was pray.

In the passing of only a few hours, I finally knew what mattered. The obvious screamed at me; I needed love, hope, understanding, patience, compassion, friends, family and God. I needed these, nothing else. Mom survived her brain surgery. I am a different person; my spirit has evolved. I have matured with what seemed the effects of years, in just a few weeks. My definition of self and life has changed.

I now value my life—and everything in it—from a different perspective. Now I am catalyzed and aware of myself. I have gained compassion, patience, understanding and love for other people. The small stresses of school, athletics or friends do not receive the worry they used to. Life is something I respect.

I now know I do not need outstanding numbers, lists or feats to show people who I am. My strength comes from God and me, not a list of accomplishments. My accomplishments continue to grow, but now they are secondary to my real self-definition. ▣

My Family's Divorce

by Michael L. Wheaton

When people talk about the past, a time before I was born, they talk about how the family was one of the strongest foundations of life. When I ponder the present and the future, I see something threatening hovering over our heads, dominating the horizon. I have heard, or maybe even dreamed, of a time in the past when men and women kept their promises to each other and their loved ones. This seems almost absurd in a decade filled with divorces of spouses, children from their parents, and even parents from children.

To the families of today who have not been touched by this tragedy, this may seem distant from their paradise, as it once was to me. When I peer into my past through the one-way mirror of life, I wish I could have told that little boy before me to enjoy his life while he could.

My life became this world of despair right before the New Year. I awoke that morning to the sound of my mother's weeping. When I asked what was bothering her, her only answer was that my father had left during the night. The truth struck my heart like a dull knife twisted into my flesh. After the initial shock, all I felt was pure anger, directed at any inanimate object that I could get my hands on.

The memory of that day now seems a blur, or just simply not to have even happened. Maybe my mind has set up its own fortification against the onslaught of anger and sadness. Maybe these past few months have just been one horrible, recurring nightmare. I can only wish. . . .

My feelings were not as complicated as some might think. I felt only one emotion—anger—toward my father, my family, myself and even God. I realize now that I have forgiven everyone, including my father.

The one complicating factor in forgiving my father was how he left. As a reminder of the many years he had spent with us, he left some typed notes, saying that he had left us for basically no reason at all. He had seemed to have become irrational over the space of just a few hours and had totally lost his mind—and all the memories of our happy times. It is equally enraging when I think of his timing. He had chosen a time when our family was spread across the country. My older brother was spending a week with his own family camping in Alabama. My oldest sister was living in California with her family. The last two people in this equation were my older sister and my twin sister who were spending the week together in the city.

We decided to tell my sisters when my twin returned. The hardest part was waiting. When she discovered what had happened, she was crushed. It was heart-wrenching to watch my mother and younger sister cry together each day.

As a son and brother, I found myself very overprotective of my family. When I saw them upset, I would strike out at what troubled them; I would rather perish than see my family experience the grief we went through during those months. This was an enemy I could not reach. This painful time pushed my anger past the critical point and so we fought many times.

This also seemed to change my life in countless ways. I suddenly lost all interest in schoolwork and groped for any friends I could find. As I did, I realized that many had a similar or even worse life than I did. I suddenly lost my ability to write that I'd had since I was small, along with my dream of becoming a writer. I also lost another very important thing, my self-control. For so many years, I had worked on containing my temper. Now it seemed that I lost it whenever I felt cheated or mocked.

I have written this in memory of the life I left behind, and to help those whose life is unaffected by this tragedy.

Movies usually make such events happen gradually. My life was torn apart within the space of one night. Only now have I just begun to put it back together. 🔳

Home Sweet Home

by Jennifer Aubrey Burhart

It was December 22nd. The blustery wind swept the countless snowflakes across my front yard. My dad was shoveling the driveway. His nose was red. With every breath he took, a white puff escaped into the air. Before you could blink, it disappeared into the cold, crisp air.

Inside my mother was packing the last of the boxes. As I entered the front door, the thought that after today I would never enter that door again burned a hole in my stomach. I picked up my dog and sat cross-legged with him on my lap on the cold, wooden floor. I had no choice but to sit there; there was no furniture in my house. I sat in a daze, just thinking. In my mind, there was just no reason for my parents to make me, a once-happy twelve-year-old, move. I had two best friends right across the street. I did well in school and always kept my room clean. Plus, this was "my house." By no means did I want a couple of strangers living here. These recurring thoughts danced around in my mind. I had so many questions, but no answers.

Out the front window I could see the orange top of a truck pull in the driveway, and I knew it was the final moving van. Instantly, three men came barreling in the back door like World War III was starting. The stale smell of nicotine encircled their bodies. I coughed silently, so as not to be noticed, for my eyes started to fill with tears. I watched helplessly as the men, my mother and my dad loaded the truck. My dog even seemed to wince as he stared out the window. I wondered if he were sad, too, or if he just longed to play outside in the snow.

The slam of the truck's doors plugged my eardrums.

My mom came in and turned off the overhead light. She zipped up my jacket for me, seeing how immobile my limbs were. A totally empty feeling filled my insides.

My mom was very solemn and spoke not a word. I imagined, for my sake, she felt remorse. I was in a semi-conscious state. For the first time in my life, I wondered what "home" would be to me tomorrow. Mom then put our dog in my arms and followed me out the back door. The sound of the bolted lock triggered more tears.

I climbed in the back seat of our red station wagon, shivering. My face stung from windburn, and my salty tears didn't help. Dad climbed in with Mom and backed down the driveway. I glanced once more at our dainty white house with black trim. I swear the big pine tree my grandfather planted in front of my bedroom window long ago was waving to me, underneath its snow-covered branches. 回

4 Love

Photo by Lisa Wojcik

One Starry Night

by Lauren Ratchford

A chill filled the air that summer night, and the stars, so visible in this country town, practically vanished under the light of the bright full moon. The sound of a billion crickets broke the eerie silence that surrounded us, and, except for the occasional plane landing at the airport, the world seemed to disappear. We couldn't even see my black car veiled by the shadow of an enormous grandfather oak.

I could hear the leaves rustling in the wind as I stepped out of my car. Closing the door, I cringed, afraid that the noise would shatter this surreal world, the way an alarm clock stops a dream before you get to the end. Looking over, I noticed that he didn't seem to care about waking up. He looked as laid-back and unaffected as ever. Nothing bothered him, not a failing grade, not even a fight with a friend. I often wondered what I would have to do to force a reaction from him.

He walked around the back of the car and wrapped his arm around me. Shoving the keys into my pocket, I enfolded my arm around his waist, and we moved, together, down the hill toward the middle of the soccer field. We stood there and stared at the night sky. From some distant corner of the park, the words of a song echoed through the fields of tall grass and groves of strong trees. He knew that I would start singing along at any moment (I did it all the time, and still do), but instead of covering my mouth with his hand or hitting my arm until I shut up, he sang along with me. Out of the corner of my eye, I saw him look at me. He turned his head, leaned down, tilted my head toward his with the touch of a finger and lightly kissed me.

My eyes widened in surprise. All we had ever been was friends. People always thought we were more, but we dated others, agreeing our friendship was too important to ruin with any sort of romantic involvement. Without speaking, we walked toward the picnic table beneath the young maple trees. We laid back and stared, in silence, at the beauty of the sky. Shivering, more from thinking about what had just happened than from the cold, I rubbed my bare arms briskly with my hands.

"Are you sure you don't want this?" he asked, pointing to his flannel jacket.

I whispered, "Yes," and rested my tired head on his chest instead. Shifting my weight, I moved so that he could wrap his strong arms around my waist. As if reading my mind, he slid his hand down my arm and rested it on my hip. He traced imaginary circles on my stomach with his index finger. The rhythmic beating of his heart and the rise and fall of his chest as he breathed lulled me into a familiar trance, like when a mother holds her baby close, gently rocking him to sleep. My eyelids felt heavy as I continued to gaze at the points of light in the dark blanket of the night, and eventually I closed them, completely shutting out the rest of the world. I could feel the warmth of his hand on my side as I slipped into the world that exists only in my imagination.

I snapped out of my trance when he moved his hand, and although he now caressed my cheek and ran his fingers through my hair, I could still feel his arm around my waist. Blinking, I tried to open my eyes, but lead weights pulled my lids down. A chill ran through my spine as his lips brushed my ear and he whispered, with hesitation, "I love you, Lauren."

I didn't know what to say! My best friend was pouring out his heart, leaving himself open to the pain and embarrassment of rejection. *Why did you have to say that?* came to my mind, but I just looked into his eyes, like an actor waiting for her cue card at the back of the stage, hoping that the answer was swimming in those pools of dark blue. Without talking or thinking, I leaned over and gently kissed our friendship good-bye. ▣

Moving On

by Brian Alessandrini

One Sunday night, my entire world changed. This was the night she left me. She had been hinting all week, but it was up to me to say we were over.

As soon as we hung up, I went to my room. The window was wide open, letting in a cold breeze. I crawled to a corner of the dark room and, before I knew it, I felt tears rolling down my face.

The following weeks were just as depressing. I went from class to class, not paying attention to anything around me. All I could do was think about her and the great times we'd had together, not just as a couple, but as friends. There seemed to be no hope.

I had friends to help me through, but it seemed most of them didn't understand. "Forget about her" was all I heard. They didn't realize I wasn't only missing the love of my life, but my best friend, too.

There were a few close friends who actually responded to my situation, mostly because they had been through it, too. They gave advice when they could, but none of it really helped. This was something I had to deal with on my own. Eventually, school came to a close and summer began. I just moped around, going along with whatever was planned, participating in activities I now regret. People would say things like, "Why do you look so sad?" or "What's wrong with you?" I had no answer.

The sun still rose every day. (I was sure of that because that was usually when I fell asleep.) The days and months passed. All this gave me time to think. There finally came a time when I could say I was over her.

When I think back to this period, I guess I learned a lot from the experience. Even with the loneliness and pain, it turned out for the best in the end. I learned a lesson of love and learned it the hard way, the only way you can. ▣

Photo by Jen Roman

Empty Love

by Olivia L. Godbee

There I was, being the complete opposite of myself, but for so long the pain was so intense and my tears were like a never-ending waterfall. Then things changed. I learned to cope, at least on the outside. But inside was different. I was lonely, hurt and depressed. I was hiding it with a smile and letting it show with fits of insanity. When I met someone with similar interests, I clung to him out of loneliness.

I, the girl who speaks only her truest emotions, was speaking a lie. I was saying "I love you," and in the process, making myself a hypocrite. It always upset me how people carelessly threw around the words "I love you," making them lose meaning. I knew I didn't mean it either, but out of loneliness I tried to make myself believe that I did.

The whole time I was hiding the truth—the truth that I was in love, but not with *him*. And against all my beliefs, I never told the one whom I really loved.

It was my good friend Jerry whom I loved so deeply. I don't know what was wrong with me, but I was so afraid that telling him would make me lose him. Two months passed and I still felt alone, and I was still saying those empty "I love yous" to others, hoping I could learn to love the other *him*. The thought never crossed my mind that Jerry felt the same way.

Then one night we were sharing poems and song lyrics we had written. He flipped through my poems and randomly selected one. It just happened to be one that was obviously about him. He asked to read it, and I objected so strongly that, being the kind of person he was, he wanted to read it even more.

After twenty minutes of arguing and mauling my notebook, I gave up, thinking, *What do I have to lose?* Then he started reading, and my fears flooded over me. I left the room, unable to look at him. Later I came back, hoping I had worried for nothing. He asked me what it meant. I couldn't tell him how I felt, so I answered, "It's self-explanatory." But that wasn't enough for him.

He wanted to hear me say it. So, finally, I did. It was a bland choice of words, but it made him smile, hearing me say, "I have liked you since the moment I first sat and talked to you, and every time we've talked since, I have become more attracted to you." His response? Just a mild, "I think we can work things out."

I ended my relationships with those empty "I love yous" and became myself again with Jerry. We would sit up late on the couch, Led Zeppelin playing on the stereo, while the whole house slept. But we would not let exhaustion win until the following day. Two souls let go on those nights to explore the depths of our minds. Nothing mattered but being close and lost in conversation.

We have been together for three months now. I know that doesn't seem like much, but with him I've finally lost the loneliness, and for the first time experienced happiness. I know in my heart that we're in love and will always be together. I have never felt so wonderful, and now the "I love yous" have more meaning than a thousand words. So, with my whole heart and soul, I can now say, "I love you, Jerry." 回

Nick

by Katherine Smith

Nick is six feet, three inches tall, a handsome, muscular guy with brown hair, brown eyes and a confidence-building comment always ready on the tip of his tongue. He's the type who would go up to an eighty-year-old woman and tell her she has great legs. He sweet-talks everyone.

We met at a conference and hit it off immediately. His charm was infectious, and soon I had Nick fever. We spent the entire two days together. When I arrived at dinner, I found him standing by my chair, waiting to pull it out. That same night he took me onto the dance floor and taught me how to dance. The next day he proposed and offered his favorite ring. We pretended to be married the whole day and walked everywhere arm in arm.

Nick was the first guy I could really have fallen in love with. Every time he walked in the room I couldn't help but grin. It was insane, overpowering and fun. After a great day he walked me to my room and gave me the sweetest kiss on the cheek. The world was spinning, my heart started pounding, nothing was more important than that moment. Then he asked if he could take me to my prom. He said he'd rent a white tux, a limousine and make dinner reservations. It sounded like my fantasy prom with a handsome prince.

The next day I was in a dream world, constantly thinking about him. I hadn't said yes to his invitation, but had promised I would tell him the following week. I returned home still floating. I couldn't wait to tell my family about my new love interest and date for the prom.

Then it hit me. My bubble of love popped. Nick, my prince, is black. I knew my parents wouldn't approve, and my grandparents would have me dragged into the street and beaten. I am an upper-middle-class white girl from the suburbs whose grandfather once told her that the most disgusting thing in the world was interracial relationships. He added that never, under any circumstances, was I to date a black guy. These were the words of a man brought up in a segregated America, but they lingered. *I'm in love,* I thought. *What does it matter that he's black?*

Reality struck me right in the gut, screaming, *What will other people think?* What happens when you show up at a private school prom with a handsome black guy at your side? How *will* you tell your grandparents? How would they feel seeing photographs of their granddaughter smiling next to a black guy?

Not only did I start to question others' feelings, but my own, too. Was I feeling something I shouldn't? Was I doing something terrible? I decided that if I had doubts it must not be true love. That's the excuse I used, repeating it every time I thought of Nick, to make myself believe it. In my heart I knew it would be too hard to love him. I told him I had decided not to go to the prom and that I was really sorry. I think we both knew it was because of race. When I had to tell him, my heart sank; I hung up and cried. I was angry and frustrated for allowing others, and even parts of myself, to influence me.

I went to the prom with a perfectly nice, well-raised white man whom I forced myself to like for the purpose of justifying going. Nick and I have never gone back to the way we were at the conference. We smile and hug when we meet, but even then I wonder if my mother, standing across the room, is watching and questioning me.

I hate myself for allowing race to dictate our relationship. Race is a subtext in my life. I, like everyone else, tuck my racism away in the back of my heart where it keeps me in check. I've tried to suppress it, I've tried to ignore it, I've tried to purge myself of it by telling myself how wrong it is, but I am not immune to it. It may have stopped this princess from being with her prince, but it also taught me a valuable lesson. When you take the "race" out of "human race," you're left with humans. ▣

Pink Elephants

by Lisa V. Atkins

I: walk the halls to class.
You: walk the other way for your morning cigarette.

I: sit at my desk daydreaming of you.
You: sit on the curb dreaming of pink elephants.

I: worry about friends and test scores.
You: worry about the cops busting your party.

I: think.
You: don't, not unless you have to.

I: have secret-keepers.
You: have "goodie" suppliers.

I: ask myself, do opposites attract?
You: ask why I ask so many questions.

I: want you.
You: wonder why.

So do I . . .

A Good-Night Kiss

Fiction by Amy Scott

The bitter January wind slaps our faces a deep pink as he slowly opens the door. He walks slightly ahead of me, and I follow the footprints he leaves in the snow as we walk down the driveway.

We reach his car; he stops and turns to face me. The moonlight dances across the golden highlights in his hair, turning them into a glowing halo that brightens the black of night. His eyes are a deep green, almost brown, and catch mine. His stare burns through my skin straight to my heart. His long, thick fingers lace through mine. He puts his hands around my waist and pulls me close enough to smell his shampoo. The scent is clean, fresh, comforting.

I close my eyes, and it engulfs me, swallows me whole. His whiskers tickle my cheek as his lips lightly touch mine. My knees go soft; I have trouble breathing. I can't remember where I am or what my name is; all I can think of is him.

After a moment, he places his hand on my shoulder and reluctantly pulls himself away, telling me he has to go, but he had a wonderful time. I want to scream, *Don't go! Stay, even if it's just for a second. Don't let this moment end!* But the words fade before they reach my lips and I am silent. I smile softly as he gets in his car.

Our eyes meet in his rearview mirror, and he smiles back at me. I wave as he drives down the road. Long after he turns the corner, I'm still standing in the street, waving good-bye. ▣

Art by Vanessa Montes

A World of Gray

Fiction by Megan Blocker

Whiteness spread around her. Snow crunched under the heels of her hiking boots, the kind with leather on top and rubber soles shaped like chains underneath. Her chains were worn to minuscule ridges, and she often slipped on the icy spots.

Hugging her thin coat, she walked slowly along the riverbank. The river hadn't frozen this year; a red flag shone against the thin layer of black ice, its surface dotted with dark holes.

Pausing a moment on the bridge to look at her warped reflection, she walked on across the field-hockey fields to the vast woods. She had entered this part of the forest before to observe nature for a freshman project. The weather had been pleasant that day and the squirrels and ants plentiful. She had experienced a heightened sense of awareness that wore off after a few minutes at dinner.

She never tried to recapture that feeling; the rush of disappointment that followed its disappearance had not been pleasant. There was only one other time she had gone to the woods. With Will. That day neither of them had concentrated on the world around them; they were devoted to each another. That day had imprinted itself so distinctly in her memory that she could recall every word, every sound, every smell; but mostly she re-membered him, his laugh and smile, a shy smile that rarely showed any teeth, even to her.

But that day they had taken a different path. And today, she had purposely avoided the footbridge that led to the playground where big cannons stood guard over the river. Late last fall she and Will had sat astride those cannons and pretended to shoot them. They had spoken of war and their childhood. The skeletal red fire engine in the center of a field had offered hours of fun; and there had been competitions on the monkey bars, jump-ing from one platform to another. Later they had walked far into the woods, so far that she had been filled with the fear of getting lost. They had crossed a rickety bridge of two-by-fours that sagged with their weight, and fol-lowed the path that ran along the river until they had come to a huge fir tree. Will had tested his strength by swinging a small log against the trunk; she had proved that it was easy by doing it herself.

It all seemed so long ago, but it had been only a year since that merry romp through the forest.

Shadows crossed her eyes, and she realized she had wandered into the forest. An icy swamp lay in front of her, its plants grown over the border of the bog, frozen and melted and frozen again by the erratic New England weather. Gazing at these gray strands that had once been alive reminded her that spring was still far off. For her, winter had started a year ago and had not ended since then; the eternal grayness had not lifted even on the Fourth of July. She hadn't been able to see the fireworks through the fog that surrounded her. Even now she felt numb, cold, although the temperature hovered around 40 degrees. Her light coat could not compensate for the chill that seeped from her insides to her fingertips.

The cold had started one day a year ago, a day in mid-February, a day much colder than this. It had started like any other day: Her alarm had rung and she had run across the hall to brush her teeth. She moved quickly, nervously; she had not slept well.

She had dreamed that she had stood in a gray shack on a gray hill; everything was gray. Her friends had entered the tiny room and said hello. They had not seen each other in years. Then an old man, hunched over and wrinkled with age, came through the creaking door. There was a yoke around his neck, and two pails of water hung down from his shoulders. The water and his eyes were the only things in the room a different color than gray; they were deep blue. Will's eyes were that color; his were the only ones she knew with that deep and pure a shade of azure. "Eyes to get lost in," her mother had once said. And then her alarm rang.

She had gone to school, troubled by her dream. By lunch, though, she had almost forgotten the tossing and turning of the night before. Later that afternoon, she sat on the bench at the hockey game, gossiping with the manager when the rumors had started. Whispers had risen over the din that filled the concrete room. Faces had turned to stare at her. Will's friend Rick came in and spoke softly with the coach. The coach had come over to her and, taking her by the arm, guided her to the spot on the floor wet with melted ice where Rick stood. Something was wrong. She could feel it.

Through the buzzing of her ears, she had heard Rick's soft voice tell her that Will was dead; they weren't sure how, it had probably been an accident. An accident. Oh, God. Her fault. All her fault. She should have told some-one . . . done something. Had he seemed that depressed? He had always been distant. Jesus, no, not an accident. No. No. Suicide. The word had made her cringe.

As she strode along the bog, she said it softly to her-self. "Suicide, suicide." It had been pills. Fifty sleeping pills and assorted others. Rick had found him on the floor, curled up, eyes closed, lips smiling. Smiling.

The next days were a blur, calls from her mother and Christina at home, nights spent on the couch in her friend's room, never resting, always lying awake until total exhaustion had pushed her into a dreamless sleep. She hated dreams now, feared them. They told too much.

The small, modern church had been crowded for the memorial service. The coffin had remained open, and the mourners had filed by for one last look. She had gone right after his younger brother. She stood looking at his face for a long time; she couldn't remember exactly how long. No, he had wanted to be donated to science, not put under the ground with the worms and maggots. He hated the dark. No, don't close him in. *Oh, God, Will, why? You should have come to me. Why? I loved you. I still love you. But you deserted me. Why? What happened to best friends?*

As they closed the coffin over his angelic face, framed with blond hair, she had wanted to scream, *No! Don't shut him in! He hates the dark! He hates being alone! It's my fault, I let him feel alone.* Instead she had gulped down her words and had allowed two warm, salty tears to run down her cheeks. *See, Will, I cried for you. I never cry; you made me cry. . . .*

Deep in thought, she looked back from where she had just walked. Behind her, a bridge rose over a narrow section of the river. Ahead of her, she saw the old familiar pine. "Why?" She picked up a stick and hurled it at the thick trunk. "Why? What did I do wrong?"

Then he appeared at her side, carefully searching the forest floor for the perfect stick. He found one and tossed it at the tree. Their faces contorted with anger and effort as they threw their pieces of wood. Her legs gave out from exertion and she collapsed to the ground. He picked her up off the carpet of pine needles and held her close. She broke out in sobs that racked her body, the first time she had cried in a long time.

Nothing, he finally replied. *I promise I'll always be here for you. Just think of me, and I'll be there.* He vanished as she wiped her wet eyes.

Glancing around, she noticed that something had changed. The sky was blue, the pine trees green.

Her fog—the fog that had blocked the fireworks and colored her entire world gray—was gone. ▣

Photo by Caycie Galipeau

Angel's Field

by Richard Kuss

We would run through the golden brown fields
as if we were the only two people in the world.
Then we would stop in a place that was only ours.
You'd lie on the ground and talk about the usual
    things that girls do,
But I would try and listen and keep track of what
    you were saying
only to get lost in your voice which
was more beautiful than angels singing.

"Brad Pitt blah, blah, blah."

I would stare into your eyes and wonder
why God didn't keep an angel like you for himself.
Then out of nowhere you pressed your lips to mine
and they connected like positive to negative.
All this time the only thing I was thinking was
    I'm in heaven.
Then you would get up and I would follow.
We would walk and talk until the sky was a dark
    violet.
Then I would say "Good night"

and you would say the same only a thousand
  times better.

And during my trek home I would only think,
  I'm cuter than Brad Pitt!

Photo by Stephen Siperstein

The Perfect Moment

by Laura Marie Rovner

What is the perfect moment? Is it the feeling you got when you got an A+ on a test, or how you felt right after you helped win the big game?

At least once in our lives we have an encounter with our own moment of perfection. For me, it occurred when I least expected it . . . in school!

That night when I walked through those old gym doors, my favorite song was playing. It was "I Care 'Bout You" by Milestone. My heart and stomach sank to my black shoes. Not only was my favorite song playing, but my crush was standing right there by the front door waiting for me, as though he knew it was my favorite song— and I couldn't dance to it with anyone but him. Slowly but deliberately he walked up to me.

He grabbed my clammy hand with his cool, confident, soft one. Our grip was loose, and I noticed a small scar on his middle finger. The moment he touched my hand I got a nervous chill through my body. Having him look in my eyes, not at anyone else, melted my heart.

We stood looking at each other for a second that seemed like a century. My hand was shaking. He must have known I was nervous, because he smiled as I started to tremble. I could feel his confidence, and he could feel my nervousness. His mouth opened in slow-motion. The words, "You look absolutely gorgeous," came rolling off his tongue and hit me like a ton of bricks. Never could I have imagined him saying anything more perfect. Once I realized what he had said, I felt comfortable and calm.

Everything else became a blur, except him, and the lyrics of that song echoing in my head. The words began to have so much meaning to me. I will never forget that moment and his words. And I will never forget dancing together to that song. This was my perfect moment. Never before had I felt more special. He made me feel like a queen, and we were meant to ride off into the sunset together with him as my king. Forever. Together. 回

A Dare

Fiction by Bat-Sheva Guez

T o the casual observer, it might seem like a typical day in Mrs. Gold's third-period study hall. But to the trained eye, it is possible to see that a real-life drama is unfolding its tentative petals to the world. Of course, it all has to be done quietly under Mrs. Gold's watchful eye, for no sounds above a whisper are allowed.

It begins in a back corner, unnoticeable at first, a slight shuffle of cramped limbs, a muffled snicker. Someone laughs only to be quickly silenced. Then the whispered words begin to carry.

"Nah, he won't do it."

"Go for it. I want to see what she'd say. . . ."

Matt replies unintelligibly, except for the bravado in his voice. Then someone says too loudly, "He's afraid."

"Shh!" says the teacher disapprovingly.

"Yeah, man. Quiet down!" comes the high-pitched, nasal tone mocking the teacher. Then it is quiet again.

"I dare you," says one boy. He is not as loud as the rest. The challenge is in his eyes, along with the belief that Matt does not have the courage to go through with it. "Her," he points across the room to a girl studiously reading at her desk.

"Her?" says Matt. The others begin to nudge each other and grin. Nobody moves.

"Now," says the first boy.

"Now?" There is a touch of fear in his voice.

"Right now. Right here."

"Fine," says Matt, unflinchingly. He stands up, conscious that the entire back of the room is watching him, and makes his way over to where the girl sits bent over her book. There is an empty desk next to her, and he slides into it, his long legs stretch out in the aisle.

"Hey," he whispers, trying not to hear the sounds of laughter drifting across the rows of desks. The girl does not move; her straight brown hair shields her face as she continues to look down at her book.

"Hey," he says again, a little louder. This time she responds, reluctantly pulling herself from the story and raising her head to meet his gaze. Her eyes are a soft gray, the kind that look as though they could easily fill with tears at any injustice. He is surprised by those eyes. She blinks at him slowly as if coming back from another world and is confused at the sight of another human being.

"Hi," she says softly. It is the first time he has heard her speak. Unexpectedly, he finds himself to be shy.

"What're you reading?" She holds up the object of her attention, and he silently reads the title, moving his lips to sound out the words. "Nice," he says. "Is it good?" She doesn't reply at first. Then she nods "Yes." They are silent for a moment. He glances uncomfortably at his desk, fingering the initials carved in the top, aware that she is staring at him and suddenly curious about what she is thinking.

"So, I was wondering if you were doing anything Saturday night?" he asks, looking over very carefully.

"I'm not," she says shyly, without facing him.

"You wanna go out then?" It is quiet for a while. He finds he cannot look at her.

"Sure," she says in a whisper so the teacher won't hear. He looks up startled to find her smiling, and at that moment he feels like smiling, too.

In the back of the room, there is a silent uproar.

"Look, he's going through with it!"

"No, he's not. He's just faking it."

"Looks like he's askin' her out to me."

"Shh! See if you can hear 'em." They all strain, listening. The forced silence doesn't last long, and soon they are laughing again.

"He sure is taking a long time," says one boy.

"Shut up," the others say almost in unison.

Finally the bell rings, and they storm out, shoving each other and shouting as they force their way into the hall where they wait until Matt emerges. He is the last one out.

"D'ya do it?" asks one.

"Yeah, I did it." This sends them into a storm of raucous laughter.

"I can't believe Matt. He actually went through with it." They grin and punch him as they walk toward their next class.

"We gotta celebrate," someone says. "This Saturday night, my old man's gonna be out." This puts them into a spirited mood, picturing the weekend.

"Wait a minute," says Matt.

"What?"

"What about the girl?"

They all stop in their tracks and look at him. Then they laugh. "It's over. You won the bet. You don't have to *do* anything."

"Oh," Matt says, a little uncomfortably. Seeing the problem, the boys eye each other warily.

"You just had to ask her out, man. You don't have to go through with it."

"I knew that," Matt says, trying to understand his sudden feeling of disappointment.

"So, we'll see you Saturday night?"

". . . I can't. There's something I gotta do," Matt says, looking at the floor. The other boy shrugs.

"Whatever. It's your loss."

The drama over, the boys walk into the classroom, all except for Matt. Instead, he takes a moment to look over his shoulder and smile at the timid, gray-eyed girl standing at the far end of the hallway. ▣

Embrace

by Matt Puralewski

The tear fell down from her chin like a single drop
    of blood flowing from a thorn-pricked finger
I approached her slowly, and reached up to
    her cheek
I wiped away the tear in a single upward motion
    of one finger
As I made the initial contact with her smooth satin
    skin, she looked up at me
I placed two fingers gently under her chin and
    raised her eyes to look squarely into mine
Her chin now up, her eyes began to dry, when
    a delicate, timid smile began to appear across
    her soft lips
But just as quickly as the smile came, it was
    now gone
She placed her hands firmly upon my shoulders,
    and slowly crept nearer to my body
I embraced her, knowing her pain, and tried as
    best I could to comfort her
She was now fully in my embrace, shaking
    with confusion
She again looked up into my eyes, and an odd
    smile came to her lips

*We stared deeply into the abyss of one
    another's eyes
She leaned forward and gave a gentle kiss upon my
    rough, unshaven face
With a smile and a giggle she again leaned
    forward, her soft lips now touching mine
This kiss seemed to melt away all of our problems
    combined
The release was like a snow-covered mountain
    shedding its icy winter cloak
All was shared
All was accepted.*

5 Imagination

Photo by Kristen Bonacorso

Undying Love

Fiction by Laura Alison O'Donnell

The warmth from her smooth hand passing through his cold palm warms his heart and fuels his passion as he gently tightens his grip. Glancing down at her, he studies her porcelain complexion, watching her pink lips move as she laughs sweetly. She breaks away and runs barefoot to the sea, a spring wind leading the way. She stands at the end of the weathered dock, her chestnut curls blowing toward the water, her eyes the green of the sparkling ocean. She faces the world unafraid. He proposes. There is nothing else his heart will let him do. He has to be with her forever. Laurel. He loves her.

A wet wind splashed Charley's weathered face, startling him from his daydream. The sun was just waking the day as he stared at the cold gray ocean. His dream faded with the translucent moon, and he was disoriented in the mist he had been struggling to climb out of for the past week. It was too early to leave for work, but trying to sleep would be useless. His nightmares had become too horrible, flooding the darkest corners of his aged memory with harsh light, forcing him to remember.

He'd left the rumpled, damp sheets of the small blue bedroom in an attempt to clear his mind with the fresh, early morning air, but it was no use. Charley's nerves were shrieking, insisting he stay home and rest, but he knew he couldn't. He had only one clear thought: Beat Laurel's cancer. She had to get better. He slowly made his way down the well-worn path of grass back to the stone cottage he had shared with her for fifty years. It was time for one more day.

* * *

"I don't know, Sandy. He just doesn't seem capable anymore!" Simon nervously clasped and unclasped his hands. "He was in the wrong classroom Tuesday, and just yesterday I found him wandering down to the shore in the middle of fifth period. He obviously needs some time off."

"I hear you, Simon," Sandy sighed. "I've tried, but he won't listen. Besides, how can I let him go? He's long past retirement, but he's good at his job and loves it. He says he needs the money." The young principal of Blue Meadow High sank into a chair in her cramped office and glanced at her second-in-command.

"I'll give him until the end of the year. Charley has been like a father to me, making sure I have everything I need, even inviting me to his home," Sandy said patiently. "It's the least I can do after all he has done for this school and for me. But he has been acting strange. He must be going through a hard time. I'll keep an eye on him, all right?"

"Whatever you say, Sandy."

Sandy smiled reassuringly, not wanting to reveal that

she, too, was worried. She saw his health deteriorating, and lately he had not been himself. But the man refused to take even one day off. She pushed open a small window to let the sea air steady her. Soon her thoughts shifted to other concerns, and Charley Jones fluttered out the window, dissolving in the mist.

* * *

The stairs towered dreamlike above Charley. His body ached from the night of restless dreaming. Even after the brisk walk he couldn't pull himself out of the haze. The dreams had been too real. He painfully began the climb to the room where he had taught geometry for forty-five years. He loved his students with their eagerness for life, and they loved him, his droopy face and bushy white eyebrows. He was a good teacher, and no one had ever told him otherwise. People had tried to explain to him it was long past time to pack up and take off for Florida, but he couldn't leave. He had been in that musty building when it was new and fresh, and had grown older with each graduating class as his vibrant tan faded into age spots and wrinkles and his once-golden hair became only a memory. Besides, he knew Laurel loved it by the sea, in their cottage made home by her touch and love for anything blue. Maine was where he would always live and Blue Meadow where he would teach. *Laurel.* The thought flashed through his troubled mind.

"Mr. Jones, would you mind going over the assignment with me before school today?" Startled, Charley glanced at the brunette looking up with hopeful eyes. Big green eyes, like Laurel's. She reminded him so much of his wife. "Of course," Charley replied kindly. "Why don't you come to my room right now?" Anything for Laurel, anything.

The bell rang. As he scanned the class a wave of nausea coursed though his body. Charley slowly sank into the worn brown chair that molded to his body. He was worse than he realized. He thought he was used to the nightmares after a week. He addressed the class differently, discovering he had no energy to teach.

"All right, class, I am going to give you the period to work on any assignments you may be missing and to discuss assignment twenty-eight in pairs. Do your best and try to be quiet." He relaxed, trying to breathe the sick feeling out of his body, but with each wheeze the room filled with a disorienting fog. He fumbled for his lesson plans, but, dizzy, he allowed his body to sink back into the chair. Far off in the hazy classroom, the green-eyed girl laughed. The melody rang in his ears long after it had dissolved, and he succumbed to the memories that haunted him.

"Oh, Charley, I do love how you can make me laugh so hard." Laurel was lying across a blue blanket on a warm spring evening, her rich dark hair blowing across her face, the fading sun illuminating her green eyes. She stretched a hand to brush his face. With horror he watched her transform; she became pale and weak, old and wrinkled, white as the starched sheets she lay on, her shriveled hand reaching out for help, pleading, "Charley, I can't take the pain, please, I can't take it, help me, oh, please, help me."

"No!" whimpered Charley, tears running down his face.

"Mr. Jones? Mr. Jones, are you okay?" the girl with green eyes asked, concerned. A pain in his chest left him numb and confused. He had to get better; he had to help Laurel. Cancer, her cancer. That's what he couldn't remember. He turned in his chair and tried to get up, shaking and wheezing. He felt his heart might break.

"I'm sorry, class, I have to go home. My wife, she needs me." His voice trailed off and he blacked out.

* * *

Sandy was in a panic. Kids were hysterical and the school was in chaos. Guilt tugged at her heart.

Once the paramedics cleared out, Sandy sent all his students home, left Simon in charge and rushed to the hospital. She waited, crying and blaming herself.

The emergency room was in an uproar. "Heart failure," the doctor said unfeelingly. "He doesn't have much of a chance," he told Sandy. Nurses scrambled to hook up IVs. Charley opened his eyes.

"Laurel, Laurel, I have to help her, she needs me." His voice melted as he succumbed to endless sleep.

A nurse came into the waiting area, startling a young child. "Sandy Paige!" she barked.

"How is he? Please, tell me he's okay," Sandy asked.

"I'm sorry, Miss Paige, but Mr. Jones passed away."

Sandy sobbed, tears smearing her heavy makeup.

"It's all my fault!" Sandy declared angrily. "I should have made him retire! His wife, what will she do?" The nurse, taken aback, patted her trembling back. "You're needed in billing." Sandy followed the nurse.

"Any information you can give us would be helpful, Miss Paige," said the young woman at the desk. Sandy rummaged through her purse for the thick file on Charley Jones that Simon had handed her.

"His wife's name is Laurel. Here's his address," Sandy shakily replied. Although she had never met her, Sandy knew how much Laurel meant by the way he talked about her. "Please, call me when you get in touch with Laurel. Here's my number. If she needs any help, she can call me."

"Thank you, Miss Paige, we'll be in touch."

Later, the loud ring of the phone startled Sandy out of her deep, troubled sleep. "Hello?" she mumbled, confused by the darkness of the room.

"Sandy Paige? This is Officer Johnson of the police department. I'm afraid I have some disturbing news. Laurel Jones passed away about a week ago. We found her at home, on a hospital cot." Officer Johnson cleared his throat. "It seems Mr. Jones was in an acute state of denial, which would account for his reportedly strange behavior. Very unfortunate case, but not that uncommon." Officer Johnson quickly wished her a good night, and hung up before Sandy recovered enough to speak.

She had chills as she thought of the horror Charley must have felt, unable to accept Laurel's death. Her heart broke, and letting the warmth of her down comforter suffocate her noisy thoughts, she wept until she saw faint pink creep over the ocean. In the dawn's light, blurred through tears, she thought she saw two figures walking hand in hand near the water, but they vanished with the brightening of day. Crawling under the covers, she slept. It would be a long time before her dreams were quiet. ▣

Photo by Karen Lee

The Summer Garden

Fiction by Eliza Larson

We had the prettiest garden on our block that summer. I would wait outside my house with the hose almost every day. Not wanting to look conspicuous, I would water every plant individually and make sure it was completely saturated before moving on. I figured the longer I took to water the garden, the better chance I had to see him. He had the most gorgeous tanned skin and soft, silky blond hair. His eyes were such an intense aqua-blue, you would swear he was looking into you and reading your mind. The neighbors thought I was really interested in botany. I spent extra time pulling out weeds and planting flowers just to be outside and have a chance to be with him.

Sometimes I would watch from the guest room to see if he was coming up the lane. When I saw him, I would race downstairs and, coincidentally, decide that was the perfect time to water the garden. Sometimes he raised his hand in a gesture that resembled a wave and yelled "Hey" across the manicured lawns. My heart would start racing and, bowing my head to hide my flushed cheeks, I would whisper a "Hi." He managed to look so cool and self-assured in his chocolate- and strawberry-stained uniform from the ice-cream shop as he strutted down the sidewalk. He would walk over to my steps and sit to watch me work.

Sometimes we talked about nothing, and sometimes we talked about everything. He'd tell me about his job, and I'd tell him about my garden. He had an ease about him that made it impossible to be shy.

I spent more and more time outside. He was the only one who listened to me without judging. But I was too shy to approach him on my own. I didn't know how to walk up to him and start a conversation. So instead I made the most of the opportunities he gave me. I always tried to be witty and show my best side. He seemed to be an angel, always the good Samaritan thinking of the other person. I had never met someone so truthful and kind. And he, open and extroverted, never needed an excuse to talk. He would stop over to say "Hi," and see how I was doing.

As the summer wore on, he came over to my garden more often. I would stop working so I could give him my undivided attention. His trust grew as I watered and tended my garden. He started telling me about some of the important things in his life; how hard it was for him to stay in one spot for long.

I talked to him about the important things in my life. He was so interested, and I never felt like I was rambling. He made it easy to talk about real things like family and philosophy. But I still didn't know how to respond to his feelings. I had never had anyone confide in me before.

After a long talk, I told him I had to eat dinner. I started busying myself with the pansies by the front tree. I dug around to check for weeds, then patted the soil back with new potting soil and watered it. I turned to him, and he reached across my arm and turned off the gardening hose. "Just listen," he smiled as he stood up. "Oh, and one more thing." "What?" I asked naively. He came over and looked in my eyes. "This," he said as he kissed me. 回

Art by Jeanette René Mayer

The Stranger

Fiction by Timothy Cahill

As the frigid wind cascaded across my face in rhythmic fashion, I could not help but chide myself for leaving my hat behind in Ridgeport. The sudden snowstorms of Mount Omeko are as near to common knowledge as the fact that seat belts save lives, but are just as disregarded. Being a particular detractor of those who neglect to use the simple safety device, I felt considerably upset at my failure to foresee the potential problems without expending the minuscule amount of time and energy it would have required to take the hat. It was little consolation that no one was presently aware of my mental lapse; I've been in the trade long enough to realize that seemingly insignificant errors often lead to dire consequences.

My trade. It would not be difficult to explain in blunt terms, but I dislike the connotation it often carries. Thus, suffice it to say that I am a nomad, a wanderer; I am a man who travels in search of compensation and then departs upon finding it.

I momentarily ceased my trudging through the dense snow when I spotted the light ahead. Temporary bewilderment soon faded into understanding as my mind came into focus. The incessant snowfall had hindered my sense of distance, and I apparently had made more progress than I previously realized. I often underestimated my hiking ability.

The light signified the location of the ski lodge, which was my preliminary destination. Though I am a wanderer, there are certain places where I take refuge, and I often return to these places in time of need. The ski lodge was such a place.

I checked my bag and, finding it secure, resumed fighting through the storm. I soon arrived at the large door, which was the lodge's point of entrance. After several knocks and a few brief words with Winters, the caretaker, I was soon within its pleasantly warm confines. The interior appearance was just as it had always been: a mess hall lined with rows of tables and an extremely large and comforting fireplace. Less obvious were the several smaller rooms, which contained emergency supplies, food and bunks for unexpected visitors. As familiar as this was, however, I was somewhat surprised to find it rather occupied; besides Winters and me, three other men were present.

"Somehow I knew you'd show up," Winters remarked lightly. "I even had a reception party ready for you." His comments were greeted by nervous smiles from the three other visitors. Not surprisingly, none of them knew who I was, nor had they expected any additional company.

"Aw, c'mon," Winters continued, raising his voice a bit. "How about a nice welcome for my friend—Drake Porter! Drake, these fellows were planning to do some skiing in the blizzard—a bunch of daredevils—but then

the weather got too bad even for them. Anyway, I said
I'd put 'em up. What are you doing back around here?
Still working for those Hiking Patrols?"

"No," I answered immediately. "I was just in town for
a visit. I was heading off toward Fiereston when the
storm hit."

"Well, no matter. Always willing to help," Winters
replied. His statement was, in fact, quite true. The caretaker of the ski lodge never hesitated to give assistance
to those who came his way, as I often did. We had grown
well-acquainted from my many visits, but Winters's use
of the word "friend" may have been an exaggeration.

I hobbled over to one of the tables and tossed my bag
upon it. As I took a seat, each man from the group introduced himself.

"Glint Williams," stated the first man sternly. He was a
heavyset fellow, but his strength was apparent. I waited
for some elaboration concerning his identity, but none
was forthcoming.

"Harvey Jacobs," the second man told me, with a
friendly nod. "I'm a banker from down in Ridgeport and
the biggest Brooklyn Dodgers fan west of the Mississippi.
It's a pleasure to meet you." I smiled kindly in response
and glanced expectantly at the third visitor.

"Narb Siluk," he mumbled softly after a moment. "I
work for the Mount Omeko Ski Patrol and know every
trail on the mountain." His introduction sounded like a
tape recorder. I suspected that he used it whenever he
met someone with whom he was not familiar.

Just when it seemed as if the three men had accepted
the odd fact that they now had company, something very

unexpected occurred: There was another knock at the door.

The man who stumbled through the door was unfamiliar to all of us. He wore an old grey coat, which, in spite of its battered look, appeared quite warm. His head was covered with a woolen hat, and he carried a large hiking backpack.

The stranger situated himself at a table, and after a moment, glanced slowly around at the eyes observing him so intently.

"Hello," the stranger stated calmly. "Thank you for providing me shelter."

"No problem," Winters acknowledged. He had a seemingly endless supply of good will.

"My name is Jake Follata," the stranger continued, apparently feeling he was obliged to give an explanation. "I was tracking a criminal from Ridgeport."

At this remark, my ears perked up. "Criminal?" I inquired. "I just came from Ridgeport several hours ago, and there didn't seem to be any trouble there."

"That's odd," the stranger commented with a frown. "I suppose you must have left before the incident. The town bank was robbed by an armed man."

"My God!" remarked Harvey Jacobs. "Was anyone harmed? How much did he steal?" he asked in response to the stranger's inquiring gaze. "I work at the Ridgeport bank. I have for the past eleven years. This is my first day off, and . . ." he shook his head in amazement and disgust.

"Well," the stranger responded, "no one was injured in any way. The teller on duty was intelligent enough to comply with the robber's demands. Unfortunately, those demands included taking every bit of cash the teller had available."

"And he got away?" Jacobs asked angrily.

The stranger nodded. "He just walked out of town with the money—all twenty thousand, nine hundred and thirty-eight dollars."

"Now, how exactly do you know all this?" asked Jacobs. "I know every resident of Ridgeport, and you sure aren't one of them."

At this remark, the stranger seemed to falter slightly. "Well, you see, I've been tracking a particular criminal for the past two months since he robbed a bank in Galtersville. I have reason to suspect that this man has been involved in a series of murders and robberies, and that the incident in Ridgeport is just the latest."

"Why are you tracking him, anyway?" I asked.

"I'm a U.S. Marshal," the man replied swiftly. "I'm sorry that I have no identification to show you, but I left it in Ridgeport in my hurry to leave. I've been chasing this man so long that when I heard about the robbery in Ridgeport, I stopped by at the bank and then immediately set out to chase him. I had no idea that I was so close on his tail."

The stranger's intriguing narration had even aroused the interest of the quiet Glint Williams. "What happened next?"

"Well, I set off along what seemed to be the most ideal escape route—the Rileston Trail. Anyway, I soon came across a trail of footprints in the snow. I began following them when the blizzard hit. At that point, I stumbled along until I found this lodge."

"Hold on," I demanded. "Are you saying that you followed the tracks to this lodge? That would mean that this criminal is here."

"Actually," the stranger explained—rather awkwardly, I thought—"after the blizzard hit, I lost his tracks in the snow. I just continued with the intent of finding shelter, when I stumbled across more tracks. In the hope that they belonged to the robber, I followed those. They led me straight here."

"You must have come across my tracks," I explained. "I arrived shortly before you."

At this point, Narb Siluk glanced up. "Are you trying to say that you've traveled all the way from Ridgeport to this lodge by way of Rileston Trail in just a few short hours? That's a tough hike."

"I'm a fast hiker," the stranger explained, a nervous edge creeping into his voice. "I have no reason to lie to you. All that I want is some temporary shelter until the storm dies down, and then I will set out again in search of the criminal."

No one seemed to fully believe the stranger's story—it seemed to have more holes than a sieve. It was not, however, as if we had a choice as to whether he could stay or not. That was strictly Winters's decision, and he did not seem to mind having the suspicious "Mr. Follata" among us.

And so the day continued, and the ferocious blizzard showed no sign of relenting. The time passed with nervous discussions of topics ranging from the possible Yankees/Dodgers World Series rematch to the recent civil rights developments. All the while, we silently grew more suspicious of the mysterious stranger and the contents of his backpack.

As dusk began to fall, Glint Williams decided to call it a day. Siluk and Jacobs followed soon afterwards, and eventually even the stranger gave up his incessant hope that the blizzard would die down. Shortly before I turned in, I pulled Winters aside, out of hearing range.

"I don't trust this Follata fellow," I told him. "His story doesn't fit, and he seems fairly paranoid. I bet that he's an escaped convict, or something of the sort."

"He certainly is an odd character," Winters agreed, "but no stranger than you or me. Besides, he doesn't seem to pose much of a threat."

"What if he is an escaped convict?" I pressed. "He might decide that he doesn't want any witnesses around to report the fact that he stayed here."

Winters eyed me curiously. "You're getting a little paranoid, Drake, but if it makes you feel better, you can sleep in the supply room. That way, before Mr. Follata can sneak into your room and strangle you, he'd have to pass my room. I'm a light sleeper, so I can come heroically to your rescue." He smiled and patted me on the shoulder. "Get some sleep, Drake. It's just been a long day."

I was not fully satisfied with Winters's response, but it would have been pointless to continue arguing. As I lay in the supply room, however, my mind could not cease pondering the contents of the stranger's backpack. Finally, after what seemed like hours of sleepless wondering, I could take it no longer. Being as silent as possible, I slowly crept out of the small room. Making my way to the stranger's sleeping quarters, I recalled Winters's comments and was especially cautious as I passed his room. After what seemed an eternity, I arrived at my destination.

The stranger had been rather careless, leaving the door unclosed. I pushed it open far enough to squeeze through, flinching at the *crrrreeeeaaaak* the old, rusty hinges made.

Trying vainly to ignore the absurdity of my actions, I examined the backpack. I carefully unzipped the compartment on the left. I reached my hand inside and pulled out . . . a comb and a toothbrush. After checking to ensure that he was still asleep, I opened the large central compartment. After pushing aside several articles of clothing, I spotted an item that caused my heart to skip a beat. Fully equipped with a silencer lay a sleek black pistol. Caught up in excitement, I picked it up. By the time my eye caught sight of the movement above me, it was too late to react.

The stranger was leaning out of his bunk with one hand around my throat and the other grasping my wrist. Eventually, my grip on the pistol gave way and the stranger snatched the gun. Seconds later, I was against the wall, staring down the barrel of the pistol.

I braced for the shot which was sure to follow, but it did not come. Instead, the stranger's attention was drawn away as Winters burst into the room with a shotgun. With surprise now on my side, I brought my knee up into my assailant's stomach and grasped hold of his pistol. As Winters looked on, the stranger and I struggled for control of the weapon, until it suddenly and unexpectedly discharged and Mr. Follata fell backward onto the ground, his eyes wide and empty.

"I'll be damned," Winters muttered quietly. "What are you doing in here anyway, Drake?"

"I . . . I was checking his bag," I sputtered, out of breath. "And I found the gun. How did you know to come?"

"I told you," Winters replied evenly. "I'm a very light sleeper."

Several hours later, the storm died down, and the three skiers left the lodge. None of them ever knew of the night's events.

Winters prepared to travel to Ridgeport to contact the police department. He left me to await his return with the authorities, at which point the entire mess could be straightened out.

Being a wanderer, however, I chose to continue on my ceaseless journey. As I got ready to leave, a curious thought struck me. I went back into the room where the stranger lay dead and again walked over to his backpack. This time I opened the small compartment on the right side, and sure enough, the hat I had left in Ridgeport lay inside.

I slipped it over my head and left the ski lodge. After several miles of traveling, I became rather warm and removed the hat. I paused along the trail for a moment to open my bag and place it inside—directly beside the twenty thousand, nine hundred and thirty-eight dollars in cash. ▣

Breaking In

Fiction by Margaret Nolan

Eighteen. He was above all this. Pressed against the side of the building behind where the super always stacked the garbage, trying to ignore the rat the landlord insisted did not exist. *Pathetic,* thought Matthew ruefully as the light in his parents' room went on. From the third floor, the sound of his father's bellowing reached his ears.

"Stop your blubbering! You're giving me a headache. If the little jerk cared about you at all, he wouldn't have left. Stop it! You chased him away with your crying. I'm not gonna tell you again; knock it off."

The rat went out of focus as guilt threatened to make him sick. When Matthew looked up again, the icy moon was reflected in his room's black windows, but a bear thrashed beyond the amber shades of his parents' room. The yelling suddenly stopped, the light in the refrigerator feebly lit the kitchen and, a man once again, his father's shape obscured the bulb. Finally, the bedroom lamp was extinguished. He would give it an hour. Hey, a street rat has all night, right?

The cold November wind clawed through the holes in his black jeans and the flannel shirt felt thinner and thinner. A long, cold hour passed according to the old watchtower clock across the street. He rose stiffly, avoiding the pool leaking from the garbage, threw a can against the wall and waited. Nothing. He broke a bottle. Nothing. Kicked a garbage can. Nothing. Fifteen minutes for them to go back to sleep.

Standing on a recycling can, Matthew crossed himself for the first time in eleven years and jumped. He caught the first rung of the fire escape and pulled himself up. Climbing to the living-room window, he sacrificed his pocketknife (stolen from a guy in a street fight) and pried it open. Moving the cactus out of his way, he stepped into the apartment. He listened with a dead man's body, afraid they would hear his breath. He knew his way through the dark, like a ghost, to his prison. The closed door sent a jolt of panic through him as he remembered the squeaking hinges. His rational mind caged his panic, and he spit on the hinges, thanking Harper Lee.

The door opened silently and Matt stepped into horrors he had thought no longer existed. Ignoring the black corners of the Marilyn Manson poster his father had torn down, he opened the closet. Matthew took his army duffle and stuffed in some more flannels, a couple of sweatshirts, two pairs of pants, his shorts and socks, a jacket and some T-shirts. He took the hardcover copy of *Catcher in the Rye* his friend had swiped from a bookstore as a birthday present, the hunting knife he'd found in the street and the photo of his mother, smiling happily in her white dress, with the ragged edge where he had torn his father from the picture. As an afterthought, he grabbed the comic books he had lovingly kept and collected, in case he needed money.

As he stole from the room, his heart nearly stopped at the faint, thunderous creak of the door. Going to the window he climbed out and threw the bag into the shadow of the garbage. Then he climbed back in.

In the bathroom, hanging on the door knob, Matt found his father's pants with his wallet. Taking twenty dollars from the wallet and a comb, he sneaked into the kitchen and crawled under the sink to get the twenty-dollar bill hidden there. Finding it, he went to the liquor cabinet over the fridge and took down the two bottles of his father's scotch. One he spat in; the other he took. On the table lay a new package of bread and his favorite Oreos.

As he picked up the cookies, he noticed the Eagles CD that lay next to it. "Welcome to the Hotel California." As he stepped from the kitchen, he heard the sound (audible only to his well-trained ears) of his father's feet hitting the floor. The old, paralyzing terror burned like cyanide through his veins. His eighteen-year-old brain lurched into action as the slippers scuffed the carpet. He ran to the window, clutching the food to his chest, kicked one leg out, dropping the cookies as he shifted over the sill. Matt jumped the ten feet to the ground, not even twisting his ankle, stuffed the liquor in his bag and ran, with his father's voice reverberating in his head, through the night. ▣

Purple Wildflowers

by Lisa Schottenfeld

Every warm summer day she could
Open her eyes as the clock chimed seven
Slip on her flip-flops
Shuffle down the hall and out to the porch
Gently tiptoe down the stairs
And dash to the tiny grassy corner
Where the purple wildflowers grew
Holding her breath
In hopes that they had magically blossomed
  overnight.
And on the magical day they bloomed
She would pluck them carefully and fix
Beautiful bouquets of violet buds
For her mother.
During the day she would
Sketch the world in colored chalk on the pavement and
Watch in amazement as
The gray squirrels cracked their acorns
Climb upon her swing and pump her legs till she flew
High above the clouds like a bird and
Could feel the air growing chilly
As she reached unheard-of altitudes.
She marveled at brilliant blue feathers

Left carelessly on the soft grass by their owners and
Enjoyed collecting sparkly quartz
Worth more than diamonds to her eyes.
On rainy days she
Splashed in puddles wearing her
Sunny yellow rainboots,
Laughing at timid earthworms come out to play.
And then she would watch fiery leaves
Fall from their delicate perches
On the branches of towering maples
And reluctantly would return to school.
She turned thirteen that year.
Quickly learned to bow to the Gap entrance
    instead of the trees
Pondering pictures of anorexic models rather than
The shapes of snowflakes,
Worried about her clothes more than
What pictures the clouds were making
Giggled over handsome celebrities and
Forgot to wish on the first star at night.
And then school was out once again.
She went to bed late and woke at one every day
Gossiped on the telephone and shopped for
    useless trinkets
Frowned at the sun and turned up the
    air conditioning,
Scorned her family and
Scowled at rainy days.
That was the year she missed
The purple wildflowers
Blooming.

A Chance Meeting

Fiction by Emily Crotzer

Maribel shuffled her feet as she sauntered down First Street. One of the sidewalk cracks bore a strange resemblance to Abraham Lincoln. They were wide and deep enough so that women who wore pointed heels would get them wedged between the concrete slabs and have to wobble and pop themselves out with furious jerks. Maribel, with her saddle shoes, smirked when these women got stuck.

"Those shoes look silly anyway. Those white ladies just want to be taller than us. At least we can walk," she said to herself, her face twisted with a mix of misunderstanding and distrust.

It was that time of year when you wear a sweater around your waist. When you put it on, you're hot; when you take it off, you're cold. Maribel chose cold, so two red and pink arms wrapped themselves around her waist, hugging her hips. Her dress was pale blue and shone brightly against her brown skin. She wore multi-colored pieces of yarn in her hair, twisting them as she walked. A green piece was wrapped tightly around her finger when she tripped on the Abraham Lincoln crack, falling to the ground. When she looked at her hand, the green yarn was still wrapped around her finger with the hair it held in bloody clumps. Her head throbbed as she pulled the string off her finger and shoved it in her pocket. She watched the tufts of black hair float to the pavement and noticed bright red blood oozing from her knee as she walked. It burned like fire, but the autumn air blew a cool kiss to flush out the dirt and pain from the wound. Her leg was stiff, and her stride was slowed.

Maribel had begun to limp down the sloping sidewalk when she felt a purring, metal presence inch up to her left. Suddenly she turned and saw an aged face through a windshield, cluttered with reflections of oak trees and telephone wires. The woman was white-haired and white-skinned. Maribel stood on the sidewalk and stared at her as she got out of the car. She circled Maribel and grabbed her hand. The woman pushed Maribel's dress from her legs. She felt the woman's warm fingers on her cold flesh as they examined her injury.

"Honey, what in the world have you gotten yourself into?" said the woman as she continued to look over Maribel with a discriminating eye.

Maribel said sheepishly, "I tripped on one of the cracks and busted my knee up and yanked a piece of hair from my head," now crying from the reality of the explanation. Maribel reached in her pocket and dug around for the piece of green yarn. She found it and held it out in her blood-stained palm. The woman looked at the child's head and winced.

"Poor dear," said the woman as she gave Maribel a suffocating hug. "You can't walk home in your condition. Where do you live, child?"

Maribel wasn't supposed to tell her address to strangers

but figured this was an exception, so she said, "1642 Rigleys Mill Road."

"Oh, I live just two roads up from there. You must be the Jackson girl . . . Maribel!" said the woman in surprise. "Nice to meet you, Maribel. I'm Mrs. Johnson, Kate Johnson." Maribel nodded with a smile, then looked down; she noticed the woman's shoes. They were the highest high-heeled ones she had ever seen. She looked at the woman and asked why she wore such tall shoes.

Mrs. Johnson replied, "They make me feel young."

Maribel smiled but didn't understand; her shoes were just there to keep her feet from getting cold or wet. Mrs. Johnson helped Maribel to the car, opening the door for her. Maribel noticed the car was smoldering. The warm air reached inside her where nothing had ever touched before. The scratchy wool of her sweater pressed against her legs and made her fidgety and uncomfortable. She adjusted her dress so she could feel the smooth blue cotton instead. Although Maribel longed to gaze at the clouds through the clear windshield, she could not force her stare from the shiny upholstery.

Maribel examined the woman's face. It was fuzzy. Her features were blurred and hard to see. She had a peach complexion and slate blue eyes. Maribel was wary of such a color. She wore mauve lipstick and peach matte face powder that gave her skin a surreal, dreamy finish. She smelled of hairspray, perfume and home. The perfume was one Maribel had smelled at the department store in town. It was lilac or lily, something like that. Oddly enough, Maribel could pick out the smell of her home in this shiny Cadillac. Maribel, once again, noticed the navy blue pumps on Mrs. Johnson's feet. She asked whether she got stuck in the cracks on the sidewalk. The woman nodded, and then motioned her closer. Mrs. Johnson, with a smile, whispered, "Yes, but I still wear them. They let me look men in the eye." Maribel giggled with her, not really understanding.

"Maribel," said the woman, "are your mama and daddy home?" Maribel shook her head. The woman exclaimed that she wouldn't let Maribel go home to an empty house without being cleaned up first. She drove past Maribel's road to her own house. Maribel was secretly happy that her parents weren't home. She wanted to see the inside of a white woman's house.

When they pulled into Mrs. Johnson's driveway, an immense white fortress patiently greeted them. The woman fetched her key from beneath the flowerpot. Maribel was bombarded with an intensely familiar smell that made her warm yet frightened. She was unable to pin it down. Maribel walked after Mrs. Johnson, trying not to disturb the silk flower arrangements that cluttered her path. She breathed the house's smell. This woman's air was thick; she must never open a window. The unidentifiable smell that lingered finally came into consciousness. Stale cigars.

Maribel remembered her Uncle Toliver, who always smelled like cigars. She thought of him as she followed Mrs. Johnson into the bathroom. He always brought Maribel and her brothers strawberry stick candy. He lived an hour outside of town and visited on Sundays after church. He kept candy and cigars in his jacket pocket so his candy would taste like cigars. Uncle Toliver drove down every Sunday in his shiny red car to eat supper with Maribel's family. After dinner, he'd pile the children into his car and take them to the nickel-and-dime store to buy them jacks or jump ropes. Maribel hadn't seen him in years; he ran off with some white lady and their car was hit by a train. He died, and she got burned when their car caught fire.

Maribel was jarred from her memory when Mrs. Johnson told her to sit and close her eyes. She held Maribel's hand as she blotted the wound with a cotton ball saturated with antiseptic. Maribel winced and squeezed the woman's hand, letting out a pained yelp. Mrs. Johnson quickly tied a bandage around Maribel's knee, cleaned up her head, then gently kissed Maribel's crown. Maribel opened her eyes as the woman leaned away. She seemed frighteningly close to Maribel.

Mrs. Johnson invited Maribel to watch television while she made them lunch. Mrs. Johnson motioned to the living room, searching for the switch to turn on the soft light of the table lamps. A glow slowly entered the room and the woman flipped on the television set.

When Mrs. Johnson left, Maribel's eyes began to wander; she was far too interested in exploring to notice the television program. Her eyes stopped at a simple photograph in a fancy gold frame. Maribel squeezed her eyes tight as she rose to examine it; she couldn't believe her eyes. There on Mrs. Johnson's wall hung a picture of her Uncle Toliver. Maribel began to cry; she didn't understand why her uncle's picture hung there.

Mrs. Johnson announced, "Lunch is ready." Maribel sat at the round, mahogany table. The seat was unyielding to her sore muscles and a perfectly browned grilled-cheese sandwich sat on the daisy-patterned plate, waiting to nourish a hungry stomach. The woman bowed her head to meet Maribel's watering eyes. She asked, "Honey, why are you crying?" in a deeply concerned voice. Maribel looked at Mrs. Johnson's face.

In the brighter light of the kitchen, her mouth gaped open with the reality of understanding. Mrs. Johnson was the woman in the car when Uncle Toliver died. She was the woman her family had searched for, loved and hated all these years. She was the last one who saw her uncle alive. Maribel realized, with a whiff of thick cigar smoke, that Uncle Toliver lived on in Mrs. Johnson's thick air and the pieces of yarn that tied Maribel's braids. He still looked a woman in the eye, regardless of the height of her heels. ▣

Daddy's Here

Fiction by Nurit Yastrow

Mom was great, but she just wasn't always all
there.

"Mom . . . Mom . . . Mom?" asked Kappie,
peering at her from across the table. Mom didn't look up.
Sometimes she drifted off into one of her worlds. Kappie
didn't understand; one minute she'd be talking and Mom
would be listening, and then a few minutes later she'd be
interrupted by an innocent, "Did you say something,
dear?"

Mom used to be perfect. She could cook, clean, talk
on the phone and help with homework without missing
a beat. She would take Kappie to museums and her soccer tournaments. They watched movies together and
cheered for the good guys. They used to talk over cups
of cocoa, and never kept secrets from each other.
Sometimes, at night, they would curl up on the sofa
under Mom's big quilt and whisper until their eyes
became too heavy and they fell asleep. But it had all
changed. It was like she had been replaced by a stranger.
Kappie missed the old mom.

"Never mind," said Kappie, slumping in her chair.

"Okay," Mom said, after a second. She still didn't look up.

Kappie got up and went to her room. She fell backwards

onto her bed and lay there daydreaming. Kappie loved her room. It was the place she went when she wanted to feel little again. The walls were white but, at the top, there was a border of tiny dusty-pink rosebuds. She called her quilt "the garden." It was just like Midas's daughter's garden, overflowing with beauty. The curtains were a pair of Mom's old bedsheets, but matched perfectly. All her furniture was white, and on top of every surface stood the tiny glass animals Kappie cherished. On the end of the bed were the dolls and stuffed animals she had had for years. When Gramma and Grampa moved in, every year Grampa offered to paint it another color, and Gramma offered to make a new quilt, but each year Kappie refused. Kappie's thoughts drifted back to Mom. *Maybe she was sick.* She decided to talk to Grampa.

"You're just being silly," said Grampa. Then he pulled out a small doll. It was made of purple yarn gathered in places to make the shape of the body. The only facial features were two black buttons sewn where the eyes would be. Kappie could tell it was old. "I don't want to hear any more silly things. Whenever you want to say something silly, tell this doll," he said. "It'll make you feel better," he whispered into Kappie's ear as if there were others around who might hear.

That night, Mom was worse than usual. She sat at the table, not comprehending anything. All of a sudden, she started to shake. Her head nodded and her hands quivered. Kappie looked at Gramma who looked at Grampa. Grampa went over to Mom.

"What is it, sweetie?" he asked. Mom started to cry. Grampa held her close. "It's okay, Daddy's here."

Grampa rocked her back and forth. Then she started to wail like a baby. Kappie got very upset and started yelling at Mom. She couldn't stand seeing Mom like that.

"Mom, stop it! Stop it! You're hurting my ears! Stop it, Mom, stop it!" Gramma ran over and held her still. Grampa picked up Mom, who was still crying, carried her out to the car and drove as fast as he could. There was no time to call an ambulance. Something was seriously wrong with Mom.

Later that night, Kappie pulled the yarn doll from under her pillow. "Why did Grampa give you to me anyway? Why doesn't he just listen to me? I wasn't silly; I was right." She talked to the little yarn doll until she heard a car pull in the driveway. She crept to the kitchen, still clutching the doll. But there was only one set of footsteps. Grampa's hair was disheveled; his blue eyes were missing their usual spark. He motioned for Kappie to come sit with him. She walked slowly; her bare feet squeaked across the floor. She climbed onto his lap and hugged his shoulders. She rested her head against his.

"I'm sorry," he whispered after a long silence. "You were right. She's staying at the hospital tonight. They're not sure what's wrong."

Kappie slipped the yarn doll into Grampa's hand. "I don't want it." She got off his lap and walked out of the kitchen. Grampa studied the yarn doll. He put it in his pocket. On her way back to her room, Kappie went to Gramma's room. She could see Gramma brushing her hair.

"Grampa's home," she announced.

"I know." Gramma forced the paddle brush through her thick hair. "He gave it to your mom when she was little. The yarn doll. He was never really good at listening. He wanted her to have someone to talk to. She hated it, but she didn't want to hurt him, so she kept it." There was a single tear on Gramma's face. She had stopped brushing, and looked as if she were searching for a memory. The tear fell, and Kappie knew she had found it.

A few days later, they went to visit Mom in the hospital. The halls were nearly empty and smelled like rubbing alcohol and anesthesia. The walls of Mom's room were white, with no chips in the paint. It was a very simple room.

Kappie thought it was ironic that she went to her white room when she didn't want to act grown up, and Mom was in this white room because she needed to act more grown up. Did Mom think about it that way? Kappie wondered if she knew why she was here in this simple white room. Did she miss Kappie?

Mom was sitting in bed, daydreaming. She was wearing a white gown with a pink polka-dot pattern. Her smile grew when she saw her family.

Gramma cradled Mom in her arms. They didn't need words. Kappie could just imagine how it was when Mom was born. Gramma must have held her the same way, holding Mom's head close to her heart.

Kappie joined Gramma at Mom's side. She climbed onto the bed and started whispering to her. It didn't matter what she said; Mom wasn't paying attention. Kappie hugged her and whispered louder, but the only response was Mom's finger running around Kappie's face. Kappie kissed Mom's cheek and left her side. Then Grampa came and slowly sat down on the bed.

Out of his pocket, he pulled the tiny yarn doll. He placed it in Mom's hand. When she saw it, she started to cry. Suddenly, Grampa seized the doll and threw it into the trash.

Mom stopped crying, like a knife had cut the sound coming from her. She looked from her father to the trash and back again. Grampa leaned over, kissed the side of Mom's head and whispered into her ear, "I'm listening."

And Mom smiled. ▣

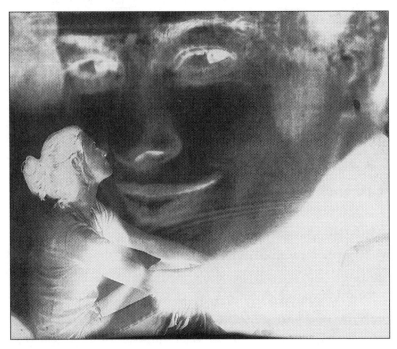

Photo by Jodi B. Heller

Railroad Blanket

by Matthew Virag

Steam-belching iron horses thundering through
   the rigid terrain in the blackness of night,
their massive amber headlights warding off
   the demons of trepidation
rushing their precious cargo of comfort and relief
speeding through the smooth valleys formed
   by my toes,
carving curves around my kneecaps,
blazing over the ripples of my rib cage,
into a terminus nestled deep inside my mind,
pistons hissing like threatened swans,
brakes screeching like knives slowly cutting
   the smoothest of glass,
engines puffing steam and forming fireworks,
illuminating the jet-black sky.

Unaware of these events,
I feel
Relaxation,
as if my flesh is melting into my doughy mattress,
Tranquillity,
like a shallow lake situated deep in a dark forest,

And Inspiration
as I pull my soft
Railroad Blanket
up to my weary chin.

Photo by Gretchen Loye

Face Paint

Fiction by Katherine S. Assef

My older sister, Andrea, had a habit of throwing up. In the car, on the school bus or on any amusement-park ride, her face turned glow-bug yellow and her eyes closed as if praying for mercy. Her throat jumped like a pinball out of its chamber, and her cheeks bulged. Then she'd spew all over.

This presented a problem for me, since I was usually the one sitting next to her. On car trips, I made puppets out of barf bags while Andrea put hers to use. We learned to drive with the windows open and kept a supply of paper towels in the back seat.

On the school bus, though, with no parents to object, I refused to sit next to her. I liked sitting in the back, with the popular girls. I admired how their slender bodies flew off the seats every time we rode over a pothole. The boys chucked wads of paper at our heads while we pouted and applied lip-gloss from shimmering tubes. Andrea had a special seat reserved for her in the front.

But when we got off at our stop, I forgot to be ashamed of her. We shared a room and I slept on the top bunk because even that height made her queasy (not to mention the ill effects of gravity if Andrea had taken the top bunk). At night, we would lie awake and choreograph flashlight dances on the walls. During the day, we explored together, searching for sunken pirate ships in the man-made lake and dinosaur bones in the sandbox.

For me, these games were not so much child's play as a glimpse into adult life. While we dug around the water pipe our plastic shovels had uncovered, I swore to Andrea I would become a paleontologist. Then at the close of a long day playing dress-up, I changed my ambition to modeling. But Andrea would always frown and say she didn't want to think about growing up.

Even though she was fourteen and I eleven, she seemed younger than I somehow. Maybe it was the way she dressed—she still wore sweaters with kittens on them—or that she often cried. I remember her sobbing for days after we saw kids throwing birds' eggs at the side of a house.

One summer, when the carnival came to town, our cousin Millie and I coaxed Andrea into taking us on the ferris wheel. She was the only one who met the height requirement, so without her we couldn't go. She tried every possible excuse to duck out.

"Let's get our faces painted again," she pleaded, looking up at a cart teetering at the top of the ferris wheel. Little green and purple light bulbs flickered on the metal spokes, calling us to enter their world.

"There's no room left on your face," I reminded her. Every time we got in line for another ride, Andrea would "take a walk" just for a second and get her face painted. Conveniently, she never came back until Millie and I were safely off the ride. She had a unicorn on her left cheek, a heart and a giraffe on her right, and an off-center teddy bear on her forehead.

"Are you guys hungry? I'm starving," she'd exclaimed as she licked her lips in an unconvincing, almost farcical manner.

"We'll buy you some cotton candy after the ride," I said, pulling her toward the line. "Or a Sno-cone or a hot dog or some mini-donuts. Whatever you want."

I knew all she really wanted was to run and hide, but I took advantage of her insecurity.

"Don't spoil this for us," I whined. "If you don't ride, we can't."

She finally agreed, and soon we found ourselves at the front of the line, stepping off the concrete into a cramped swinging cart with plastic seats. Millie and I sat on one side and Andrea on the other.

When the cart began to rise, Andrea reached to buckle her seat belt, but there wasn't any.

"No seat belts," she groaned.

Millie, who was a year younger than I and extremely hyper, began rocking the cart just inches off the ground as if it were a hammock. Andrea paled and wrapped her gangly arms around her stomach.

"You're going to be okay," I told her. "Just close your eyes."

We had a gorgeous view of town, with the houses stacked like building blocks and the cars gliding easily along the highway. But I looked at my sister turning green and knew it wouldn't be so gorgeous if you were leaning over the side, sick.

When our cart reached the top, it stopped. Millie quit

rocking, but the cart kept teetering back and forth. Andrea, with her eyes closed, appeared well on her way to throwing up. Her brown hair was held back with a thick teal headband, and the worry lines on her forehead made the painted teddy bear look deformed.

A droplet of rain fell on my nose, and, at the same moment, the door swung open. I heard the springs creak as if it was going to fall off.

"Oh no, oh no, oh no!" Millie screamed. The two of us huddled against the other side of the cart. It was tilted so that we were sliding toward the open door. I looked down, but the view of thirty seconds ago had changed drastically. The houses had tumbled on their sides and the cars seemed to be veering off the roads. Like them, we would capsize and fall, our arms and legs still flapping in an attempt to fly, like wheels still spinning after a wreck.

"Somebody shut the door!" Millie yelled, staring at me. Our legs were sticking to the plastic seat, and I could feel Millie quivering next to me.

"You shut it!" I protested.

"You're older!"

"So?"

"So, shut the door!"

"No!"

"Don't argue," Andrea interrupted us, her voice raw, as if she couldn't swallow. We grew quiet, like a married couple caught fighting in front of their child. "I'll shut the door."

Millie and I remained silent, our hair dampened by the rain. Neither of us had expected Andrea to be so brave.

I knew that she not only had a weak stomach, but she also had no sense of balance. Although her long, thin legs might have been a dancer's, there was something gawky about the rest of her. She always seemed to be standing at a slant, leaning toward something just past her nose.

She rose slowly from her seat. I wanted to make her sit down and tell her I would close the door. But as she bit the insides of her cheeks to keep from crying, I could only murmur the prayer "Our Father," although I couldn't even remember all the words.

"Hallowed be Thy name . . ."

She let herself slide toward the open door, then grabbed onto the railing. She looked up at the darkening sky, brown hair blowing into her mouth.

"Deliver us from evil . . ." I prattled on, thinking of all the reasons God might have to send me to Hell. I remembered what I'd said to Andrea—"Don't spoil this for us. If you don't ride, we can't."

She reached out, the eyes of the kitten on her sweater glowing. She grabbed the rim of the door. It was rusty and splotched with white bird droppings.

"And lead us into everlasting life."

She put her free hand over my mouth before I could get to the "Amen."

"We're going to be okay," she said. "Just hold still." *Hold still, hold still, hold still,* I chanted the new mantra in my head. Millie and I squeezed hands as Andrea pulled the door toward her, curling her feet to grip the floor. But the cart began moving again, and her feet slid toward the door.

"Andrea!" I screamed.

Just as her feet reached the edge, she slammed the door shut, and we heard the reassuring click of the latch. The air around us softened and we began breathing through our mouths again. But Andrea's teal headband had blown away, and she stood craning over the edge of the cart, watching the wingless bluebird plummet to the ground.

None of us spoke for the rest of the ride. Our cart moved three or four more times around the wheel. It was raining harder now, and we could hear each drop against the metal spokes. I watched Andrea's yellow, red, brown, white and blue face paint smear away. ◫

Photo by Tess Morton

6 School Days

Photo by Megan Galipeau

Okay, I'm Up

by Talin Aprahamian

6:40. Okay, I'm up
I'll get up. I'm coming—here I come!
No, I'll sleep. Uh!
I have to get up. Zzzz . . .
Uh oh, maybe I should
have gone to bed earlier—
Bed? Sleep?—wait, huh?
SLEEP? Is this some kind of new concept?
Do I have time to sleep anymore?

Arrgh! I'M UP!
Toothbrush? Need some clothes maybe . . .
(That would be good)
Keys. Got the keys? Yes.
No. Where did I put them?
Oh, breakfast. I need food—
THE BODY NEEDS FOOD!
Okay. Jacket? Oh, yeah
It is about ten degrees outside, isn't it?
Thanks, Mom—love you, bye

Oh, school, oh . . . Oh! I have
a math test today! I hope

I remember all I studied
last night. Last night
Batteries in the pencil?
Did I sharpen my calculator?
What's that? Solve for WHAT?!
Did we learn that?
Oh, oh, brain freeze
Where's my . . . did I . . .
Huh? Oh hola . . . yea, yea . . . bien
(I suppose)
Quiz? What? Tomorrow? Oh no
Not another project—no, I can't
Not again. Please not again.
Hey—did something change
about the Civil War
since the last time I learned it?
Ah, yes, and isn't college
right around the corner?
I hear you loud and clear—
Yes, it has been made known
to me that my grades are
very important.

No, I can't. Yeah, I'd like to
go home and take a nap, too.
I have track. Till when?
Oh, eternity.
No. This Saturday I have
a meet. A big one.
Sorry. Tonight I have
a piano lesson.

Yeah, but remember that three-
page paper we have to write?
IN SPANISH
So? everyone leaves things
till the last minute sometimes.
Or all the time
That's my style.
My style.
It's my style.

Dinner? Shower? Oh, God—
Homework? The phone—
What? Who's on the phone?
No—I can't figure out the
physics homework either. But
I'll give it another try.
Oh, yeah? I know—vocabulary
test on just 240 words?
Sure, no sweat (whatever!)
What makes this year so much
harder than last year?
Can I do it?
Will this stress ever go away?
I'm trying to do it all.
I want to make everyone happy.
Happy?
Or do I want to hide
in my bed? Hide from school,
But life?
No. I want to be happy. I'M UP!
I want to be happy

even if it is 11:30
As I finish my homework
and put my head to my pillow.
I can do it! I want to do it!
I want to be happy ...
Zzzzz . . . I want to be happy,
successful, I want to please
Everyone ...
I will make everyone happy
Because I want to be happy
. . . zzzzz . . .

Photo by Amy Annino

Prom Night

by Erica Doughty

I would be lying if I said I haven't day-dreamed about my prom since I learned what glamour was. Honestly, ever since I was old enough to appreciate princess dresses, sparkling jewels and passionate romance, the prom seemed a mystical and royal event. In fact, I have been mulling potential hairstyles, makeup, slippers and gowns for twelve long years. My prom fantasies have evolved dramatically during the time I spent anticipating the magical night. When I was very young, only a pink gown studded with diamonds would suffice. Arriving in a horse-drawn carriage with Donnie Wahlberg (of New Kids on the Block) on my arm, I'd make a grand entrance and immediately be crowned Queen among cheering and confetti. But, by the time the PA at school started blaring announcements about the prom, I was willing to settle for a clearance-rack dress, costume jewelry, a rusty Honda and my boyfriend, Josh. It's both a relief and a tragedy how we lose our childish idealism.

After a decade of plotting, I had failed to work some possible liabilities into my Prom Equation for Perfection, including big feet, the body of a hippo, absolutely no money and a long-distance relationship. That's why three hours before I was going to be picked up for the Big Night, I found myself sprawled on my bedroom floor, sobbing like my heart was breaking. My long-lost idealism had decided to make a surprise visit in a flood of nostalgia. Every time I lifted my head, I was forced to see my cheap dress and hideous, spray-painted sandals. The world might as well just have come to an end.

There was an irritating knock at my bedroom door, and I peeked out hoping to see my Fairy Godmother or at least Josh. I couldn't have been more wrong; my mother, who possesses the sensitivity of a sunning rattlesnake, stood with her hands planted on her hips. I was too hysterical to recall our exchange. (That's a lie—I remember it verbatim. I'm just too embarrassed to repeat what we screeched at each other.) Strong words were exchanged, and I ended up slamming the door in her enraged face.

A few minutes later she reappeared to apologize, and I managed to explain my plight between choked sobs. Trying to make peace, she offered to try her hand at my hair. Since I was ready to shave my skull clean of my blonde rat's nest, I threw my shoulders back and cried, "Sure! Why not?"

I often complain about my mother, so I'm going to take this opportunity to say that even though the woman can't cook a decent pork chop to save her soul, she can really do hair. While I was waiting for her to wind my impossibly fine tresses around hot rollers, I nervously picked up the package of false eyelashes I had bought on a whim the day before. It's amazing how our latent talents show themselves in desperate situations. Within seconds I was viewing the world through thick black lashes.

My hair was finally done. Mom clipped it high on my head, and cascading blonde curls brushed my shoulders. I took one glance in the mirror to admire my 'do and lush lashes, and burst into tears again. I looked ridiculous.

But it was too late to do anything about it. My friend, Tracey (my chauffeur), had arrived wearing silver slippers, a lavender princess dress and a wrist corsage. I glared at her hatefully. With a smirk and wave for Super Mom, we were off to the prom.

There was a huge line of couples waiting outside the ritzy club. My friends stood together in a tight herd trying to make the best of our pathetic, dateless states. Then there was a ruckus and my friend Steve burst through the crowd coming toward me. A few days before, he had informed me he was going to be my date. I had laughed, thinking he was kidding. I acquire most of my male friends by being loud and obnoxious in class; basically, they like me because we feed off each other. So when Steve scrambled through the masses with a corsage, I was beyond shocked.

A few words about my history with Steve: In seventh grade Mom, The Dark Queen of Domesticity, poured sour milk into an innocent bowl of oatmeal one morning. Unknowingly, I shoveled it into my mouth and hurried off to school. Soon my gastrointestinal system had a few irate comments about my choice of breakfast and decided upon an immediate and complete evacuation of the foul Quaker Oats. Steve happened to be present, and later complimented me on my ability to puke soundlessly. Not everyone who witnessed this atrocity handled it so compassionately. Thereafter, certain people would announce my approach by clutching their stomachs and emitting an enthusiastic cry of "BAAAARFF!"

"Stable" is not a word I'd use to describe Steve. He has severe mood swings, and unfortunately happened to be on an extreme high the night of the prom. He couldn't stop squirming, and he was talking as if he were auctioning off livestock. I was exceptionally tolerant, though, and when he grabbed my arm and dragged me around the room for the sixth time, I obliged. Just for kicks we decided to take random pictures of people we didn't know. By the time dinner was served I'd worked up quite an appetite crying, mingling and ordering the "in-crowd" kids to "strike a pose." We stuffed ourselves and waited with excitement for the partying to begin.

Eventually the buffet was cleared and the music started. Soon half my class was out there grinding and writhing, and my date also felt inclined to take me out for a spin. Wearing dress shoes and standing on an anthill, Steve is five feet, three inches. Barefoot, I am five feet, nine inches of Amazon warrior woman. Facing each other, he is eye level with my cleavage. But did I let this ruin my night? Of course not! So in a group of my closest friends, I jived away. As we got more confident in our dancing ability, I realized Steve was getting wild, very wild, and waving his arms as if trying to fend off a swarm of killer bees. During one song, he even attempted an Irish jig, and the class jerk sauntered over to tell Steve not to hurt himself.

Where was I? Weaving through the huge mass of squirming bodies to escape my date, who kept grabbing my wrist and pulling me back. A popular song came on and Steve whooped, jumping excitedly. I edged away, but he allowed me no respite. He leaped high in the air, and his patent leather shoes came down hard on my vulnerable, naked toes. As I reached down to make sure they weren't bleeding, the delicate white rose on my wrist corsage plopped to the ground and was instantly crushed. My face crumpled, but Steve picked it up, tore it apart and showered me with rose petals. My friends were also getting trampled by Steve and began dancing away from us.

Soon we had a four-foot clearance in every direction. With this added space, Steve started trying out new dance moves. Meanwhile, a group of chaperones had assembled in our corner to gawk. "Shoveling" consists of gripping an imaginary shovel and attempting to dig a hole in the dance floor while galloping from side to side. When Steve started "shoveling," my health teacher bent over, screamed with laughter and started pointing us out to other teachers. Soon they were all snickering. I prayed for an early death. And then . . . a miracle. The song changed to "Lady in Red."

With a sigh of relief I ran off the dance floor, but heard him scream, "No! This is Brook's song! We have to—for Brook!" Brook is our mutual best friend who moved to Texas last year, whom we both miss terribly. Only for her would I submit myself to further humiliation. With a sappy grin, Steve went to put his arms around me gently until I grabbed his wrists and insisted we just hold hands. I didn't think the night could get worse until he started to serenade me at the top of his lungs, changing the lyrics to "Lady in Blue" to describe my prom attire.

Because he could not see over my shoulder, he kept pushing me into other couples.

Combined with the fact that he was also ruining their romantic moments with his bellowing, we were getting looks that could kill (which would have been fine with me). At one point he started to lay his head on my chest. With an angry gasp I pushed him away. Glaring hatefully into his glazed eyes, I growled, "Forget it!"

Soon the deejay flipped on the strobe lights and played techno music. I was sweating, and now the lights were flickering, the music pounding. I felt like I was stuck in a psychedelic blender and started having a panic attack. I stumbled out of the room and begged some teachers to let me go outside for air. Frowning, they agreed with the stipulation that I remain in their sight.

The fresh air didn't help, and I continued to become increasingly disoriented and dizzy. Almost in tears, I asked my friends if anyone was leaving early. Luckily, one of my friends jumped at the chance and dropped me off at home twenty minutes later.

I was home—and safe at last.

Today is Senior Skip Day, and I took it off hoping that people might forget what happened if they don't see me for awhile. But I swear one thing: Someday I will have my princess dress, carriage, silver slippers, diamonds and fabulously handsome date! Even if I am just an eccentric old woman by the time I am able to afford it . . . I will have my fantasy! I will have my Perfect Prom! ▣

Senior Year

by Mindy Bruce

I could not have imagined a few years ago being the person I am today. Looking back, I remember how I would look up to people my age. The seniors were so cool. They were the ones who had it all together. I couldn't wait until I was a senior to be just like them. It didn't seem real that I could ever be like that. In my eyes, I saw them as perfect. Everything just fell into place for them. They had the car, they played the perfect game, and they were graduating. It wasn't one particular graduating class; it was every year's seniors. I watched the classes ahead of me take their turn. Each year I came one step closer, never really believing I would ever get there.

Now that I am a senior, it still does not seem real. It doesn't feel at all as I thought it would. The truth is that the seniors are really no different from the rest of the students. We are all still stressing about grades, and realizing that the car comes with a price and playing sports is only for the few who are good enough. Mom and Dad are still sticking to the curfew idea, and we feel as lost in the world as we did a few years ago. The idea of leaving our cozy home and going to a strange college doesn't seem as exciting as it used to. It now seems like a scary dream. It is something I want, yet fear.

I am in shock. My body feels numb. I am left wondering when I will reach this dream life. I can't help but question what the seniors ten years ago were really like. Did they have it as together as I thought? Were they as perfect as I pictured? Or did I admire people who were actually no different from me? I wonder if younger kids look up to us, the seniors, as I used to?

Am I going to live my whole life waiting to reach a point, imagining my life will be perfect when I get there, and then have reality kick in? I know one thing for sure: Growing up is scary. I used to think seniors didn't get scared, but the fact is they do. I am more scared now than I have ever been. I am scared I will no longer have someone there to catch me when I fall, or tell me it is just the wind. I can't just pretend to be grown up. I will be. ◙

Photo by Jessica Shaw

Mr. Svensen

by Meredith J. Hermance

Freshman year we feared him. Sophomore year we began to realize that our fright was more like respect. By junior year, we had come to the conclusion that he might actually be more than just another authority figure. But senior year, when we finally realized how important he was to us, he was gone.

He was a teacher, a coach, a role model and a friend. He was someone we looked up to and admired. He gave us encouragement and support and always believed in us, even when we had given up on ourselves. He was always there when we needed him, except for the one time when it meant the most. He was Mr. Paul Svensen, our field-hockey coach and history teacher, and on December 7, he passed away.

I will never forget the way my head felt on that chilling winter day. I remember sitting in my first-period history class waiting for the teacher. But when he walked in, I suddenly wished that I wasn't there to hear what he was about to tell us. It was obvious that something was wrong. His face was flushed, and his eyes were red; he looked as if he had just been shot. Time stood still as he uttered those unforgettable words, "Mr. Svensen is no longer with us. He suffered a heart attack last night and . . ." I didn't even listen to the rest of his speech. All I could hear was the phrase: *Mr. Svensen is dead, Mr. Svensen is dead,* running through my mind. I was in complete shock. This could not be happening. My field-hockey coach for three years, a man I admired, was gone. It was impossible to comprehend.

I ran out of the classroom to find my teammates, and luckily I didn't have far to go. Two of my co-captains were standing at my locker, crying. I had promised myself that I would keep my composure, but this was too much. My emotions overwhelmed me, and tears rolled from my eyes and splattered onto the cold, hard floor. The three of us hugged and tried to console each other, but it was no use. How were we to deal with such an immense and unexpected tragedy?

It has been more than ten months since Mr. Svensen left us, but the pain remains. He meant so much to all of us. He was an inspiration to everyone. He made you want to work hard and try your best, even if you doubted yourself. He was the first one to congratulate you on a job well done or to point out what you could improve. He made people want to give 110 percent all the time. He was a great motivator, a wonderful person and always knew how to get the best possible effort from everyone.

One of my fondest memories happened during my sophomore year. It was my first year as a member of the varsity field-hockey team, and we had just won our first game. While we were stretching at the beginning of practice, Mr. Svensen walked over to me. He said calmly and confidently, "If you continue to play like that, you'll be a league all-star someday."

My goal this year is to fulfill my coach's vision. He always had faith in me, and I intend to live up to his expectations. I know that I may not be the most skilled player on the field, but mentally, I am prepared to contend with anyone. The belief that Mr. Svensen instilled in me pushes me to do my best. I am inspired by his memory, and I want to prove that I am capable of all that he imagined. Each day as I walk onto the field, I remember him and think, *This one's for you, Mr. Svensen. I'll show everyone that you were right to believe in me.* And I know that wherever he is, he can hear me and is smiling. ◙

Art by Ana Raba-Mickelson

The Race

by Justin Toohey

The dotted chalk line extended into darkness like a lonely highway at night. I stood with my cross-country team in the starting box, dreading what was to come. The rain had stopped just long enough for us to stretch out, and the sun had actually peeked from behind the thick clouds, but more clouds were rolling in from the west.

All I could think was, *This is going to be a terrible race! Why didn't I just stay home?* Every year the race against the Academy was a joke. Some upperclassmen hadn't even bothered to show up. But I was a freshman. In the box to our left, the Academy team seemed unaffected by the foul weather. They knew they would lose even with a tailwind and a three-minute head start.

"Runners, thirty seconds!" shouted the balding starter with a limp.

Thirty seconds. I was already at the front of my box; there was no turning back now. I wished there was. *No,* I corrected myself. *That's not a good attitude. You have three miles ahead of you!* Coach had warned us never to underestimate any team or give less than our best. "Don't think of this as an easy win—earn it," he'd said. "If you get cocky, that's when they'll bite you from behind."

"Ten seconds!" the starter called.

I did a final stretch and moved into position.

"Runners, on your mark!"

I knelt to the cold, wet grass.

"Set!"

My muscles tensed, ready to propel me over the five kilometers. Out of the corner of my eye I saw the small man raise the pistol.

I was off. I dodged and maneuvered my way toward the front, hurdling puddles of water and avoiding flying elbows. The first mile went by in an instant. I heard my name yelled from the sideline and realized it was my coach. The runners on my heels kicked up debris that zipped past my face as I spun quickly around a red flag. *Those guys were right,* I thought. *This is gonna be a piece of cake.* There was only one boy in front of me, and he was from the Academy.

I followed his green sneakers under a set of bleachers that bore only two dedicated parents. *Wow, Green Shoes, you're pretty fast,* I thought. *What are you doing running for the Academy?* While one part of my brain cursed him for making me work hard on a day like this, another thanked him for the challenge. We swerved around baseball diamonds and soccer nets while the gap between us shrank. Somehow I had forgotten there were runners behind me as well.

I groaned as I slammed to the ground and the next runner landed across me. I wriggled free of the body that had tripped me. I felt, rather than saw, Green Shoes running ahead without me. *Wait!* I wanted to say. *Time out!* Instead I lay there like a slug. A sharp, searing pain tore at my thigh, sending waves of agony to my brain. I knew almost immediately I had been spiked. The boy who had tripped me stepped on me as he got up. He hadn't meant to, but it felt like I had been wounded in the Battle of Gettysburg. All I wanted to do was lie there in the brown water.

"Get up!" I heard. It was my coach, running up to me. "C'mon, get up!" He wasn't allowed to touch me during a race; he stood six feet away, mentally picking me up by my bootstraps. "It's just a scratch!" he encouraged. "Now, go get 'em! Let's go, son!" Then I said something that made Coach furious. "Don't you ever say 'I can't' again!" he roared. "Now you get up!" His words injected new life into me, and I sprang to my feet, all the pain vanishing.

Only a few seconds had passed, and Green Shoes wasn't as far ahead as I thought. I made up my mind to catch him. Energy powered my legs as I sped past the kid who had tripped me (keeping my distance this time) and accelerated toward Green Shoes. The flapping of his ponytail counted my steps like a metronome. For a moment Green Shoes dipped out of view over the crest of a small hill, but when I ran over it a second later I was suddenly upon him.

I felt droplets of his sweat as I pulled alongside him. I could hear the heavy rhythm of his breathing, and I knew he could hear me, too. We ran past the three-mile mark, side by side.

"Two hundred yards, Justin. Kick it from here. This is a sprint!" Coach's voice seemed distant. I had to do it. I couldn't let my coach down.

There were one hundred yards left when we emerged from the trees. Green Shoes and I seemed to share telepathy now. Both of us knew that in another few moments one would emerge the winner of the battle. *Fall back,* I willed him. *Just fall back!* Most people do at this point. He didn't. *I am going to win this,* I knew he was thinking. *No, you're not,* I thought back.

Sixty yards. Green Shoes and I ran at our mutual limits, rounding the last yellow flag and sprinting the home stretch. My muscles turned red-hot and begged me to stop. I refused. I had to beat those green feet. I just had to.

Forty yards. We were now openly swinging elbows at one another, and we were lucky not to have been disqualified. Could they call it a tie? Probably not. I had to win.

Twenty yards. Green Shoes and I entered the column of screaming parents that led to the finish line, but I couldn't hear them anymore.

Ten yards. I was moving forward in leaping bounds now, desperately reaching out with my mind to pull me in faster. The wind against my face made my cheeks flap uncontrollably and my eyes squint in the excruciating pain that accompanied every step.

Five yards. Green Shoes was a blur in my consciousness, and I floated forward without any thought.

Four yards. The world around me turned gray like the static on a TV screen.

Three yards. My lungs ached and my legs burned from oxygen debt.

Two yards.

One yard. I barely felt myself slip into the chute with Green Shoes clinging to my back.

I had done it! I walked down the tunnel to the recorder; the same bald man with the limp. "Eastern, one; the Academy, two," he said. I was too exhausted to be thrilled, though I thought I should be. As the clouds overhead drifted eastward, I spun to face my adversary. It was the first time I had seen Green Shoes' face, and there was sadness in his blue eyes.

We looked at each other, gasping for breath and unable to speak, and shared a mutual respect. I extended a hand, and he shook it with his sweaty palm.

"Good job," I choked out.

"You, too," said a hoarse voice. He was not ashamed. He had given his best, just as I had. I left Green Shoes, and my thoughts reverted to my coach. The realization hit me: Were it not for Coach, I might still be lying in the puddle where I had fallen. If I'd waited even one more second, I could not have caught Green Shoes. I owed it all to Coach. I didn't even hear someone walk up behind me through the mud. "Hey, bud," I recognized my coach's voice. He loomed over me, beaming as if I were his own son, and said calmly, "I knew you could do it." That was all that needed to be said. □

Obituary

by Kathleen McCarney

I don't know you
but there you lay
in black and white
a paragraph
of your sixteen years

they forget about the time
your gum got caught in your hair
and you cut off
your only golden curls

or that time you flooded the laundry room
and missed your softball game
cleaning up the mess

but wait
that was me
and this is you

a tiny, printed section
on my page
next to an ad for America Online
"You can talk to anyone, anywhere"

but you can't
I can't
and that's what happened

had you planned it out?
like I had
what happened to you?
did you crash your mommy's car?
did you crack your porcelain smile?
did you get a C in science?
did you try to talk?
But were silenced
or worse
ignored?

you could have been like me
or me like you

sisters
in a cruel situation
fighters
in that high-school hypocrisy
but I blinked
and never saw you in the halls
eyes never met
paths never crossed
life's little joke
on you
no more
than an ink stain
on my paper

The Great Goddess of Sleep

by Devin Foxall

ince the dawn of time, mornings at America's high schools have been plagued by an evil presence—a presence so horrid and widespread that it threatens to ruin the minds of students quicker than listening to bad music. A presence which, unless contained, threatens to dismantle America's schools in a thick, gray haze.

Fortunately, I have come up with a plan to do away with this devious force—a plan so simple, it makes the act of chewing gum seem complex. Let's bring nap time to high school.

Ah, yes . . . the wonderful, carefree days of kindergarten, so restful, so peaceful. From these orange-painted walls comes our savior, riding on the frothy wake of warm apple juice. In all its glorious splendor, the great goddess of sleep will come drifting down the halls, a feather pillow in one hand and a rubber mat in the other. With a silent, motherly kiss, all tired students will soon be resting peacefully in their designated homerooms.

Today, students are bogged down with overflowing amounts of stress. The days are crammed with various duties, obligations and responsibilities. Having nap time will give each student one hour in the day to put all this aside and succumb to the gentle stickiness of a rubber mat. Nap time will also help boost student performance. Everyone knows that a well-rested student performs better than a tired one.

With lack of sleep, a student's brain capacity begins to drop faster than the stock market. And without the occasional visit to lullaby land, students' incoherent ramblings begin to make rap music seem intelligent. Is this the school we want? Of course not. Who knows, students might discover great bursts of creativity in their dreamy hour. Often the answer to a problem or dilemma will be revealed in a dream. As my friend and great philosopher, T.R. Wetrieb, once said, "It is upon the sleeping hour that one will receive divine intervention in the form of clarity and a newfound spirit."

Nap time would also serve as a way of raising money for our under-funded schools. Many scientific research companies pay people to allow them to monitor their sleep. Some pay as much as $50,000 a month. If a high school had 700 of their students participate in a nine-month nap time experiment, they would raise over $315 million—enough to buy every member of the math team a new protractor.

In my dream, I see a school where students don't look like they've just chased three tranquilizers with a quart of warm milk, a school where the students don't stumble around like my cousin on New Year's Eve. When the windows of sleep are cleansed, the students will see things as they truly are: infinite. 回

One of the Guys

by Cara Tibbits

I have always loved football. I started playing in third grade on a flag football team. There were several girls on each team, so it was not unusual. I continued to play through the sixth grade, but by then, only three girls were playing. The next year, I coached a third- and fourth-grade team. Then, at the end of seventh grade, they announced a meeting for kids interested in playing football the following year. Since I had really missed playing, I decided I would go.

Before the meeting I was extremely nervous and a little scared about what everyone would say, or how they'd react to my playing football. After school, I walked down the hall to the meeting. When I looked in the window, I saw over sixty guys. My stomach dropped; I was so nervous and intimidated that I felt like being sick. I opened the door, looked around and sat down. I tried to ignore the snickers. I could hear them saying how stupid I was to think I could play. I wanted to crawl under the desk, but it would have been too humiliating to walk out. I didn't want them to think they could make me give up something I loved.

Somehow I got through that and the next few weeks of rude comments and laughs from guys who thought I shouldn't play. As the first day of practice approached, I started getting really nervous. I didn't want to be there because I felt so uncomfortable, but by now it was too late to turn back. I did love the game, so I figured I should make the best of it. The more practices we had, the more comfortable I felt. My coach was great. He gave me a fair chance, and after a while, the guys got used to me playing. The ones who didn't want me there realized they couldn't make me quit. I still felt a little awkward being the only girl.

When we got into the season, the other teams were shocked to find a girl out there with them. Some wouldn't hit me; others thought they could teach me a lesson, so they'd hit me harder. Once they found I could hit just as hard, they gave up and played. By the middle of the season, I was having a lot of fun. My feelings of intimidation were gone, and I liked playing with my team.

At the end of the season in a game against a private boys' school, I went to tackle this kid and one of his teammates hit me to try to stop the tackle. He landed on my knee and brought me down with him. Although my knee didn't hurt as I lay there, once I got up, it wobbled and the tears started to roll down my cheeks. My coach and the referees didn't realize how badly I was hurt, so play continued. I did the best I could from a kneeling position. Then it was over. A few people helped me off the field.

Once we got home, my mom took me to the hospital where they took X rays, and put me in a brace and crutches. I had torn ligaments. My football career was over. The local newspaper wrote a story about me being the only girl in the town's history to play tackle football.

I loved playing football, and I love the game. My coach, parents and teammates were all terrific. It was a great experience, and I'll always be glad I did it. ▣

Contemplation

by Beth Anne Nadeau

The classroom is cold
Good thing I brought a sweater, *I think*
as I take notes frantically
because bad grades won't
get me to college
get me a job
get me a life.
I picture my pencil smoking
from all the overwork,
the way it would if I were
on some sitcom.
I picture what it will be like
to hear the 2:15 bell ring and
know that I am free
for the time being, anyway.
I picture you at college,
great big campus,
little tiny dorm room.
My teacher talks of homeostasis
enough to fill a notebook to the brim
with notes, but
my pencil stops moving.
I miss you, boy,

more than I expected I would.
Each day I pray that you
will call or write, and
when I do hear your voice
or see your familiar handwriting
I am again alive
the way I was before you left.
I never thought I'd be so lost,
not knowing what to do with myself,
who to call at night,
who to make weekend plans with.
I miss your shy eyes and
constant blush
the way someone misses shelter
when caught in a storm.
The classroom is colder now and
I pull my sweater tightly around me.
My lab partner is looking at me,
touching my arm, trying to
understand
but I know she can't feel what
I feel.
The one she loves
sits with her every day
at lunch.
The one she loves
loves her back.

The New Teacher

by Jen Beachley

My junior year in history was meant to be a joke. I found myself, an honors student, in a normal-level class due to a missed signature. As I entered the classroom that first day, I observed my new classmates. They were proud to get D's; you know the ones I'm talking about. I took my seat and began to dread the course. Then the new teacher walked in.

He was twenty-seven years old. I could tell he was new by how he eyed the class and nervously sorted the papers on his desk. I heard he was working on his master's thesis. I imagined a room full of wild teenagers, never getting anything done, and this helpless young man frantically trying to make them pay attention. As an added incentive for my cynical viewpoint, I hated history with a passion. I saw it as boring with stale facts about famous dead people. Then my new teacher spoke.

Benjamin Adams introduced himself while closing the classroom door, and then he took a seat on his desk. Literally, on his desk. For a teacher to sit on anything other than a chair was different. He said he wanted to tell us about himself so we'd be familiar with each other. He declared that his goal was to be a teacher, but also to be our friend. He wanted to make the classroom a place where everyone felt equally respected, with everyone treated as young adults.

So, Mr. Adams told us about how he became a teacher. After high school and chasing his dream to become a rock legend—and failing—he joined the military and became a sergeant, ranger school graduate, and trained to be an airborne ranger. He still skydives. After receiving a history degree, he decided he'd have a bigger impact by teaching students about the country they live in. That was why he became a teacher.

This impressed the class. Here was a man who listened to the same music, liked the same hobbies, and chased his dreams. He was younger than most teachers, and was willing to admit the mistakes he had made in life.

Soon the learning began, and we took notes. I had never seen a teacher more passionate. He paced around the room, excitedly waving his arms and recalling the hidden tales of our heroes of yesteryear. He would come alive as he spoke about his love for the United States and how great this country was. His enthusiasm was contagious, and it inspired me to do extra assignments just to learn history in my spare time! Even slacker students who hated school were excited and shouted answers to his questions. They were actually taking pride in their work, and suddenly these students were getting good grades on tests. I was amazed.

He never gave up on those students who weren't the quick learners, and would willingly repeat information in different ways to help them understand. The man never quit, even when the rest of us were all confused. His class felt effortless, and his teaching was exciting, stimulating and caused everyone to have a newfound national pride. His class inspired me to take Advanced Placement American History, which I hadn't planned to do.

Mr. Adams isn't just the most amazing teacher I have ever known, but a true giver as well. Not only is he finishing his master's thesis, but in his spare time he is a coach for the varsity volleyball team, as well as the head coach of the junior varsity team. (By the way, both teams went undefeated and won state titles in his first year of coaching.)

He may not be the oldest teacher, or the most experienced, but to me he was the most inspirational teacher I have ever had. ▣

Photo by Erica J. Hodgkinson

Who I Am

by Kristy R. Davis

October 27, 6:45 A.M.:

I knock my buzzing alarm clock onto the floor, and I wearily roll out of bed. Wow, what a night! I was up until 2:00 writing an English paper, and there's no way I am going to be able to make it through calculus (a.k.a. Boring 101). But have no fear, thanks to Dolly the sheep and her friends, human cloning is possible. I haul myself over to my Closet o' Clones (only $99.95 at Clones 'R' Us, the only place for clone shopping) and contemplate which Me to choose for the day. I rule out No. 5, the laid-back, nonchalant slacker. I use No. 5 on those rare occasions when I don't have any responsibilities and when I need a time-out from life. But because I have a Biology II test on cellular respiration during seventh period, No. 5 will stay in the closet today.

How about No. 4? The fourth Me is the ambitious extrovert who loves to lead. "Lead, follow, or get out of the way" is the motto of No. 4. She recently attended a seminar for young leaders, and she's still in drill sergeant motif. She'll maintain order in the closet today. Do you think that I'd actually send her out for the public to see? Down to three choices, and catching a basketball with my face really hurt the chances for No. 3. I need to save No. 3 anyway. The District Championship is tomorrow, and my team is counting on me. Okay, so now I have a 50 percent chance of being the right Me for today. I can go for the Personality clone, or the Diligent Student clone. No. 2, Miss Personality, is sensitive to those around her. She often takes it upon herself to be responsible when others aren't, and she cares about everything. Whether it's a friend who's whining after her latest boyfriend's rejection, or just Sis asking for advice, No. 2 is there. She sacrifices her time, her feelings, herself, for those she loves.

Still, thinking about that biology test, I choose No. 1, and send her off to school like a kid vacationing at Disney World. So far, No. 1 is doing okay. She sits on the edge of her seat diligently copying calculus notes about derivatives. The only bad part of the class is that she actually enjoys it. She types and revises my English paper in the computer lab during the social break between classes (what a social life). And like any good student, she hands it to Mr. Newton before the bell sounds.

Now Kristy No. 1 is intensely reading the U.S. History book in the library. So she doesn't see the young girl approaching her table. "Hello, Kristy," Jackie yells in her slurred speech. No. 1 slowly lifts her head, and looks at Jackie indifferently. Jackie's eyes lose their shine.

Time Out, Substitution!

No. 2, Miss Personality, replaces No. 1, the Diligent Student. As soon as No. 1 disappears from the library, time ticks again. "So, Jackie, have you stolen anyone's shoes lately?" No. 2 asks. And Jackie's sweet, angel-like

grin reappears—Jackie was born developmentally chal-
lenged. I met her when I was a counselor at basketball
camp. Although Jackie realizes she will never be able to
play sports, she appreciates the opportunities we give to
her to learn. I was Jackie's favorite counselor. I didn't
have the chance to pick a pet—Jackie chose me first.
During the week, wherever I went, Jackie followed. She
was always into mischief. She once hid my shoes. And I
can't let a clone handle her.

I realize that I can never live my life with the help of
clones. Sometimes I have to be more than one Me. I can't
just call a time-out and hope that the world waits for me.
I am a Diligent Student. I am Miss Personality. I am a Jock.
I am a Leader. And sometimes I need to take a break. I am
all of those clones in one. That's who I am. 回

Fitting In

Photo by Patrick Michael Baird

Still Me Inside

by Mai Goda

I need a change!"

And so on that single whim, I cut my long black hair, streaked it bright red and, to top it off, pierced my eyebrow. I had gone from dorky to punky in a week, and as trivial as it seems, this transformation has had a great effect on my life.

As long as I can remember, I had always been a good girl. In school, I got decent grades and never was in trouble. At home, I tried not to give my parents too much grief. But more than that, I had the "look" of a good girl. People always saw me as a quiet, studious, Asian girl. Friends' parents often asked if I played the violin or the piano. "No, the flute," I'd say, and they would nod, not surprised. Walking around with my long black hair over my face, I hid behind my image. I felt somewhat obliged to appease the stereotype imposed on me.

Needless to say, heads turned the day I walked into school sporting a new, short, bright red hairdo. I enjoyed the reaction and attention I received from my friends and teachers. I didn't listen to my friends' warnings about people seeing me differently, people who frowned on a "rebellious punkster." After all, I was still the same person inside, so why should this change matter? I soon found out how naive I was.

One day, I was late for school and needed a pass from my vice principal. I was met by a surprisingly stern look. Writing one, his voice and stare were cold and condescending. Mistaking me for one of those punk delinquents, he left me with a warning: "Don't make a habit of it." Had I come late to school a week before, he would have said nothing. I was not used to this discriminating treatment, and I felt angry, embarrassed and somewhat defeated. Now when I went to the mall, suspicious eyes followed me—store clerks keeping a cautious watch—but the worst was yet to come.

It was the night of our music recital for advanced students. For weeks I had prepared my piece and was excited. The room was packed with parents waiting to hear their children. But as soon as I walked into the room, all attention was focused on my head. As I sat waiting my turn, I felt the critical eyes of parents.

I performed well, but felt awful. Afterwards, I still saw those disapproving looks as they walked out with their children. I even overheard a friend being lectured on how she shouldn't color her hair or pierce her face, and not to become "a punk like Mai." I was ready to go home feeling angry when my friend's father stopped me.

"You were very good tonight. At first I didn't recognize you," he said, looking at my head.

"Oh, yes, I look very different from last time, don't I?"

"Well, you played even better than last year. Look forward to hearing you again."

I went home feeling good, as if I had finally won a battle. Now the stern look of the vice principal, the suspicious stares of the store clerks and the disapproving eyes of my friends' mothers didn't bother me. I was still the same person inside, punky or not. There was nothing wrong with me; it was the judgmental people who had the problem. I regained my confidence.

I still get looks and stares, but they don't upset me. In a way, I traded in one stereotype for another, but this time I enjoy proving them wrong. People are surprised to see me getting good grades and applying to good colleges. They're surprised to hear me play the flute so well. And they are absolutely shocked to see me standing in front of the football field, red hair shining in the sun, conducting the marching band!

As for my red hair, I re-dye it occasionally to keep it bright burning red. It seems to give me the power to fight against the stereotypes forced on me, and gives me the confidence that I never had before. ▣

I Don't Understand

by Jessica A. Melillo

I thrust open the main door and pushed my way through the congested hallway. We had just come from an assembly about Black History Month. As I popped open my locker I heard a voice behind me say, "You know you ain't nothin' but a n _ _ _ _ _ lover." I whirled around to utter a string of profanities. A familiar face greeted me. At the sight of this longtime "friend," I froze and swallowed my ready slur. The offender simply laughed in my face and walked away.

Dizziness and nausea overwhelmed me. I slammed my locker shut and ran to the bathroom to splash water on my face. All through my next class I kept replaying the incident in my mind. This supposed friend since first grade no longer spoke to me, unless making derogatory statements. I just didn't understand why people placed so much value on the color of skin.

Exiting the room as the bell rang, I spotted my boyfriend leaning against my locker. I walked over to him and found myself welcomed in his strong embrace. We engaged in a short conversation and then parted to make the next class on time. He had restored my confidence and rebuilt my security with his caring words.

Then another tidal wave of prejudice crashed and washed away my security. "Once you go black, you don't go back. He'll probably pull another O.J.," sneered a boy I had never seen before.

My best friend walked by and told me not to forget the party tomorrow night. I wouldn't forget—how could I? Everybody was going as couples. But my boyfriend wasn't allowed in the house because his skin had more pigment than mine. I yelled back that I had other plans with my boyfriend.

My mother raised me to believe that all people are equal. For fifteen years I had never directly experienced racism. I knew it existed, but I never knew what it felt like until I started going out with a black male. I've been in this relationship for a year and have never been happier.

Some people say it's only our parents' generation who disapproves of interracial dating. They say it's only their parents who won't allow me in their house. But as I walk through the halls in my school and hear racial slurs, I know they're wrong. I don't understand prejudice, and I never will. My encounters with racism have left me wondering if America will ever be truly the United States. ▣

Temptation

by Eileen Carlos

People look at me as "a good kid." I get along well with my parents (sometimes), and do better than most in school. I don't drink, smoke or do drugs. But no one knows that I've been close to trying all three.

Things at home aren't as good as they seem. I fight with my parents almost every night. They complain about everything I do, or don't do, while my little brother sits back and runs the entire house. I've seriously thought about running away many times.

School demands much of me, too. Sometimes I think I just can't handle it anymore. That's when I start to think about having a smoke, getting wasted or high.

Smoking isn't as bad as the others. But for someone like me with asthma, it could lead to serious lung problems. Besides, once you start, you don't stop, right?

My friends drink and do a little pot, so it wouldn't be hard to have a beer and smoke some weed. It's that easy access that scares me. I worry about my friends a lot. I worry that some day they'll just get too drunk, or too stoned, and it will be too late. I've tried to tell them that they're hurting themselves—that I care about them and don't want to see them hurt. But they don't listen. They don't know that their lives are too good to be doing that stuff. But, at the same time, I can see what drives them toward it.

The temptation is there. I've felt it many times, and I've seen my friends give in to it. I don't know what to do about them—it hurts me to see the kids I grew up with slowly killing themselves. For me the temptation is strong, but I've managed to rise above it, and I know I'm not alone. All of you out there who also feel the temptation, don't give in, no matter how bad things get. I know that alcohol and drugs may seem like they'll make everything better—but they'll only make things a lot worse. Now all I have to do is take my own advice. ◙

Photo by Marissa Meerbach

My Brown-Eyed Girl

by Emily Kate Peloquin

It was years ago, really, when the event occurred. It was a junior-high bus-stop argument. The circumstances seem trivial now. It could have been anything—a dirty look, a slightly broken heart, a bruised ego.

I had met three of my friends at a playground in the afternoon. We had been released early from school, and we were celebrating our holiday with Pepsi and Twinkies. At thirteen we knew all too well that we were the coolest seventh-graders in our school, possibly the world.

It was then that the trouble started. A group of ten eighth-graders approached our territory. Normally this would not have been terribly upsetting, but at first sight, I knew I was done for. At the center of this posse was a boy with whom I had long been engaged in a verbal conflict. The week before, we had a loud and upsetting argument in the school hallway. He was winning and making me out to be a fool. In that moment of desperation I threw my ethical and moral values out the window and called him the most insulting name I could think of. I felt awful about it. I knew I had let down my closest friends and made myself into an appalling hypocrite. I even considered apologizing, but I was far too frightened even to speak to him after my ghastly slip of the tongue. I knew that my enemy was coming to the playground this afternoon in order to make me pay for my mistake.

The riotous crowd approached, making slanderous remarks about me. The boy whom I had scorned came out of the crowd to yell and cuss directly to my face. One of his group, a girl, emerged from the mob and pushed me to the ground. From my position on the muddy lawn I could see her imposing figure. She was the tallest, heaviest, most frightening girl I had ever laid eyes on. She had the highest hair and the most hateful, glaring eyes. I thought for sure that I would die at her hands. She walked slowly toward me, stepped over me to a dry patch of grass, and then sat down next to me, staring into my eyes the whole time. Once she was seated, she did not touch me, nor did she speak. She simply looked into my soul.

I stared back in awe, and for those few moments I could see all the horrors of the world. Emanating from her dark brown irises was the hatred and sorrow acquired in a lifetime of being an African-American girl. In the intensity of her glare I could see the pain and death of millions—the Crusades, the Spanish Inquisition. I was trapped in visions of trails of tears, holocausts, and hundreds of years of discontent and submission. She sat there, her unspoken rage upon me.

The girl then stood up, still silent. She reached out her hand to me. There was no emotion in her gesture, no pity or understanding. She simply offered her hand. I took it, and she hoisted me back onto my feet. I began to cry. I knew I was safe; I had not been beaten, and yet I was completely devastated. I had seen all the evils within me. I felt psychologically crushed.

My friends gathered around me. As my rivals dispersed, we gathered our belongings and started home. As we walked, my friends talked about how wonderful it had been. They thought I had stared her down. They saw her as the one who was frightened. I knew that they were only trying to make me feel better and so I just laughed. I could see that they did not understand. That girl had destroyed me. With just her eyes, she had torn me apart. In doing so, she had laid a foundation for an entirely new person—someone who would now have strength, integrity, understanding, compassion—a bigger person than I had been. I never learned her name, but there are times when I think back to her and the peaceful war that she waged . . . my brown-eyed girl. ▣

One Boy's World

by Kathryn D'Angelo

There he sits
enveloped in a world of his own
created by the precious authors
of the fiction he so happily reads.
The girls across the library
haughtily snicker and giggle
as they tear apart every inch of him.
He hears, he knows.
The librarian ashamedly stares and sighs.
She hears the comments of her own daughter,
she knows.
The football jocks laugh wildly
while they cruelly degrade
the country he calls home.
The small, quiet girl
standing by book stacks angrily frowns at her ex.
She hears, she knows.

All the while he sits tranquilly.
He's no longer in the library,
he's gratefully on a perilous journey
through treacherous foreign lands
fighting off evil lurking around every corner
just waiting to pounce.
In these battles it's different
from his everyday life.
In these battles, he wins.

Photo by Marwan Kazimi

Color Lines

by Barry Floyd

My mother always told me not to judge a whole group based on the actions of a few. My understanding of my mother's words was put to the test one night.

My friend Thanu and I were sitting in the back of an empty bus, coming home from the movies. The bus usually dropped us off on the corner of our block, so you can imagine our surprise when the driver suddenly stopped the bus and said, "Last stop."

"What do you mean 'Last stop?'" I asked. "Doesn't this bus go to the airport?"

"Nope," he answered, as he pushed a button to open the doors. "The ten o'clock bus goes to the airport. This bus only goes to 65th and Elmwood."

There was nothing else we could do but get off. "What are we gonna do now?" Thanu asked, as we watched the bus pull away, leaving us in the cold.

"We might as well walk," I said. "We don't live that far. It's either that or wait for the ten o'clock bus."

We must have walked about two blocks when we saw a group standing in front of a restaurant. There must have been ten or fifteen of them. The skunk-like smell of marijuana filled our nostrils. None of them spoke, but they eyed us strangely.

We continued up the street when I realized we were being followed. I glanced over my shoulder and, sure enough, there they were—not close enough to be a threat, but definitely following us.

Thanu noticed, too. "Let's keep moving," he suggested. If they wanted trouble, they could follow us right into our neighborhood. To get into a fight here—while outnumbered—was just plain stupid.

A voice rose from the crowd and made its way to my ears; only one word: "N _ _ _ _ _."

I stopped dead in my tracks and turned around.

"Come on, man. Let's keep movin'," Thanu insisted. I knew what he was saying made sense and I should listen, but I didn't. It was like someone had lit a match inside of me that sparked a flame of anger. "Nah, I ain't runnin'. I'm waitin' right here."

Looking back now, I don't know what I was thinking. We were outnumbered by at least eight people, and we weren't close enough to home to expect help. I stood there and waited.

When they caught up to us, I asked angrily, "Why are you followin' us?"

The tallest one answered, "My bud here said that you were talkin' trash about him. I don't care who you think you are, but you don't come around our way and disrespect us."

"Man, you better back up out of my face. I don't even know any of you. What would I talk trash about you for?"

Believe it or not, I was trying to calm myself and think about my mother's words. But all I could feel was that spark of anger spreading into an inferno. It made me feel invincible. I felt like I could literally take on all of them. Before I could do anything stupid, Thanu jumped into the conversation. "Look, man, we don't want trouble. We're just passing through."

"Well, keep on walking, then."

I stood there for a few seconds, wondering whether I should just ball all of my anger into a fist and unleash it. But Thanu grabbed me by the arm, and we left.

We walked for a few blocks in silence. I stopped at a streetlight and began ramming my fists into the metal pole, screaming in anger, until my knuckles turned numb from the cold. Still angry, I sat on the curb and tried to calm down. I closed my eyes, but all I could see were their faces, taunting me with that word.

Thanu spoke up. "If we had more people with us, they wouldn't have tried that." His words were supposed to comfort me. I was thinking back to my elementary school when I was one of the only black kids in my class. Even then, when we were young kids, I had put up with this nonsense. "I hate them all," I said angrily.

But as soon as the words were out of my mouth, I wanted to take them back. I remembered my mother's words and I realized that if I allowed this incident to turn me into a racist, I would be no better than those who caused this to happen. ▣

Coming Home

by Julie Schultz

Going away to college for the first time can be both scary and exciting. You are leaving your friends, family and familiar surroundings and moving on to a foreign environment. Your schedule changes and your eating habits do, too. It can be a very difficult transition, but it is really exciting. You meet all kinds of new people. You can take courses you like, stay out as late as you want, and explore yourself and your limitations beyond the bounds of family life.

You hear a lot about going away before you leave. You may have talked about what it would be like and shared your knowledge with those in the same situation. But what people tend to neglect is the importance of coming home.

When you come home from college the first time, it is like nothing you've ever imagined. Your family may have seemed to have adjusted surprisingly well to life without you; your town looks a little different and your friends have begun to change as a result of their different experiences. The shock of being home can be just as scary as leaving for college.

Here's my analogy for coming home: When you live at home, you are part of a brick wall that is made up of your family. When you leave for school, you take a few of these bricks with you and use them to build your own wall at school, a wall that is uniquely you. When you come home, you find that your old bricks don't fit quite as snuggly into your family's brick wall. Just as it shifted when you left, the family wall needs to shift again to fit you in when you come home. By the same token, if your family comes to visit you at school, even just for a weekend, there is no place in your school brick wall for them. Everything has been rebuilt to suit the new situation.

If you and your family understand that things are bound to change when you leave for school, you can be prepared to plan for this uncomfortable shifting of bricks. Before you leave, talk with your family and friends about your fears of coming home as well as your fears of leaving. Brainstorm ways to make these transitions easier and to avoid the tensions of these shifts. You know that you can always come home, but the sacrifice you make for spending these years away at school is that you never come home the same way twice. Your feelings about your friends and family change and grow, and you may be surprised at how nice these changes will be if you understand that they will happen. ▣

Photo by Courtney Miller

Stop Making My Baby Gray

by Melissa Thornton Keys

A child
Born into a world
A world of hate and despair
Nowhere to go
No one to cling to
No one to look up to
Seen only as a disaster
Grandpa T. calls her a n _ _ _ _ _
Grandpa D. a damn slave driver
Names engraved on her side for life
She is only a baby
A newborn
And already, only being moments alive
She is an unwanted misfit of society
Looked upon as an outcast
As if this child had chosen to be half black and half white
She must learn to live in a world of gray
Where she is made to pay
For representing two people's forbidden love
People are so selfish, so blind
Unopen to differences

Unopen to change
People say that they make these remarks because
they are superior to the other
But I think we both know the truth
The truth is—they are scared
Scared that maybe
In these differences
These people are just as good as they
So I say to you, Father
I'm on to you
Maybe you aren't selfish
And I know you're not blind
You're scared
And I think you know it
I wish you could understand
there's no need to be scared
I will always love you
And, if that's not enough, I'm truly sorry
But, please, stop making this world GRAY
Stop ruining the lives of others
Just because you feel your life has been a failure
Please, I beg of you
Stop making our children GRAY
I LOVE YOU, DADDY

The Fall

by Alissa Deschnow

We are all interconnected in the web of life.

That spring was gorgeous. Persephone, goddess of spring's return, walked the earth, waking it from its sweet slumber. The trees were in bloom, and the flowers ran wild. I was immersed in a world of beauty and that is when I noticed Jane. We had been friends, but that spring we became inseparable. On those clear blue nights, we would talk about everything. Friends, school, boyfriends and a love of life drew us together.

Summer came; it was hot, too hot. I was bloated with heat, and a wildfire blazed through my mind. I was absorbed by Jane. She became my life. I only felt normal—loved—with her, yet I also felt inner disgust with my happiness. She was my best friend, I loved her—but more that that, I was in love with her.

For months, I had battled my emotions. I had a war raging in my head. I tried to ignore this growing attraction. Lord knows I couldn't talk about it. Jane at that time was my only connection to the real world, the straight world. I was isolated and starved when I finally surrendered and decided to tell her.

Fall was early that year. The temperature must have

dropped 65 degrees in one week. I remember so clearly the cold moving in. It was mid-August; Jane and I had spent the day playing cards and watching TV. I was waiting for night, for everyone in my house to go to bed. I was extremely tense. We were finally alone in the kitchen. I looked directly at her for the first time that night. I said something like, "I want you to look at something. Please don't laugh, and please don't hate me." I went to retrieve a book of poetry, poetry I had written to her.

We sat in my living room. I knew I was shaking. With her pale, thin fingers, she began flipping through my flower-covered book. It was too much for me to bear. I paced in the kitchen. That had always made me feel better, although it did not make time go any faster. My palms were sweating. It was the longest fifteen minutes of my life. When I returned to the living room, she said, "We have to talk."

The rest of the night is a blur. We talked and walked for about two hours. There was nervous tension, an ominous feeling not present before. She left, confused, and the next day I left on vacation. I did not have the best timing, but it made sense at the time. Sometimes I wonder what would have happened if I had not left her alone and confused for the week. But insomnia is built upon "what ifs."

The last time we talked was a week after I returned. We talked on the phone for three hours. She said that she did not want to see me. She asked me not to call her or even talk to her in school. I was desperate; I pleaded and begged and even cried. But she hung up. Connection terminated.

It was a hard fall. My sanity grew crisp and fell like leaves, piece by piece upon my soul. I placated myself with school and sports. I was drowning in my own sorrows and in my own tears. There was no one to turn to.

Fall was hard, but winter was far worse. Like many trees that lay dormant in the cold, I hung to life by a thread. Cold wind whipped through my head.

We are all interconnected in the web of life. Whether we like it or not, nature is all around us. And if you hang on, just hang on, spring always follows winter. It was a beautiful spring. ◙

Photo by Chris Parsons

Different

by Kerri Lynn Morrone

If you were blind you'd hear my voice and
* call me musical.*
You'd touch my hand and call me clean.
You'd feel my heart and call me friend.
*   Yet you can see.*
*   And just because your eyes see my colors,*
*   I am*
*   no longer*
*   musical.*
No longer clean.
No longer called friend.
You hear my voice and call me loud.
You touch my hand and call me filthy.
*   You crush my heart*
*   and call me different.*

The Longest Hallway

by Kendra Lider-Johnson

Most people I know like to have gym late in the day so they aren't sweaty in all their classes. I prefer it in the morning, so it's not hot when we're outside, and the bees aren't active. I am lucky this year, because my schedule allows me to have gym first period. It is good to get my least favorite class over with early.

Today, Monday, is one of those ambiguous spring days. It is warm enough to wear shorts if I want, but it might be better to wear pants. This is what I worry about as I say good-bye to my friends and leave homeroom. Do I change into sweat pants or wear shorts? I don't forget to keep an eye out for Peter, but he must have gone the other way today.

The locker rooms aren't too far from my homeroom, but to get there I must walk down a hallway that stretches forever past the art rooms, cafeteria and outside doors. I hate to walk it alone, but I have no choice. Three seniors, the kind of guys I can't picture as adults with jobs and families, lean against the wall to my right. I will not be afraid; they can't hurt me. I have trained myself to walk past them without making eye contact. I pick a spot farther down the hallway and stare at it. Eye contact with them is deadly. I would become a victim; I would become vulnerable.

I concentrate on walking, swinging my arms casually, and already I am past the first senior. Coming upon the second one, I fail. They have laughed, and I lose my focal point. Worse, I look at them, opening myself up for attack. It's too late to undo; I must wait for whatever they choose to heap on me. The middle kid, kind of goofy-looking, smiles. I am almost relieved. I can almost breathe again, but there is a little corner of me that remains wary: A smile means nothing in the hallways of this school.

That suspicious, scared little person inside of me is proven right. When I am a few feet beyond the last guy, I hear more laughter. My heart sinks, and I wait for the words—rather, the missiles. And they come.

"Black Afro . . . frizzy head . . ." I do not hear the rest; I don't need to. I have heard these words before, and they are no longer a shock. I am not angry; I feel no rage. No, I am sad, and worse, I am ashamed. I feel guilty for my shame, want to kill it, but still my face burns. No matter what I do—perms, curling irons, hot combs, curlers, hair gels—I cannot get my hair to lie flat; it is thick and wild. I want to tell that kid, the goofy-looking one, that he is wrong—it's not an Afro. But I don't turn around, because I know that under these chemically treated curls, loathed and loved by me, the roots are already growing in, and that I will wait as long as possible before perming them again. Plus, I am late for gym class. 回

8 Milestones

Photo by Maya J. Krolikiewicz

Kind Stranger

by Olga Tsyganova

The cold air nipped my face at the train station that early morning. Half asleep, I stared into the distance, watching for the train to take me to my class in the city. The world was serene as the sun rose; pedestrians were few and kept to themselves, minding their steaming cups of coffee.

The distant sound of the train startled me. Reaching into my pocket, my numb hand searched for the twenty-dollar bill to pay my fare. As the train approached I became impatient; the pocket was empty. Frantically, I searched through my bag. Leaning my head on my hand, I was desperate. I sat on the frigid bench. Unless the money dropped from the sky, I'd be stuck here for eight hours. I felt so stupid.

"What's the matter?" a rough voice asked. A short, elderly man stood in front of me.

"Oh, nothing. I'll be all right," I mumbled, trying to push back my despair.

"Did you forget your money, kiddo?" he asked.

"Well, yeah—sort of. It was really dumb of me, and now I'm stuck here. I'm going to miss my math class, and the train is leaving."

"Calm yourself. Here," he said. "Use this."

The man held out a twenty-dollar bill. I looked up, amazed. People just don't do that anymore. People worry about their own problems, rarely stopping to think about others, especially teenage strangers. But there he stood, an elderly man in the middle of a train station, handing me money.

"Thank you, but no, I can't."

"I'm not asking you what you can and can't do, just take the money or you'll miss your train!"

"Well . . ."

"None of that—go!" the man said, pushing me toward the train. I bought a round-trip ticket and tried to give him the change.

"Keep it. You need some spending money." I did not know what to say—a million thoughts raced through my mind, yet I stood silently.

"Thank you so much—this is really amazing. Thank you so much. I really appreciate it," I babbled. He just stood there in the stairway to the train.

During the trip I was silent. I was overwhelmed, seeing the world through changed eyes. That man made a difference with such a simple act.

A week later I was at the station again, with an extra twenty dollars in case I saw him. And there he was. I wasn't sure it was the right person, but intuition pulled me toward him. When he saw me coming, I saw tears in his eyes. I flashed a shy smile.

"Excuse me, sir," I said. "I believe I owe you this," and handed him the money. The man opened his mouth to say he didn't need to be paid back, but I did not let him speak. "No, I insist, sir, that you take this." I pressed the money into his hand. "I'd feel bad otherwise." He smiled.

"Just remember to do the same for someone in your shoes someday. You have a good day, kiddo," he said.

I smiled, content. I will never forget his kindness. The system worked that day, the system of trust. ◙

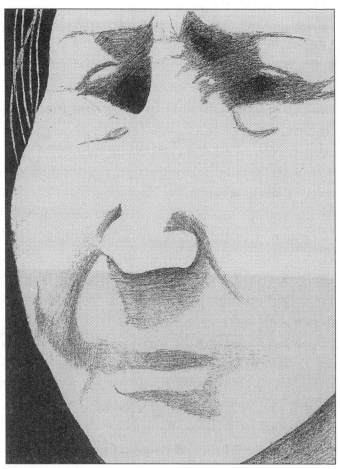

Art by Amber Delphine Hall

Changing Times

by Jennifer Fusco

Y̧ou know how you feel awful for people if bad things happen to them? You feel really sorry for them, but you don't really know how they feel—until it happens to you.

It was a Wednesday night, and I had just gotten home from my volleyball game. We had finally won, so I was in a pretty good mood. I grabbed some chips and a soda and sat down to watch TV. My mom called me into the living room; I was annoyed she had interrupted my show, but I went anyway. To my surprise, my dad, mom and little brother were all sitting around the fireplace. "Sit down, Jen," my dad said. Although his voice was calm, his eyes were glassy and his hands shaking, as they sometimes do when he's nervous. I took a seat next to my brother.

"Dad has something he wants to tell you, and he wants everyone to be here," my mom said. I started to get nervous—my parents were acting really strange and I couldn't understand why. I knew my dad had a lump on his knee, but no one really thought anything of it.

"I went for a biopsy on that tumor today, and well, I have cancer." I just sat there, staring at the wall. You never notice how interesting chipping paint is until you stare at it to avoid eye contact. All I could think was, *No, not my dad, he's too young. There's so much he wants out of life; there must be a mistake.* Before I realized it, I was crying hysterically. I couldn't stop. The tears just kept coming. Mom hugged me, telling me everything would be okay. *No!* I thought. *Everything won't be okay.* My dad, the one I laugh with, the one I go skiing with, the one I sit in the kitchen and eat nachos with until I'm sick, has cancer. I remember asking a lot of questions, but I don't remember many of the answers. He needed to go through ten months of chemotherapy. He'd be living in the hospital most of the time, and we wouldn't see him very often.

I have learned to deal a little better during the past few weeks. I know I have to be strong and help hold the family together through this. I've also learned to take advantage of the time I spend with him. I believe my dad will beat this and will live to be an old man who has had a great life. Every step of the way, my family will be there to give him the love and support he needs to pull through. ▣

Too Late to Cry

by Robert Dixter

I did not cry. They say that it is all right to cry, that it is not being a wimp. Then how come I did not cry? Perhaps it is not cool, but who cares what is cool and what is not? We are talking about my grandfather here.

Every Friday night my parents, sister and I would go to my grandparents' place for dinner. We used to call my grandfather Paps, because that is what I called him when I was a baby. Paps would always debate politics at this meal. He would make me laugh by saying things that I was never allowed to say. I loved him, but of course I never told him that to his face. It is not that I was not allowed. It just seemed like a corny thing to do. He would take me fishing and to baseball games. These were times I looked forward to, because I knew that it would never be boring and Paps could always make me smile.

Then I remember one day as if it were yesterday. The phone rang, and my mother answered it in her usual way. I remember hearing a lot of whats and wheres, and then my mother said something to my father and raced out of the house. My sister and I were told that Paps had suffered a bad heart attack. We rushed to the hospital with my dad. Paps was hooked up with all these wires. I held his hand in mine for a while and I wanted to tell him that I loved him, but I didn't. Later a nurse came out to tell us that Paps had died. I sat there stunned. What do I do? What do I say? I said nothing and did nothing. I did not cry.

Afterwards we took my mother home. She was sobbing the whole way. My entire family was crying. I wanted to cry but could not get my body to do it. What was I afraid of? Why couldn't I cry? I loved Paps and wanted to cry for him, but I could not. The following week was the funeral. As they lowered his casket into the ground I felt a tear, but it still did not come. Everyone wept but me.

I loved Paps. They say that it is all right to cry, that it is good to get it out. Every night since the funeral, I lie in bed and cry. I cry for Paps. Now it is too late to cry, but I cry anyway because it is too late. ▣

Photo by Dan Zaslavsky

My First Kiss

Fiction by Kelly Dean

We're going to play Spin the Bottle?" I asked, shocked. "I can't play that! I don't know how to kiss!"

"So, practice. That's what I've been doing," Adrianna said, calmly. I knew why she was so calm; she'd probably kissed millions of guys by now. Even though we were only eleven, more than half the guys on the football team we cheered for liked her. I glanced at my friend again. After an hour of trying, her hair was finally in a perfect ponytail. Her blue eyes shone brighter than usual, thanks to eyeliner and mascara; her tanned skin glowed and her cheeks were flushed, partly from the excitement of our cheerleading competition, and partly from the blush her mom had applied. We were wearing our uniform: green and white sweaters with "Hawks" across the chest, short green pleated skirts and saddle shoes.

"Girls, are you ready?" Adrianna's mom asked from the bottom of the stairs.

"Coming, Mom!" Adrianna yelled back and continued to talk to me in a low voice. "If you practice, you'll be fine by Friday. That's six days away."

* * *

"Hello?"

"Sean, guess what? We got first place. I'm so excited; we did the cheers perfectly!" I was talking a million miles an hour, the adrenaline still rushing through me.

"Wow, Brianna, slow down. You guys won? Congratulations! I told you your team was the best." Sean was my closest guy friend; we'd practically grown up together. I could trust him to do anything for me. Then a plan started to form. It was probably the best idea I ever had.

"Hey, Sean, you've never kissed anyone, right?" My mind was focused on the party with Spin the Bottle.

"Nope, why?" he asked. I'd known the answer before I asked, but figured I should lead into the plan, not just spring it on him.

"I was thinking that when you get a girlfriend, you're gonna have to kiss her eventually, and you want to be good at it, in case she's experienced, right?" Tricking him into wanting to do this was the key.

"Yeah, I never thought of that. I'm guessing you have a plan, so let's hear it."

"Considering that we both need to learn how to kiss— me for this party on Friday, and you for when you get a girlfriend—I figured we could practice with each other!" I knew he was gonna go for it; he had to.

"Alright, I guess this could work. It wouldn't be considered our first kiss either because we're just practicing, right?"

"Exactly!"

*   *   *

"Brianna! Sean is here!" my mother called; I had invited him over for our first practice.

"Okay, Mom, tell him to come down," I yelled back. I was excited, but scared. So many questions ran through my mind. What if he is really good, and I'm horrible? He walked down the stairs; he seemed as nervous as me, which made me feel a little better. His skin was pale, and his lips were stained red, probably from an ice-pop.

"So, how do we start?" he asked. I shrugged.

"How about we just kiss, and however it happens we just go from there?" I suggested. That was what my cousin did, and she practiced a lot with her boyfriend.

"Okay, here goes nothing." He leaned in and tried to kiss me, but as I watched him get closer, I started giggling, so he backed up.

"What? What did I do wrong?" He looked even more nervous.

"Nothing, you just look weird so close up. Maybe I should close my eyes."

He started to kiss me again, and I closed my eyes. I felt his lips push against mine and quickly pull away. I tried to figure out what was wrong with the kiss. Maybe it should last longer. Whenever I watched my cousin and her boyfriend, they kissed for almost half an hour straight. Of course, we wouldn't be able to do that the first time; we'd have to build up tolerance.

"So, now what?" Sean asked.

"That was good, but let's see if we can hold it longer, okay?"

I watched him shut his eyes, then closed mine. Again I felt his lips gently press against mine. They stayed there longer this time, thirty seconds to be exact. We opened our eyes and decided we should practice a few more times before stopping for the night. By the time he left an hour later, I was beginning to like it.

We practiced every night that week. By the time Thursday night came we both felt ready for other people and to have our first real kiss.

*   *   *

As I was leaving the house Friday night for the party, the phone rang.

"Hey, I'm just calling to wish you good luck tonight. Call me when you get home, so you can tell me how your first kiss was," Sean said.

It seemed forever to drive to Adrianna's. She was waiting at the door, wearing almost the same outfit as I was, as we had planned: a short black skirt with a tank top. When we got to the party, a lot of people from the cheerleading and football teams were there. Jackie was having the party in the basement because it was her birthday. Her parents had agreed to stay upstairs.

We had dinner and danced, then someone dimmed the lights. Someone else grabbed an empty soda bottle and everyone made a circle. Adrianna sat next to me and tapped me on the shoulder.

"So, did you practice?" she whispered.

"Yep, I practiced a lot, actually."

The room became hushed as people started spinning the bottle. Three people went before me. Then I spun the bottle and watched it go around and around. *Who will I have to kiss?* I wondered. Before I could think, the bottle stopped, pointing directly at Bobby. I'd had a huge crush on him since football season began. I felt butterflies in my stomach. What if I forgot everything Sean and I had practiced, or even worse, what if we had practiced wrong? Everyone was waiting for me to kiss him. I knew Bobby had experience, so I decided to follow whatever he did.

He came over to me, and we closed our eyes, then his lips were on mine. It wasn't soft or gentle like kissing Sean. I decided he wasn't a very good kisser, so I pretended it was Sean and just kissed the way we had practiced. After twenty seconds, it was over. I thought my first kiss hadn't been very good, but at least I'd had it, and could stop practicing. I couldn't wait to tell Sean he was a better kisser than Bobby. Boy, would he be happy.

"Wow, you were amazing," Adrianna whispered.

"I told you I'd been practicing," I said.

"You learned how to do that on a pillow?"

"On a what? No, I practiced with Sean. Who said anything about a pillow?" I asked.

"When I said to practice, I meant on a *pillow,* not a *guy.* So, this was your second kiss, not your first. What's it like?"

Wow, I kissed a guy before Adrianna did? Wait until I tell Sean! ▣

A Small Cheese Pizza

by Rachel Svea Bottino

It was an intensely cold November day with a biting wind. My mom and I entered the first restaurant we saw in a hurry to get away from the harsh weather. Mom ordered a pizza and I found a cozy booth near the heater. As I gazed around, I saw a homeless man sitting at a corner table. For some reason—I'm still not sure why—he intrigued me.

I studied him, absorbing every detail. Growing up, I was taught never to stare, but the temptation was overwhelming. Because of the way his knees grazed the bottom of the tabletop, it was evident that he was tall. His clothes were filthy. Even though he was wearing endless layers of clothing, he looked as though he weighed nothing. A mass of tangled hair, thick as a lion's mane, covered most of his face and a shaggy, knotted beard covered the rest. I focused on his eyes because they were the only part I could see.

His eyes were transfixed, almost hypnotized by the steam that curled up from the coffee cup sitting in the middle of the table. An employee came over and gave him a small cheese pizza, and what I saw next would change my whole perspective on life.

The man looked at that pizza as if it were the most

precious thing in the world. He didn't touch it at first, almost like a person who has a priceless object he is afraid might break. He stared at that pizza as though it were made of gold. When he finally decided to eat it, he didn't grab a slice and devour it like we do. He ate unusually slowly, savoring every bite.

When we got our pizza, my mom placed it in the middle of the table and started eating. She couldn't see the man from where she was sitting and asked me why I wasn't eating. I nodded toward the man and she turned. When she saw him, she understood. That circular piece of dough in the middle of our table suddenly looked different. It was no longer just an inexpensive supper. People think of pizza as a matter-of-fact thing that has no significance whatsoever. But now, after seeing this man, something as simple as a small cheese pizza was suddenly so much more complicated.

I was drawn to this man not out of pity, but curiosity. I wanted to know who he was. I wanted to know what was going on in his mind. He is a human being, like everyone else, but is viewed as though he is incapable of having thoughts and feelings. When people look at him, they see a lost cause. But I saw a soul waiting to be found.

I watched him as he got up to leave. He finished the last of his coffee and headed toward the door. As the door opened, a gust of frigid air rushed into the store. Holding his collar tightly around his neck and bowing his head against the snapping wind, he walked through the parking lot and out of sight. ▣

You're Hired

by Kerry Elizabeth Miller

After looking in my wallet and finding nothing but ticket stubs and a library card, I had a revelation: I needed a job. I applied to half a dozen places, filling out paperwork about my past work experience (none), background-check release forms and quizzes which I guess were supposed to determine if I was a moral and literate person. Example: "Question 78: Can you count past fifty?" I never got a call back from any of these places. All this for minimum wage? Give me a break.

Finally, I had a breakthrough and actually had an interview with the manager of a restaurant. He looked at me and said, "Come back in the fall." The next week, I talked to the other manager. She looked at me, I smiled and she said, "You're hired!" I entered the world of the working.

Since I was sixteen, I was too young to be a server, but I could be a hostess. Fortunately, my job did not require a name tag, hair net or anything in the neon color scheme. I just had to dress nicely. I did have to wear pantyhose, however, which has to be the most despicable leg covering known to humankind.

I showed up for my first day of training properly

clothed and ready to work. Apparently, though, my trainer wasn't. It was a Friday night, one of the busiest nights in the restaurant business, so they couldn't afford to go without a hostess. The manager grabbed one of the waitresses and told her to "show the new girl what to do." This was the extent of my training: "Um . . . like, this is the seating chart. When people come in you like, seat them, and—I don't need to tell you any of this, do I? You read the manual and stuff, right? Okay, good. I'm kinda busy now—have fun!" With that brief introduction, I was on my own. *Okay,* I thought. *This hostess thing can't be that hard. I can smile, I can say "Smoking or non?" I'll be fine.*

Fine? Well, that depends on what you mean by "fine." If you like being screamed at by servers, cooks, busboys, bartenders, little old ladies and not-so-little bikers, then I was fine. If you like being hit on by old men with hair pieces, I was fine. If you like being called "little lady" by thirteen-year-old chain-smokers, then I was fine. If you like going completely out of your mind . . . then I was just peachy.

That first night was one I'd like to forget. Luckily, though, I got a more in-depth (that's not saying much) training session the next day, and after a few nights, I was practically a pro. I could wash windows, bus tables, clean menus, restock mints and inflate balloons with the best of them. I could lie through my teeth ("Sure, it'll just be about five to ten minutes"), I could program the juke-box with fifty of my favorite songs in ten seconds flat and I knew the answers to all the puzzles on the kid's menu. By my second week, I was a trainer myself.

While I know a lot, I don't know how to get to the restaurant from Pennsylvania or which gas station has the cheapest cigarettes. I am not a cook, server, cashier or manager.

I make $5.50 an hour, so, Buster, don't push it. Please don't brush off the seats like they are infected with some contagious disease. Don't give me dirty looks when I can't give you a window seat. It's not my fault the kids at the next table are screaming. I can't help it if you don't like ribs. And, please, don't expect me to sing the restaurant's theme song. I am hostess, hear me roar. Smoking or non? ▣

Photo by Stephanie Quinn

My First Party

by Cassie Warren

My brother, Brandon, whom I idolize, taught me many things. For instance, he taught me how to wrap a rubber band around the sprayer on the kitchen sink, so when some poor unsuspecting soul turned on the water, he got quite a shower! Then there was one important lesson I learned from being with him—always be myself and never pretend to be something that I'm not. I never knew how much of an effect he had on me—until I went to my first high-school party.

It was the fall I turned fifteen. Most of my friends would be there. A few days before the big party, my two best friends asked if I would like to go with them. I half-heartedly asked my mom's permission. To my surprise, she said yes.

The night of the party I took a long time to get dressed, partially because I wanted to look cool, although I had no idea what awaited me. As I kissed my mom and dad good-bye, I felt a new kind of independence. It was as if this were a milestone in my growing up.

When we arrived, I stumbled out of the car in a state of shock and disbelief. This was it! My very first high-school party! I walked through the clusters of people, many of whom I knew. Some were as surprised to see me as I was to see them. Gradually, I began to loosen up and started to laugh and joke. Pretty soon, I grabbed a bottle of beer from a cooler and began to drink. No one made me do it; it was my choice. I knew that when I took that first sip, I was responsible for everything that happened.

It didn't take me long to figure out that the drinking part was not what was making this night wonderful. I returned to the cooler, this time for a cola. Five minutes later, one of my drunken friends came up to me with a cigarette in one hand and a beer in the other. She slurred an invitation to come smoke with her. As ridiculous as it sounds, I was willing to drink, but I was (and still am) opposed to smoking. I told her no and wandered into the older group of party-goers. Even without the alcohol, I was having an incredible time.

All of a sudden, out of the corner of my eye, I saw my brother. He stood with a group of guys with his arms folded and a half grin on his face. As I stood in shock, he eased over to me.

"Having a good time?" he asked. I nodded. He leaned in toward my mouth and took a sniff. "Ah-ha!" he said. I wanted to tell him how I had wanted to try drinking, but that I'd figured out that it doesn't take drinking to have a good time. I also wanted to tell him how I had refused to smoke, but all of these ideas started to blur. I didn't know where to begin.

When I opened my mouth, he stopped me. "I saw you taking a beer from the cooler." I opened my mouth to defend myself, only to be stopped again. "AND I saw you visit that cooler again. Only that time you came back with a cola instead. I also saw you give up the opportunity to have a cancer stick rammed down your throat."

I smiled and felt proud. As if he knew I would, he grabbed me by my shoulders and playfully disheveled my hair. He looked back at me and said, "I'm proud to have a sister like you, so don't ever change." 回

Photo by Jessica Mazonson

The Making of a Man

by Rob Dangel

It was the beginning of gym class, and I set my belongings down in the most secluded area of the boys' locker room. I felt my simple, undeveloped body was inferior to the libido-loaded adolescents who ruled the locker room, and I wanted to avoid confrontation with them. My worst fear had always been that someone was going to sneak up and pilfer my undergarments, which would then force me to chase after this B.V.D. bandit in my birthday suit.

I was stripping off my clothes in the process of changing into my uniform, when the glistening incandescence of a single chest hair caught my eye. I paused for a moment and looked down at God's gift. There it was: dark, silky and beautiful, the only one of its kind. And I thought, *After one, more are sure to follow.*

I was at that age when boys suddenly change from a boy to, well, not a man, but something in between the two—a demented, terrifying creature known as an adolescent. By the time I entered this stage, most of my friends were well underway in their journey toward manhood. All around me droned the chorus of squeaky, semi-low-pitched male voices, and I, with my soprano voice, came to the realization that I, too, would be dragged to the same fate as the others. I was, however, what is considered a "late bloomer" and, unlike my classmates, had not yet developed.

A few months after my chest hair sighting, my voice began its gradual and cruel change. Whenever I spoke, an embarrassing, indescribable chirp would escape from my mouth. Usually, I could not even speak a full sentence without my voice jumping an octave or two. But, I realized that all of us guys go through this, so I could deal with it.

The last drastic change from boy to adolescent that I encountered was libido control. Because I was late in blooming, I had witnessed the drastic effects libido had on other males. No longer were the boys happy with each other's company. They were in search of something else: the sexual unknown. The devil of puberty turns every young male into an uncontrollable mass of hormones whose every waking moment is occupied by the thought of the female gender.

I, too, succumbed to this natural fascination with women, but in a different way. Once I developed an interest, I, like many others, wanted a girlfriend—but I was certainly unprepared for the role of being a boyfriend. I remember the tumultuous experience of my first girlfriend. At the end of English class, all corners of the room were filled with the drone of students packing up to hurry to their next period. I was leaning over my belongings when I felt something grab at my behind. To my surprise, my future girlfriend was standing behind me with the look of a criminal who had just gotten away with murder. My face turned a deep tint of scarlet as I searched the room for a witness to her crime. Luckily, nobody had noticed.

I attempted to say something, but all that came out of my mouth was a stutter. Feeling embarrassed, I ran for the exit, books and papers all jumbled in my arms. My only thought was to escape from that room and find a secluded stall in the men's bathroom to see if she had inflicted more than superficial damage. Whenever anyone touched me, I had the habit of checking for an out-of-place ruffle in my clothes. Thankfully, I was unscathed.

Later that month, I somehow got dragged into a relationship with that same girl. The night I went to meet her mom and dad was another incident that I will never forget. I was in their guest bathroom combing my hair, since I was about to meet her parents, and I wanted to look presentable. Out of the corner of my eye, I saw the door creep open and my girlfriend enter. "What are you . . . ," my voice jumped an octave, "doing?"

"Oh, nothing," she replied, with the same look on her face she had had the day she accosted me in English class. For weeks, she had hinted that she wanted to engage in the ritual of kissing, even though I was completely terrified of her intentions. At that moment, I felt like a lost mouse being stalked by a great owl.

I had never been alone in a bathroom with a girl before, and I had no idea how to go about kissing. I had read many magazines on the topic, but they were no help. I was worried that my inexperience would cause me to falter. I wondered, as she edged closer and closer, when our lips come together, what then? My heart began to beat faster and faster. I looked around for a way out, but she had me cornered. I let out the loudest scream I could humanly produce and then jumped under her legs in an attempt to escape. Crawling the length of the bathroom, I scrambled to the exit as quickly as I could. My way was blocked by four knees, two covered with pants and two bulging out of the top of red-and-green argyle knee socks. I looked up to see her parents staring down at me.

"Hi," again my voice cracked. "I'm Rob," I said while offering them my trembling, sweaty hand. They received it politely and asked if everything was okay. The door opened behind me and my girlfriend exited. "Hi, Mom, Dad," she said as she blithely walked around the corner and disappeared from view.

Looking back, I learned that behind every cracking voice, sweaty palm and sexually accosted boy, there is a mature, honest, responsible man in the making. The memory of the lone chest hair sighting that I so gleefully discovered in the locker room is a savored memory tucked away with the squeeze on the behind and my first kiss. Maybe adolescence was not so bad after all. ▣

Car Talk

by Nicole M. Docteur

I've been the proud owner of a driving permit, a small plastic card verifying my right to drive with a consenting licensed driver, for the past year. I am also, unfortunately, a very poor driver. Thanks to my abilities, the rear end of our station wagon has seen pine trees, poles and snow banks, all up-close and personal. It's embarrassing, actually. I am supposedly a bright, well-rounded student who should be able to sail through this one teenage rite of passage with no problem. Alas . . . I cannot.

The problem all started a year ago when that now-aging permit first found its way into my eager hands. Mom and I took our first trip around an empty parking lot. I was totally unaware that my mother was most definitely not the best teacher for me. It wasn't that she yelled, or told me I was doing poorly. No, actually my mother told me I was doing quite well while digging her nails into the seat and trying to brake for me. As you can imagine, my mother's "helpful instructions" only managed to make me more nervous. A quick evening run to the drugstore, where I nearly plowed over a small, parked car, brought an end to any hopes of learning from Mom.

Since it was obvious that I could no longer practice with her, the job was placed in the hands of my father. The idea of learning from Dad was not one that thrilled me. I loved him dearly, but I just did not see Dad as someone I could be comfortable learning from. He almost never yelled, which was an advantage. And Dad also almost never talked. We shared a typical father-daughter relationship. He'd ask how school was, and I'd say it was fine. Unfortunately, that was the extent of most of our conversations. The prospect of spending hours alone with someone who might as well have been a stranger really scared me.

As we got into the car that first time, I was not surprised at what happened. Dad and I drove around, saying almost nothing, aside from a few instructions on how to turn. As my lessons wore on, however, things began to change. Dad would turn the radio up so I could fully experience, and thus appreciate, his favorite Stones music. And he actually began talking. It was a bit scarier than silence, at first. I was soon hearing about past failed dates, "basic bod" gym class, and other tales from his past, including some of his first encounters with Mom.

Dad's sudden chattiness was shocking until I thought about why he was telling me so much. In the car, I was a captive audience. In order to learn to drive, it was a requirement that I sit and listen to his every word. In all the years that I had wondered why my father never spoke that much, I had never stopped to consider the possibility that it was because I had never bothered to listen. Homework, friends, and even TV had all called me away from him, and, consequently, I never thought my quiet father had anything to say.

Since I began driving with him, my dexterity on the road has greatly increased. More important, though, is that my knowledge of who my father is has also increased. Just living with him wasn't enough—it took driving with him for me to get to know someone who was a mystery. ▣

Cartoon by Kate Bosco

First Choice

by Jamie Bleiweiss

I have always wondered what it would actually be like living at college, going to classes every day, partying at night and maybe studying a little in between. Now, as senior year comes to a close and my college years rapidly approach, the ideas are becoming realities. Questions keep circling in my mind: *What will my roommate be like? Will we get along? Will there be a variety of guys on campus?* I can only begin to speculate on the answers and pray that my college nightmares will not become realities.

When I was younger, I always imagined myself at a prestigious school like Harvard with beautiful old buildings lining the quads. When I got into high school, I realized my dream of an Ivy League school was just that—a dream. I never took into account SAT scores, AP classes, ACT tests, honors classes, extracurricular activities, all of which basically determine where a person goes to college. I naively believed that everyone went wherever they wanted.

Once my junior year was complete, my list of schools had narrowed considerably. I applied to the usual state schools like everyone else in my class, and a couple of safe schools (just in case things didn't turn out quite as I hoped), and I applied early decision to my reach school, which happened to be the one school I desperately wanted to attend.

I waited three months to hear from my first choice. Every day I took trips to the mailbox praying the letter would arrive. Finally, on a rather unassuming day, as I innocently wandered to the mailbox, I saw a small envelope with "my" school's emblem on it. My hands began to shake, my mouth went dry and my pulse began to race. I darted into the house and ran into my room. I wanted to tear open the letter, but nobody was home. I knew I could not let it just sit there and wait until someone came home. If I waited, I would die of anticipation.

Finally, I took a deep breath and slowly opened the top of the envelope. I was nervous, because I had been told that if you got a small letter, that probably meant bad news. I didn't care; I had to know. I tried to reason with myself; I kept saying, "If you don't get in, it's not the end of the world." (Yeah, right.) Carefully, I pulled the letter containing my future out of the envelope. I rubbed my good-luck stone and began to read.

My heart began pounding, and tears came to my eyes. I tried to scream, but words would not come out. I had to re-read the letter to make sure I saw it correctly. I quickly grabbed the phone and called my father to tell him the good news. My dream had come true; I was going to my first-choice university! ▣

The Chinese Test

by James T. Kalil II

I cannot think about Christmas without remembering the year of the robot and the Chinese letter. When I think of all these events, this memory still makes me smile. It wasn't until years later that I was told "the rest of the story."

Like every year, the commercials marketed new toys in early November. I can still picture myself sitting and spooning cereal into my mouth when this four-foot robot appeared on television. This robot did everything—at least that's what the ads said. It played ball, sang songs, even served drinks. Right then and there I knew this would be the brother that I had always wanted. My mother kept telling me that the robot was too big and too expensive for Santa, and she was quite sure that he could not load it on his sleigh. Like most eight-year-olds, I did not believe her. After all, this was Santa Claus she was talking about.

So there I sat Christmas Eve writing my note to Santa. I was in a confused state. I had just heard from my friends that Santa was a charlatan and my parents were the gift buyers; I was baffled. If this were true, I would not get a robot. Only Santa could fulfill such a dream. I had to put Santa to a test. I asked him to answer my note in Chinese. This letter would prove to me that he was authentic and the awful rumor about him was untrue. I placed my note on the mantel with milk and four cookies (three, after I ate one—funny, I still feel guilty about that little transgression).

I went to bed early, but the robot kept popping into my mind. I had all sorts of visions of what we would do together. I even planned that he would do my homework. These thoughts seemed to stall the sleep process, but finally Mr. Sandman got the best of me.

Morning came early that Christmas—about 3:00 A.M. When I woke my parents, they promptly ordered me back to bed. I could hear the chimes of the grandfather clock: 3:00, 3:30, 4:00—until what seemed like eternity finally came to an end. The clock finally counted out seven o'clock. Down I went, two stairs at a time, to search for any colossal package. I was not worried. I figured that the robot had to be assembled, which meant it would be in a smaller package.

I rushed to read Santa's letter; he had written to me in Chinese. It didn't surprise me. After all, my eight-year-old faith could produce minor miracles. We started to unwrap the gifts and I tore into them like a crazed lion looking for her cub. After making a mountain out of the unwrapped presents, my body started to tremble. Where was my robot? I could feel the tears trickle down my face. No amount of force could stop the flow of lost hope. *Why had Santa let me down? What had gone wrong? Was he angry because I ate one of his cookies?* My thoughts were broken when I heard a muffled voice say, "Jamie, where are you?"

My dad opened the foyer door and out walked the robot. I stood dumbfounded. The spell I seemed to be in was not broken until the flash on my dad's camera made me blink.

"The rest of the story" is that my parents didn't see my note to Santa until 10:00 P.M. Christmas Eve. My mother said that it had been snowing that night and the weather was dreadful, but she wasn't ready to see me lose my faith in Santa. So, out she went in search of anyone who could write Chinese. After five restaurants and asking a dozen or so Chinese who could not write in their native language, she found a little man who wrote in Chinese that there was a Santa Claus.

The robot is long gone, but the letter in Chinese is tucked away in my drawer. Whenever I come across it, I think of all the emotions that swept over me that Christmas morning. I carefully refold the letter. I don't really want to throw this memory away. ▣

When Two Worlds Collide

by Gwen Steel

I was born in Minneapolis. The city is in my blood. But I live in the country and have been forced to cope. One thing I've always had trouble with is birds. How could anyone enjoy staring out the window for hours at these feather-brained creatures? My mother had always been one of those ridiculous birdwatcher types. She tried to raise her children with a respect for wildlife, but this had not been too effective with me.

One evening, a hummingbird caught my mother's eye. I'd heard the facts before: "One of nature's most fascinating creatures is the ruby-throated hummingbird. Its incredible wing speed allows it to hover in midair. Its miniature size . . ."

What made this particular "hummer" so odd, however, was that it had been sitting on the same perch, frozen in time for ten minutes like an icicle on a still winter morn. My mother got a stepladder and retrieved the bird from his perch. She inspected him. It appeared his tongue was paralyzed, and he was unable to drink the red liquid from the feeder. My mother handed the injured creature to me while she went inside for an eyedropper.

Never in my life had I felt as frightened as when I held

that tiny life in my hands. Within the silky, smooth, green shell, the miniature heart beat so fast that I thought it literally might explode. I placed the eyedropper inside the long, graceful beak, and prayed that he would swallow.

At first, he only shuddered, but finally he managed to swallow. After a few minutes, he glided gracefully to the ash tree on the front lawn. Although it appeared that the bird was cured, something urged me to keep watching.

Within minutes, a second, slightly larger hummingbird appeared. He did not alight on the feeder, but instead hovered within a few feet of my face. He would fly to the ash tree, then back to me. It didn't take me long to realize that he was sending me a message, a sort of "S.O.S."

I crept to the base of the tree where I found the tiny creature's form quivering in the evening air. I slowly reached into the dewy grass to scoop up the bird. His feathers were damp now, his eyes closed. It seemed his heartbeat had slowed to a dull thud within his thumb-sized body.

"Please, please, be okay." He had asked me for help. Now he owed me a favor in return. I was asking him to stay alive.

It must have been a very tragic picture: a child, wiping her tear-stained face with her one free hand, while the other palm was cupped around a tiny, dying creature. Fate was taking its own course. It seemed hopeless.

The pulse from its heart was hardly recognizable, and the body was growing colder. Its throat, which moments before had been so brilliantly bright, was fading to a dull gray.

As a child clawed at the ground that evening, digging

a grave for a creature she'd tried so desperately to save, she felt at first that she had proven herself correct: Her world and nature's were separate, not to be interfered with by outside forces. She had given all the comfort she could, but to what avail?

Yet she realized there are some things she could change and some she must simply accept. Either way, sometimes two worlds collide, and strangers must ask for, and be willing to receive, help from others. Without this, survival is not only impossible, but meaningless. ▣

9 Memories

Photo by Lisa A. Bourgeault

The Perfect Present

by Dawn Marie Cullinane

lmost twenty years ago, my brother, Shawn, died in a freak accident at the age of ten. Even though I wasn't born, stories of him still linger, and I'm reminded of him every day. This year as Christmas approached, I felt that before graduating I wanted to find the best gift for my parents. There had to be one that would repay them for everything they had done for me.

As always, when I asked my mother what she wanted for Christmas, she said, "There's nothing you can get me that I don't already have." But, I recalled her describing a picture Shawn's classmates had raised money for and hung in the lobby of his elementary school. My mother had mentioned many times that she wanted it. I didn't even know where Shawn had gone to school, since we'd moved since then, so I had to stop several times to ask for directions before finally finding the building. I could feel my temperature rise as I pulled up next to the only car in the parking lot.

Horrible thoughts of an empty building and the possibility that they'd gotten rid of the picture danced through my mind. I looked in the lobby for it, but didn't see it. Then I found a young janitor and tried, with tears in my eyes, to explain Shawn's accident of so many years before. I looked at the floor, trying to control my feelings. He explained that they had recently remodeled the building and put many items in storage. He was patient, offering to look, but without any luck. Then God answered my prayers. A teacher appeared, and I repeated my story.

She had been both of my sisters' music teacher. She remembered them, and the picture that hung in the hall. Through her tears, she told me she'd been trying to find my mother for years to give it to her.

"You still have it?" I asked. She pointed and there it was: a little boy flying a kite in a pasture. At the bottom was a small brass plaque engraved with "To our classmate, Shawn, May 1981." The teacher wished me a Merry Christmas and then insisted that an angel must have sent me.

I wasn't going to ask her why, but she quickly explained. She had already left for Christmas vacation, but had come back, having forgotten something. It was a miracle that she'd run into me.

When my mother opened her present, she started to cry. "This is the best present anyone could ever give me," she said. Now I know the true meaning of Christmas. ▣

Photo of painting courtesy of Dawn Marie Cullinane

Cootie Monsters

by Kymberly Anne Terribile

Every day during recess my friends and I would gather near the jungle gym and discuss typical second-grade stuff.

"Did you know that Jimmy still wets his bed?" Kara announced.

"Ewww," we all yelled.

"I heard that Sam picks his nose and then he eats it!" Jamie giggled.

"Gross!"

Kara and Jamie were my best friends. I told them everything. Well, almost everything. In second grade it was unacceptable for a girl to like a "cootie monster" (a.k.a. a boy). Ryan Anderson had been the boy of my dreams since he pushed me into the mud in kindergarten. I had eyes for this blond-haired, blue-eyed, freckle-faced kid, but I couldn't tell my best friends for fear of public humiliation. For almost two years I withheld this information. Then, one day, I decided to tell them.

We sat in my room after school eating homemade chocolate-chip cookies.

"Hey guys, guess what," I said. "I like Ryan!"

"Ewwww!" Jamie shrieked. "You can't like a cootie monster!"

I stared into her dark brown eyes and hoped she wouldn't tell any of our classmates.

"Promise not to tell?" I begged, fearing this information would ruin my life. They promised, and the discussion came to a close. I felt relieved I had told them, but a little nervous that they might slip and tell.

The next day when I arrived at school, everyone was laughing at me.

"Kym, is it true that you like Ryan?" Amanda asked.

"No! Why would I like him? He smells bad!"

"Well, Jamie said you do."

I felt my world shatter. I couldn't believe my friends would betray me. "No! No! I don't like him! I hate him!"

The entire class began to gather around me. "Kym and Ryan sitting in a tree, K-I-S-S-I-N-G!" They all sang and taunted. The yells and giggles were more than I could handle. I darted out of the classroom as fast as my little legs could carry me. When I got out to the hallway, I began to cry; salty tears trickled down my bright red face. I never wanted to go back to class again. I couldn't face the kids. I hated Jamie and Kara. And what would Ryan think? Just as these horrible thoughts began racing through my confused mind, I felt a hand on my shoulder.

"Kym," said a familiar voice, "are you okay?" When I turned I saw none other than my crush of two years.

"Why are you crying?" he asked. "If it's because of those nasty kids, forget about it."

"That's easy for you to say," I said, trying to wipe the tears. "They aren't teasing you."

"Well, they *are* teasing my future wife." What? What

had Ryan said? Had I heard him right? Did he say that we were going to get married?

"Come on," Ryan said. "Let's go inside." I took Ryan's hand, and we walked back into the classroom together.

After that day, Jamie, Kara and I never talked again. The terrible laughter has almost faded completely. Ryan moved away that summer, and I never heard from him again. But I will never forget what happened that day when I was seven. Most of all, I will never forget Ryan and my first marriage proposal. ▣

Photo by Caycie Galipeau

Join The Young Authors Foundation and get a monthly subscription to **Teen Ink** magazine.

Only $25 per year!

Foundation Members Receive:
- Ten months of Teen Ink magazine
- Members Newsletter
- Partner in Education Satisfaction – You help thousands of teens succeed.

SUPPORT TEENS' VOICES!

The magazine includes stories, poems and art plus music, book and movie reviews, college essays, sports and more.

If you like Teen Ink, then you'll love Teen Ink magazine.

Join the Young Authors Foundation with a minimum donation of $25 and you will receive 10 monthly issues of *Teen Ink* magazine.

We will start your monthly subscription when we receive your check or credit card information.

Thanks for your support!

BUSINESS REPLY MAIL
FIRST CLASS MAIL   PERMIT NO. 9974 BOSTON,

Postage will be paid by addressee

TEEN INK
Box 610097
NEWTON, MA 02461-0097

NO POSTAGE
NECESSARY IF
MAILED IN THE
UNITED STATES

Repentance

by Jonathan Levine

*Varroom went the little brown bottle of
Grandma's perfume
as I rolled it down the table
Up and down I kept rolling the brown bottle
ignoring her request to put it down.
She was right, as usual, and the bottle smashed:
on the floor it went
in a million pieces.*

*My grandma fell along with that bottle
as if she were broken in a million pieces
Her father had given that bottle to her,*

*and I was very young
and afraid;
my body prevented me
from saying sorry.*

*She died
and at her funeral
I drew her a picture
of how I felt:*

it was a picture of a perfume bottle
with me trapped inside,
waiting and hoping
to be let out
onto a lady's coat
to be admired by everyone
like the smell of fresh banana bread
that someone's mother just baked
I wanted to be a scent
with nothing holding me back
Because that was how I felt—

filled with so much grief
I couldn't say sorry
It's like I was trapped in a stretched balloon,
and would never see the light of day
How I wish
I could have said
sorry.

Morning Ritual

by Marissa Nicole Lefland

Let's try this one more time, sweetie. Put the larger part over the smaller part and flip through. Wrap the large portion around the back—no, not the front—there you go. Then back around to the front. Bring it up through the opening. Put the long part through the loop. Let me do the slipknot, Marissa. That's the daddy's job."

I was always sure to wake up before my sister on school days. It was important to see my dad off to work and spend as much time with him as I could. We'd always go downstairs and munch raisin bran, which I detested, but ate because he loved it. After we drank the last sips of orange juice, we'd stretch and make a sound from the back of our throats that sounded like "Ahhh." Whenever we did, my mom would shoot my father "The Look." He'd just laugh as we raced up the stairs to their room for the ten-minute tie-tying lesson.

To this day, I don't understand how my dad had so much patience with me. I must have choked him many times, yet he was always willing to show me exactly how it was done. While tying a necktie wasn't an essential skill, it was imperative for me to be able to do what he did, exactly as he did it. Somehow, Daddy knew this;

we've always had an unspoken understanding about everything that happened in our lives, even today.

My dad would fold up his collar and tell me I was ready for my lesson. I remember climbing onto the bed that seemed so huge, tumbling over to him and feeling triumphant that I was almost as tall as he. As my mom watched with amusement from the doorway, I meticulously grasped the ends of the tie while my dad gave instructions. When my masterpiece came out a mess, I knew Daddy wouldn't be upset. Eventually, with his help, the knot would be perfect.

Looking back, I know it wasn't tying his necktie that was significant. It was that something so insignificant could bring a father and daughter so close. ◙

Photo by Benjamin P. Quigley

House on Miry Brook

by Allison E. Casazza

Maybe because I was so young back then I don't remember things the way they really were. I know the house on Miry Brook was the first home my grandparents owned. They bought it in 1950, and their five children grew up there. In a way, I did, too. A good portion of my early years was spent at my grandma's house. We called her Grandma KittyCat because we couldn't pronounce Casazza, and she had two cats. Grandma KittyCat lived fifteen minutes away, on a narrow road only one car could drive on at a time. We always honked the horn to warn oncoming cars.

That house was large for a widow, but perfect for her large family, which at one time had filled the rooms with laughter. It was a two-story, dark-brown bungalow with a front porch full of rockers. The porch was the best place to sit on cool July nights to watch fireworks. I used to pretend it was a stage and dance for hours. My dad mastered the unicycle there.

After my grandfather died in 1967, my grandmother raised her family there. Apart from her family, her home on Miry Brook was her greatest love. As a single working mother, she tended to her home with the help of her sons. The grass was always mowed, leaves raked and leaks fixed. When her last child was grown and moved away, the chores didn't end; she did them alone and never complained.

The time I spent at the house on Miry Brook was always a joy. It started when my parents honked the horn, and my grandma would be on that porch waiting for my brother and me to run across the lawn to hug her legs. One of the best things was that lawn: Our yard was a steep hill, but hers was flat and large. My brother and I could play all the games we wanted. There seemed to be endless hiding places, and on warm days we ran back and forth through the sprinkler, growing tired from so much laughter. We would go inside for Grandma's sun-brewed iced tea. The two of us would sit at the kitchen table, listening to Grandma while she sang along with Frank Sinatra.

In the backyard, there was a bush so huge it was more like a tree. I would crawl through the first layer of tiny leaves to the branches inside that were strong enough to hold us. We would run to this bush when our parents told us it was time to leave and hide there, covered with leaves. Every time, my brother and I would crouch, perfectly still, and peer through the leaves to watch our parents until one of us would giggle and blow our cover.

At family gatherings Grandma would bring her crystal punch bowl set into the dining room. The delicate cups with tiny handles hung on the rim of the bowl, and if I reached high enough, or stood on a chair, I could touch the glasses with their intricately carved patterns. I would stir the ladle round and round until the punch spun like the water draining from my bathtub. I would do this until my mother caught me and told me not to touch it again, unless I wanted the punch to spill all over Grandma's beautiful carpet.

I was afraid of one thing in that house: the window in the downstairs bathroom. I feared that a brown bear would sneak up and watch me. I was so afraid that I would always pee as fast as I could and then run to the safety of the kitchen.

My grandma moved out of her house when I was seven because this was no longer the same family neighborhood where she'd raised five children. Now she lives on a quiet street; her house is much easier to maintain. The yard is not as big, but she says there are "plenty of things to keep me busy. There are thirty-seven shrubs in this yard, you know." My grandma is not a short drive away anymore. I only see her a few times a year now.

I drove by the old house on Miry Brook a while ago. It was in the worst condition. An old, worn-out couch and rubbish were strewn on the once-grand front porch. I went to the back and honked the horn. The backyard looked like a junkyard, covered with trash and old cars. ◙

First Snow

by Selena Lu

orn in China, I had never seen snow before I stepped off the airplane in America. I was nine, still a little girl who knew nothing about the world.

"Mom, rice is falling from the sky!" I said, thinking, *That's why Chinese people think Americans are rich.* Mom did not hear me. I wondered, *Why isn't anybody picking it up?*

That night, while my parents slept, I went outside with all the bags I could find, believing that if I filled them with rice, my parents wouldn't have to work hard anymore. I grabbed a handful of rice—it was very cold. I thought, *Americans are different from Chinese, so their rice must be different, too.*

I put all the bags in my room and fell asleep. I dreamed of how happy my parents would be when they saw the rice. The next morning, my mom woke me. The first thing she asked me was, "Why is your room wet? What are these bags filled with water?"

I replied, "That is the rice I got from the street." My mom laughed in a funny voice, and said, "That is not rice. That is snow. In America, when the weather gets cold, the rain changes to snow."

Oh! Now I understood why the rice was so cold, and why the Americans did not collect the rice. Oh, well. I guess I learned the critical difference between rice and snow. ▣

Art by Hart Sawyer

Close Shave

by Emily L. O'Brien

Shaving is the only thing I have completely given up trying to do correctly. I managed to get through *Walden*, the chapter on interactive processes in my math book, and mastered the intricacies of walking and chewing gum at the same time. Somehow the art of leg hair removal remains elusive.

I began shaving the summer I turned eleven. The reason why still remains clouded in my memory, but I think it had something to do with my mother. She had not permitted me to shave, citing the hassle and stubble connected with the operation. Being an obstinate kid, I did not believe one blessed thing she said.

So, I had just gotten off the bus (where the younger kids were belting out the tune of choice) from day camp and was alone in the house. For dinner, Mom had left a package of macaroni and cheese, but had neglected to realize we had run out of milk, rendering the meal inedible until she returned to remedy the situation. Who told her she had the right to starve a poor little girl who had been almost fricasseed on the volleyball court that day? Anger and resentment rose high in my young spirit; I was going to be rebellious, do something I had wanted to do for a while, but was told by the same woman who forgot

THE essential ingredient of macaroni and cheese, never to do it until SHE voiced her consent. HA!

Off I trod to the bathroom, got her razor and pulled out the shaving cream from beneath the sink. It was then I came to my first block: How was I going to go about this procedure? Should I hop into the shower and shave while balancing on one leg or sit on the edge of the bathtub? The latter seemed the safest since I would not trust my sense of balance while holding a blade in my hand.

So I sat on the edge and spent a good three minutes trying to find a semi-comfortable position on the three-inch-wide surface. I shook the can and rubbed on a good inch of cream. I was ready. After the first attempt, which was stalled by my head of hair, which had landed in the cream, I ran the razor up my leg and shook off the excess. I continued this until all the hair was removed, then started on the other one, nearly clogging the drain with the mess. By the time I was done, the once half-full can was empty. It was then I heard my mother's key in the lock, causing me to skitter off to my room and put on a pair of jeans, even though it was a damp ninety degrees.

Mothers, I find, have this inexplicable sixth sense, which they must pick up in childbirth classes. I had jumped into bed with the covers pulled up to my chin when she came in. She walked in and a grin oozed over my face.

"You shaved your legs," Mom stated.

I laid in my bed, dumbfounded. How did she know? I merely nodded, expecting a barrage of chastisements, but instead received a smile which gave the message she knew something I did not. I was not able to sleep much that night.

The next day I thought I knew what she had smiled about. Running my hands down my formerly smooth legs, I found that my fingers encountered tiny pinpricks on their upward journey. Stubble. *Well, no matter,* I thought, *I'll just shave again tonight.* The second time I made the mistake of shaving in the shower, stumbled a little and gashed myself. Now, a shaving cut is a lot worse than a normal one because the water spreads the blood around so it looks like you are losing half your blood. It took ten tissues and five Band-Aids to stop the bleeding.

Since then, things have not improved. Mom always shakes her head, claiming I look like I have been beaten because of the large number of scabs. Mom says she wants to sit down and tell me how to shave properly. All I can do is wish her the best of luck in correcting years of blood-letting. ▣

Did You Ever Wonder?

by Erin Temple

Did you ever wonder what
It would be like . . .
If children ruled the world?

Skyscrapers of building blocks
Streets of chalk-o-late bars
And toys on every corner.

The world would be perfect
No wars, no jobs, no school
And everyone would gather . . .
At the plastic swimming pool.

But ah, this is only fantasy,
Because adults seem to think
That the only way to think
Is the way they think
But, if everyone thought the way they think
I would be inclined to think
That we could not think . . .
At all.

It sort of makes you wonder
Why adults make life so hard
And exactly what would become of us . . .
If children ruled the world.

Army Men

by Mark Baker

Everyone remembers getting up very early to watch the dynamite, anvils and cheap jokes of Saturday morning cartoons. You raced around the house in your pajamas, the sugar from two bowls of Lucky Charms coursing madly through your veins until, as the chaos reached its peak, your groggy parents roared, and you sat quietly and got out toys.

For some, it was blocks or Legos, for others, Barbies. Mine were plastic army men in their classic positions, unchanged since who-knows-when. Their faces were stern and serious, always ready for a scrap with the enemy. Modeled after America's finest, they had a variety of weapons: The infantry gripped their rifles and machine guns tightly; heavy artillery, flame-throwers or bazookas lined up ready to fire at your command.

Our house was their battleground, a field of never-ending possibilities. Piles of laundry were trenches and bunkers for troops to hide in. On the kitchen table, they hid behind glasses and cereal bowls (missile silos and toxic-waste dumps). The backyard was one of my favorites, where soldiers battled for control of the sand-box or swing set. On a few occasions my troops became MIA due to the blades of the lawn mower or teeth of the dog. The best parts were the unending possibilities. It was a giant role-playing game, and I was commander.

In our world of political correctness, violent toys may now be considered improper. But to me, there was no greater joy than a plastic bucket full of these small men, who got me into an occasional heap of trouble. There was the time several fell off the PT boat patrolling the kitchen sink. They disappeared into the disposal and were mauled by the whirling blades. When my brother and I got the idea that our set needed casualties, we took a big heap of soldiers and melted them one by one, ruining my mother's candle. If you have ever seen plastic melt, you know just what they looked like. They were, to my youthful mind, cool, with their bodies twisted and appendages charred. We painted them with red model paint and then set them up to look like the opening scenes of "Saving Private Ryan"—and my mom went crazy!

These soldiers are part of the American tradition. Every boy who has grown up in America probably has memories of these soldiers modeled after those who fought in battles of freedom including D-Day, The Bulge and Iwo Jima. They're still in my basement. Sometimes I play with them when I feel down. I know they will always be at attention, waiting for my next order. ▣

Sassy

by Amy Hochsprung

Chink. Clank. Chink.

That sound always reminds me of one day when I was eight years old, and it was a cold, dreary afternoon at the end of February. The dregs of a recent snowstorm were still on the ground, brown and slushy, and the sun, its light bright and cold, was playing hide-and-seek among the dark clouds.

The school bus had dropped me off at the corner, and I remember walking home, my cheeks red from the biting wind, and my thin legs straining to jump over puddles and avoid the cracks in the sidewalk. I had my special purple lunchbox in one hand, and in the other I clutched some crayon drawings of my family I had proudly made in school. As I approached my house, I broke into a joyful skip, and frolicked up the front steps and through the door. In the hall I shed my purple coat and matching boots, and, leaving them carelessly on the floor in a wet bundle, I ran through the foyer and into the kitchen. There, the sunshine was filtering down through the many windows with square patterns of light playing tag on the wooden table where my mother sat. Oddly, she was in shadow: The sunbeams danced around her, but not near her, as if something kept them away. My mother's fingers were wrapped tightly around a half-empty coffee mug. I recall those hands with strange clarity: the skin stretched thin and drawn into a straight line. Her eyes, usually merry, looked glassy and swollen, and I saw the tracks of dried tears on her smooth cheeks.

Sensing that something was wrong, I forgot about the drawings I clutched and stood in the doorway, looking at her with apprehension. She attempted a smile, failed, and then pushed back her chair and rose. She crossed the room and squatted down in front of me, and, looking straight into my eyes, began to speak in a low, gentle voice.

Thinking back on it now, her words escape me.

All I recall is thinking, *No . . . this isn't true—Sassy CAN'T be dead!* I ran from the room, ran from my mother and the words she had spoken, ran from the death I saw dancing with the sunbeams in the bright kitchen. I raced up the front staircase and down the hall to my bedroom where I grabbed my favorite Slinky. Filled with sudden urgency, I raced down the hall, almost tripping over Sassy's favorite toy mouse, and stopped, breathless when I reached the top of the stairs. There I sat, pulled my knees to my chest, and wrapped my thin arms around them, a small voice inside my head repeating, *She's alive. She's alive. She's alive.* I sat up straight and reached for my Slinky, the familiar feel of its cool wire coils calming me, for I knew Sassy would come. I set the Slinky up against the top of the step and gently pushed it, my hand quivering, and watched as it began its downward descent.

Chink. Clank. Chink.

I kept my eyes riveted to the silvery metal blur, waiting for Sassy to come scampering to catch it as she had done unfailingly thousands of times over the years. No matter where she was, Sassy always heard that distinctive sound and came running, determined to catch the toy before it reached the bottom.

Chink. Clank. Chink. I looked over my shoulder and down the hall. Empty. "She'll come," I whispered.

Chink. Clank. Chink. I peered down the stairs to the front foyer. Empty. *She'll come*, I thought.

Chink. Clank. Chi . . .

The Slinky stopped, its silvery music interrupted by the bottom of the staircase. It sat still. For a moment nothing stirred, and then, in the too loud silence that followed, I began to weep, for Sassy had not come. ▣

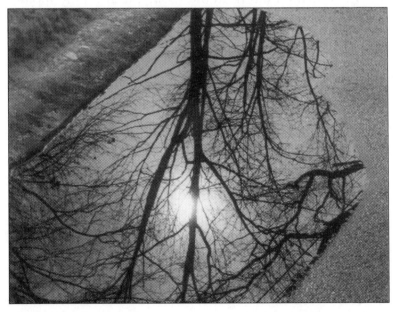

Photo by Melissa-Jeanne Aucoin

Words from Within

by Ellie Roan

Hey out there! I bet you thought I was gone, having perished in the shadows of your mind after all these years of neglect. Well, surprise, I'm still here. You haven't forgotten about me, have you? Ever since you started growing up, things haven't been the same. You never listen to me anymore. Long ago, if I didn't feel like cleaning our room, we'd go outside and play on the swings, shouting or overflowing with giggles. Now, we hardly ever play. I can't even remember the last time we went to the park! These days, you're so busy. You have time for other things: school, sports, and your big friends, but I'm feeling pretty neglected. I hate to say this, but I'm a lot smaller than I used to be.

Years ago, I was in control, free to do spur-of-the-moment activities, without worrying about the effects of our actions. Remember the time we knocked down that bees' nest with a baseball? Now *that* was exciting! I mean, sure, we ended up with a few stings, but we're still alive, aren't we? If it weren't for me, would you ever have had the chance to study a furiously buzzing, yellow, swarming wall of bees? All those hours of science homework you struggle through will never compare with that experience!

Consequences, consequences, consequences! That's all I ever hear. Remember the hot summer evening we drenched Mom with the garden hose right before she went to that party? Did consequences get in our way then? Of course, I didn't enjoy being grounded for the rest of the month, but it was worth it, wasn't it?

You often try to lose me, but I find a way to live on. I still see a small part of me inside you—dashing around like a maniac during a downpour, playing foolish games while baby-sitting. . . .

I'm not such a big part of your life anymore, but I'm right there with you as you gaze into the night sky with that same childlike wonder I remember so well. I was there as you memorized *How the Grinch Stole Christmas* last year for no apparent reason. I know you aren't going to make up stories as you play with Legos anymore, but you still use your creativity to think how things should be or could be. I gave you that imagination. Don't forget the good parts of me—my spontaneity, my innocence, my inquisitiveness.

Hold on! Don't tune me out yet. The reason I'm disrupting your big-person life is because I want to make a deal. I know there are parts of me that you don't like, but there are others you could use in that "mature" world of yours.

So, here's what I propose: I promise to think a little bit about your precious consequences before I act (not a lot, mind you). In return, I want to be a bigger part of your life. Try not to care so much about what other people think; be spontaneous! Don't be afraid to do strange things; you know weirdness is one of your best qualities.

And most of all, be inquisitive! Too many adults just accept what they're told without thinking. No wonder they get annoyed when little kids ask so many questions. I know this plan will work wonders. What do you think? Is it a deal?

Hold on—is that the ice cream truck I hear? Let's go! ▣

Photo by Colleen Fitzgerald

How to submit writing, art and photos for the monthly *Teen Ink* magazine and future *Teen Ink* books:

You must be twelve to nineteen years old to be published.

- Include your name, year of birth, home address/city/ state/zip, telephone number and the name of your school and English teacher on each submission. Most published pieces are fewer than 2,500 words.

- Type all submissions, if possible, or print carefully in ink. We can't return any submissions, so keep a copy.

- Label all work fiction or nonfiction. Be sure to include a title.

- Affix name and address information on the back of each photo or piece of art. Please don't fold.

- Include the following originality statement in your own handwriting after each submission: "This will certify that the above work is completely original," and sign your name to affirm this is your work.

- Request anonymity. If due to the very personal nature of a piece you don't want your name published, we will respect your request, but you still must include name and address information for our records.

Other information:

If published in the magazine or book, you will receive a free copy together with an environmentally sound wooden pen and a special *Teen Ink* Post-it pad.

All works submitted become the property of *Teen Ink* and all copyrights are assigned to *Teen Ink.* We retain the non-exclusive rights to publish all such works in any format. All material in *Teen Ink* is copyrighted to protect us and exclude others from republishing your work. However, individual contributors retain the right to submit their work for publication elsewhere, and you have our permission to do so.

Writing may be edited, and we reserve the right to publish our edited version without your prior approval.

Send all submissions to:

Teen Ink

Box 97 • Newton, MA 02461

E-mail: *Book@TeenInk.com*

617-964-6800

To learn more about the magazine and to obtain a free sample copy, see our Web site at *www.TeenInk.com.*

All the royalties from the sale of this book are being donated to The Young Authors Foundation

Established in 1989, The Young Authors Foundation, Inc. is the publisher of *Teen Ink* (formerly *The 21st Century*), a monthly magazine written entirely by teens for teens. This magazine has been embraced by schools and teenagers nationwide; more than 3.5 million students read *Teen Ink* magazine every year.

The magazine empowers teenagers by publishing their words, giving them a voice and demonstrating that they can make a difference. *Teen Ink* is also dedicated to improving reading, writing and critical-thinking skills while encouraging creativity and building self-esteem. The editors have read more than 300,000 submissions from students during the past twelve years, and more than 25,000 of them have been published. There is no charge to submit work, and all published students receive a free copy of the magazine plus other items.

In keeping with its mission, the Foundation distributes thousands of class sets and individual copies free to schools and teachers every month. In addition, more than twenty-five hundred schools support the foundation by paying a subsidized fee for their monthly class sets.

From its beginnings as a small foundation with a regional publication, The Young Authors Foundation has grown steadily and today is a national program funded with donations, sponsorships, grants and advertising from companies and individuals that support its goals. In

addition to funding the magazine, the foundation under-
writes a number of other educational programs:

- *Teen Ink Poetry Journal* showcases more than one
  thousand young poets and is distributed free to sub-
  scribing schools.

- *Teen Ink Educator of the Year Awards Contest* wel-
  comes nominating essays from students to honor
  outstanding teachers with cash awards, certificates
  and publication of their essays in the magazine.

- *Teen Ink Book Awards* program donates thousands
  of free books and award materials annually so
  schools can recognize students who have shown
  "improvement and individual growth in the field of
  English."

- *Teen Ink Interview Contest* encourages thousands of
  teens to interview family and friends. Winners per-
  sonally interview national celebrities including Hillary
  Clinton, Colin Powell, John Glenn, Jesse Jackson,
  Martin Sheen, Maya Angelou, George Lucas and
  others.

- *Teen Ink Web site (www.TeenInk.com)* includes
  more than 13,000 pages of student writing, art, photos, resources, contests and more.

The Young Authors Foundation, Inc., is a nonprofit
501(c)3 organization. See next page for details on how
you can support these programs and receive a monthly
copy of the magazine.

Join The Young Authors Foundation and get a monthly subscription to Teen Ink magazine.

Only $25 per year!

Foundation Supporters Receive:

- Ten months of Teen Ink magazine
- Annual Newsletter
- Partner in Education Satisfaction – You help thousands of teens succeed.

The magazine includes stories, poems and art plus music, book and movie reviews, college essays, sports and more.

SUPPORT TEEN VOICES!

☐ **Annual Dues $25***
I want to receive ten monthly issues of **Teen Ink** magazine and become a supporter of The Young Authors Foundation!
(Enclose your check or complete credit card information below)

☐ I am interested in your foundation. Please send me information about The Young Authors Foundation.

☐ I want to support the Foundation with a tax-deductible donation for: $_____
(Do not send copies of the magazine)

NAME_____PHONE_____

STREET_____

CITY/TOWN _____ STATE _____ZIP _____

PHONE_____E-MAIL_____

M/C OR VISA *(CIRCLE ONE)*#_____EXP. DATE _____/_____

Send a gift subscription to:
NAME _____

STREET_____

CITY/TOWN_____STATE_____ZIP _____

Mail coupon to: Teen Ink • Box 97 • Newton, MA 02461 – Or join online: www.TeenInk.com

* The Young Authors Foundation, publisher of *Teen Ink*, is a 501(c)3 nonprofit organization providing opportunities for the education and enrichment of young people. While all donations support the Foundation's mission, 75% is designated for the magazine subscription, and no portion should be considered as a charitable contribution.

Acknowledgments

We want to give special thanks to all those who have worked with us to make the *Teen Ink* book series a reality. When we started this project in 1989, we never imagined we would work with such wonderful, talented and dedicated people. Many played a large part in the overall success of our nonprofit Young Authors Foundation (which helps fund all our projects); others work tirelessly on our monthly magazine that is the source for the *Teen Ink* books; and others contribute their time, skills and insight to make these books the best representation of teen writing available. We are most fortunate to have all of these people as family, friends and coworkers:

Our Children:

Robert Meyer, Alison Meyer Hong and her supportive husband, Michael, have been our constant source of strength throughout the entire process. Their love, support, encouragement and wisdom have helped guide us every step of the way.

Our Staff:

Julie Chen has been our book project manager, assistant editor, organizer and that special go-to person who makes it all come together. Most of the authors, teachers and others involved in this project have come to know about her caring concern for their individual needs. We are most grateful for Julie's insight and attention to detail that have made their mark on these books.

A special thanks to the rest of our most incredible office staff, filled with young, energetic voices that are always there with advice and assistance: Kate Dunlop Seamans, Karen Watts, Tony Abeln and Elissa Gershowitz, as well as our long-time volunteer, Barbara Field, who has been a support in so many ways through the years. In addition we appreciate the extra effort from our extended staff, which includes Paul Watts, Denise Peck, Larry Reed, Jim Brown, Michael Seamans, Scott Saltus, Bob Kuchnicki, Ray Hebert, Steve Gilbert, Frank Chase and Tyler Ford.

Our Family, Friends and Foundation Board:

Our extended family and friends who always listen to our voices and offer their support on many different levels: all the Raisners, (Barbara, Debra, Jason, David and Amy), Joseph Rice III, Jennifer and Rick Geisman, Alison Swap, Barbara Wand, Molly and Steve Dunn, Timothy

Neeley, Glenn Evans, Marty Kaplan, Jeanne Cole, Filis Casey, Zick Rubin, Paul Chase, Paula and Lowell Fox, and Stewart and Jackie Newland. And the even larger family of Foundation Board Members: J. Robert Casey, David Anable, Richard Freedberg, as well as our Advisory Board: Beverly Beckham, Michael Dukakis, Kay Fanning, Milton Lieberman, Harold Raynolds, Susan Weld and Thomas Winship who have served with us through the years.

Our Publishing Family at HCI:

All the incredible folks at HCI who respected our belief in this project, and then supported it with their energy, talent and resources: Peter Vegso, whose voice is always supportive and insightful; Tom Sand for his business acumen and sense of humor; Lisa Drucker and Susan Tobias, our editors with such amazing eyes for detail; Terry Burke and the entire sales gang, whose tireless energy helped launch the *Teen Ink* series; Kim Weiss and Kimberley Denney, whose ideas gave us constant encouragement as we worked together to spread the word about the book; the innovative Kelly Maragni and her talented staff; the amazing Randee Feldman, whose book events were such an inspiration to all; and, Larissa Hise Henoch and Dawn Grove for their continued commitment to make the book design and graphics so inspiring for our entire series.

In addition, we want to thank the following teachers and more than twenty-five hundred students who read and evaluated sample chapters of *Teen Ink 2: More Voices, More Visions.* Their feedback and ratings were invaluable in helping us select the final pieces for this book.

Alabama School of Fine Arts, Birmingham, Alabama—Anne Black and Denise Wadsworth Trimm

Albright Middle School, Houston, Texas—Catherine Busald and Leslie Scarborough

Ashtabula County Joint Vocational School, Jefferson, Ohio—Debra Cary and Suzanne McCune

Auburn High School, Auburn, New York—Preston Wilson

Bay Port High School, Green Bay, Wisconsin—Michael Roherty

Bellport High School, Brookhaven, New York—Glenn Hadzima

Black River High School, Ludlow, Vermont—Colin McKaig

Bourgade Catholic High School, Phoenix, Arizona—Marianne Moriarty

Brunswick High School, Brunswick, Maine—Jeanne Shields

Cortez High School, Phoenix, Arizona—Diane Bykowski and Tom Helms

Destrehan High School, Destrehan, Louisiana—Lynn Thompson

Du Bois Area High School, Du Bois, Pennsylvania—Carole Roberts

Eufaula High School, Eufaula, Oklahoma—Gale Applegate

Exeter Area High School, Exeter, New Hampshire—John Ferguson

Framingham High School, Framingham, Massachusetts—Peter Galamaga and Kate Greene

Gabrielino High School, San Gabriel, California—Robin Solid

John Dickinson High School, Wilmington, Delaware—Tara Dick

Kamehameha Secondary School, Honolulu, Hawaii—Ruth Canham

La Mirada High School, La Mirada, California—Andrea Wood

Mandeville Junior High School, Mandeville, Louisiana—Lee Barrios

Memorial High School, Eau Claire, Wisconsin—Debra Peterson and Fred Poss

Mercy High School, Middletown, Connecticut—Adrienne Lovell

Notre Dame Academy, Hingham, Massachusetts—Roberta Devlin

Papillion LaVista High School, Papillion, Nebraska—Margaret Shanahan

Patrick Henry High School, Ashland, Virginia—Sallie Bedall

Pilgrim High School, Warwick, Rhode Island—Susan Dillon

Pine-Richland Middle School, Gibsonia, Pennsylvania—Susan Frantz and Aleta Lardin

Randolph High School, Randolph, New Jersey—Elizabeth McConnell

Rippowam Cisqua School, Bedford, New York—Kendra Gilder and Cathy Greenwood

Royal Palm Beach High School, Royal Palm Beach, Florida—Kim Grinder

Shoreham-Wading River High School, Shoreham, New York—Kevin Mann

St. Albans High School, St. Albans, West Virginia—Bettijane Burger

St. Mary's Jr./Sr. High School, Lynn, Massachusetts—Lisa Spinelli

Stephenville High School, Stephenville, Texas—Jennifer Muncey

Stoughton High School, Stoughton, Massachusetts—Judith Hamilton and Tracy Hurley

Ward Melville High School, Setauket, New York—Faith Krinsky

Washington High School, Phoenix, Arizona—Jill Green

Watertown High School, Watertown, Tennessee—Lynda Jellison

Whitehall High School, Whitehall, Montana—Lee Ann Gallagher

Wichita East High School, Wichita, Kansas—Jennifer Fry and Lisa Kellerby

Williamsville North High School, Williamsville, New York—Daniel Greiner

Williamsville South High School, Williamsville, New York—Lisabeth Pieters

Winnisquam Regional High School, Tilton, New Hampshire—Barbara Blinn

Wyoming Park High School, Grand Rapids, Michigan—Jeremy Schnotala and Mary Van Vuren

Contributors

Brian Alessandrini is a senior in high school. He enjoys reading and writing, which is one reason why he's looking forward to college, which he sees as an opportunity to celebrate and respect something many take for granted: education. Brian is grateful for his ex-girlfriend in his story. Even though the experience was difficult, "It taught me so much. If it hadn't been for this, I wouldn't have the strength I have today."

Amy Annino shot her photo as a "roving reporter" for her high-school newspaper using her old Pentax ME with a flash. While in high school, she won an award for her photography, and she played in both the concert and jazz bands. Having graduated from college with a degree in biology and chemistry, Amy is currently pursuing her Ph.D. in plant physiology. She still enjoys photography, especially during vacations, and is trying to turn some of her photographs into postcards.

Talin Aprahamian wrote her amusing poem about high school as a senior. She is now finishing college and studying accounting. She works as a resident advisor, campus lifeguard and is an active member of the Armenian Youth Federation. In her free time she enjoys playing the piano (which she's done since she was four) and swimming with her friends. Talin is happy to say that life has been less crazy in college, and she is glad her mom was always there encouraging her.

Katherine S. Assef has been writing since the fourth grade as "a way to forget my ego and discover the world." Her favorite writers include Amy Tan, Raymond Carver, Margaret Atwood, Alice Munro and Toni Morrison. Now a high school freshman, she loves to sing, act, dance and draw. She also enjoys taking long walks by herself and spending time with her family and golden retriever, Duchess. Katie dedicates her short story to her friend Sarah, who "always makes roller coasters less scary,"

333

and to Mr. Littell and Kelly, "two one-in-a-million teachers who helped me grow in so many ways."

Lisa V. Atkins is a freshman in college interested in studying psychology. Right now she is being "a typical college kid—trying to figure everything out." She loves to read and listen to all kinds of music. She also enjoys writing, singing and dancing, and has studied tap, jazz and ballet for years. Lisa has lived in Washington, Florida, Louisiana, Texas and Germany (where she and her family return to visit each summer). She thanks S.A. for inspiring her poem which she wrote as a sophomore.

Melissa-Jeanne Aucoin graduated from college with a degree in creative writing and French, and is pursuing a career in publishing. She enjoys writing, reading and shooting photos. One of her most memorable experiences was the semester she spent in France and visited Italy, Holland, Germany, Spain and Belgium. She writes, "Those moments with new friends in Europe helped me discover a lot about myself, and traveling alone at times was definitely an educational experience—about myself and other cultures." Melissa took her photo as a high-school senior. She thanks her photography teacher, Mr. Berube, for "his patience with me and for his encouragement to pursue my dreams."

Patrick Michael Baird took his photo while a senior in high school. Now a college freshman studying photography and psychology, most of his time and energy go into his school projects and photography. In his spare time he likes to visit galleries and enjoy city nightlife. Patrick took his photo using a Canon Rebel G. He thanks his former photography teacher, Ms. Demetrious, for being a huge inspiration, as well as all his friends and especially his family for their love and guidance.

Mark Baker is currently in the eighth grade. He has played ice hockey for the last eight years and is an active participant in Odyssey of the Mind at his middle school. He has a paper route and enjoys playing the piano, reading and writing fiction. He also likes hanging out, playing football with his friends and spending summers at the beach. Mark's reminiscent piece was published in *Teen Ink* magazine last year.

Dan Baldwin took his photo as a senior in high school. After graduating, he was appointed as a call firefighter for his hometown and also became an emergency medical technician for the state. Now a college student studying fire science, he plans to be a firefighter and paramedic. He currently works as the manager of an independent supermarket, and enjoys boating and snowboarding in his free time.

Jillian Balser has come a long way since she wrote about her family during her junior year in high school. She is now a college sophomore studying fine arts, communications and theater, and she writes, "I am proud of the person I have become and the opportunities and obstacles that await me. . . . I am fascinated by and fully intend to experience everything the world has to offer." Jillian thanks "Mum and Dad for giving me my life story, to *Teen Ink* for helping me share it and to the kids of the world for listening."

Natascha Batchelor graduated from college with a degree in urban forestry and currently works as a tree expert. She enjoys working outdoors and helping people understand the plant life around them. She believes that like many things, there is more to trees and plants than meets the eye. Natascha's piece about her mother was originally published in *Teen Ink* magazine when she was a senior in high school.

Jen Beachley wrote her piece about a very special teacher as a senior in high school. Now a college junior studying business and computer science, she is active in student government and her school's horsewomen's association. She still enjoys writing and is working on a young-adult horse-racing series. Jen plans to pursue her MBA, and then she hopes to write and work in marketing in the horse-racing industry. She also dreams of owning a farm to raise thoroughbred racehorses.

Brandy Belanger is a freshman in college. She enjoys photography and reading. (Her favorite novel of all time is *Gone with the Wind*.) In her free time she enjoys going out for dinner, playing pool with her brother and watching movies. Brandy wrote her personal piece as a sophomore in high school. Writing served as an outlet for her and she's happy to say that she's now enjoying college and doing much better. She credits her mom with helping her through those difficult times.

Teresa Bendokas took her photo during her junior year in high school. She and two close friends, Jason and Nathaniel, were walking on the beach and climbing rocks when she started to take pictures for fun. After high school, Teresa studied photography. She is now a college sophomore majoring in human services, hoping to help children with special needs. She loves the outdoors, and especially enjoys snowboarding and kayaking.

Jamie Bleiweiss graduated from her first-choice college with a degree in biology and psychology, and works with young children who have developmental disabilities. She plans to pursue a Ph.D. in psychology. In her free time, she works out and spends time with friends. Jamie wrote about applying to college as a senior in high school. She dedicates it to her family who have always been so supportive.

Megan Blocker wrote her poignant short story during her sophomore year in high school. She is currently a college senior studying religion. She still loves to write, although her interests now lean more toward essays and seminar papers (which come with the territory!). She is president of a school choir and has directed and produced a number of shows. After graduating she plans to spend time living in Europe.

Kristen Bonacorso took her photo as a sophomore in high school. Now in her second year of college, she enjoys hanging out with her friends and "could spend hours looking at photographs." She is a big fan of Ansel Adams and especially appreciates black and white photography and the use of contrasting textures. After eating only grilled cheese and French toast for seven years, Kristen has learned to appreciate food as an art in itself. She also loves the beach and going for drives to enjoy the ocean scenery.

Kate Bosco drew her cartoon as a high-school junior when she was learning to drive. Now a college freshman studying graphic design, she hopes to work in advertising. She loves to play softball and has been the pitcher for her high school and college teams. She also enjoys drawing, inline skating and going to the movies. Though she almost received the title of "Worst Driver" during her senior year, Kate is happy to report that her driving has since improved. She especially thanks her dad for "getting me into art when I was little and for teaching me how to drive."

Rachel Svea Bottino entered college this year as a sophomore with a major in English. The poignant experience she wrote about as a junior in high school had a lasting effect: "I've become more appreciative of what I have and what many people don't have. . . . [It] opened up my eyes to a serious problem that not only our nation faces, but also the whole world." Rachel dedicates her piece to her former English teacher, Ms. Sullivan, "who was so supportive and influential in my life."

Lisa A. Bourgeault took her photo of her sister, Anna, during her senior year in high school. Now a college junior studying apparel marketing, she is active with her sorority and has been studying dance since she was little. She spends summers studying modern and jazz dance and has even danced with Savion Glover and Jeannette Neill. Lisa still enjoys photography and collecting anything by Anne Geddes. She also loves going out to eat and spending time in the sun.

Andrew Briggs wrote about his grandmother as a senior in high school. He has since graduated from college with a degree in psychology and currently works for a large E-services consulting firm. In college he played in the orchestra for musicals, participated in Habitat for Humanity and was a member of a fraternity. Andy expresses his creative energies through photography and playing the cello, which he has done since he was nine. He still has a passion for creative writing.

Mindy Bruce is a college junior studying communications and public relations (and starting to feel the way she did when she first wrote her piece as a senior in high school!). She is involved with the public relations club and helps with special events for Kids Across America. She also works as a cake decorator at a bakery. For fun she writes and spends time outdoors, hiking and camping. Mindy says her former English teacher, Mrs. Jennings, "showed me I have the ability to write, something I have always wanted to do."

Jennifer Aubrey Burhart wrote her piece as a high-school senior about a move that happened when she was very young. After graduating with a degree in math education, she taught math for a year and now is enjoying her graduate studies for a Ph.D. program in counseling psychology. She has done some writing since high school and recently discovered that she loves to read. She is even attempting to learn to cook and has resolved not to eat cereal every day! Aubrey dedicates her poignant piece to her dog, Benji, who was such a big part of her life.

Timothy Cahill is a college sophomore majoring in English. This past football season he was an officer of the marching band and was responsible for co-writing scripts for the halftime shows. He is also a member of the film society and mock trial team, and in his free time he enjoys politics and Ping-Pong. Tim wrote his engrossing piece as a freshman in high school. Tim also created the Preface of *Teen Ink 2*.

Eileen Carlos wrote about being tempted as a junior in high school. She has since graduated from college with a degree in psychology, and currently works as an office administrator for a large securities firm. She is active in community service, serving as the United Way coordinator for her office. In her free time she enjoys reading business and self-help/spirituality books and going to the movies. She is proud to say that to this day she has never smoked a cigarette (or a joint) and has never drunk to excess.

Allison E. Casazza is a freshman in interior-design school. She loves many of the creative arts, including art, writing and dance, and has studied ballet, tap, jazz and modern dance for ten years. She also enjoys traveling and hopes to visit more of the United States and Europe. Allison wrote her reflective piece as a high-school senior. She thanks Julia and Erica for always encouraging and teaching her, and Ms. Heyd for all her love and support.

Kristi Ceccarossi wrote her humorous short story as a junior in high school. She is currently a college junior studying English and journalism, and she serves as the arts editor for her college daily newspaper. In her free time she still loves to read and recently has chosen to write poetry, mostly due to a lack of time for creating fiction. Kristi hopes to travel and would love a job in travel writing or photojournalism that would allow her to experience different communities around the world.

Lara Chard still clearly remembers the day she drew her first artistic masterpiece in kindergarten. Ever since then, she has "concentrated on creative expression and grown through every piece I have created, whether it was drawing with a stick in the sand as a child or spending countless hours on a painting." Now a freshman in college studying fine art, Lara has been active in Girl Scouts, varsity cheerleading and playing the drums. She is also an environmental awareness and animal rights advocate. Her photo appeared in *Teen Ink* magazine last year.

Paul Constant was published in *Teen Ink* magazine many times while in high school. Since then he has studied English and sociology, and self-published four comics and three journals. His most memorable experiences include visiting Graceland where he wept at Elvis's grave, meeting both the President of Ireland and Scotty from "Star Trek," and being shoved aside by Hunter S. Thompson while working as the mall Easter bunny.

Lucy Coulthard wrote her poignant piece about her uncle as a senior in high school. Currently a college junior studying wildlife biology, she plans to pursue a masters and work in biology conservation. Lucy loves the outdoors as well as spending time with her family, boyfriend and friends. Another favorite pastime is reading; her favorite authors include Kurt Vonnegut and Chaim Potok. Lucy credits her high-school English teacher, Mr. Marshall, "for teaching me how to be a good writer, for exposing me to a variety of great literature, and for urging all his students to get their work out there and published."

Emily Crotzer enjoys photography and even though her evocative piece is fiction, she prefers writing poetry. Her favorite poets include Gwendolyn Brooks and her friends who are fellow writers. She also loves to travel and hopes to visit Cuba or Costa Rica this summer. Emily wrote her short story as a senior in high school. Now a college sophomore interested in international relations and psychology, she thanks her mom, dad, Jennifer and Jessica, her former creative writing teacher, Mrs. Bedall, and her college professor, Mark Wood.

Dawn Marie Cullinane believes her most memorable experience will always be the Christmas she presented the painting of her brother, Shawn, to her parents. Now a freshman in college studying journalism, she became interested in writing through her high-school teacher, Mrs. Minton, who was killed in a car accident when Dawn was a junior. Dawn writes, "She was my teacher, friend and mentor. I loved her for believing in my writing and always being there for me. I know she's looking over me and smiling for all my dreams that have come true."

Kathryn D'Angelo, a dedicated horseback rider, often competes in shows. As a junior in high school, she is involved in the student council and also works as a legal secretary. The most significant events in

Kari's life have been "those of revelation and understanding." These small experiences have contributed to who she is today and will continue to shape the person she sees in the mirror every day. Her caring poem was first published in *Teen Ink* magazine last year.

Rob Dangel, a college graduate with a degree in business/MIS, currently works as IT manager for a software company. In his free time he loves to play computer games, travel, scuba dive, take care of his ninety-gallon marine reef tank and do home improvements. Rob wrote his hilarious essay as a senior in high school. He now looks back and wishes he could be that age again, when going through puberty was his greatest worry. He writes, "Ferris Bueller (my personal hero) said it best: 'Life moves pretty fast; if you don't stop and look around once in a while, you might miss it.' That rings true every day of my life."

Kristy R. Davis wrote her pensive piece as a senior in high school. Currently a college junior studying politics, she is president of her class, chair of the college Republicans and a student ambassador. She also works as a legislative aide for her local board of supervisors. She loves sports, politics and volunteering for political campaigns. Kristy thanks Mr. Newton "for teaching me the importance of noticing others."

Kelly Dean is a high-school senior. This summer she and her friends are planning a trip to Florida to celebrate graduation. She hopes to study psychology and secondary education in college. Kelly enjoys reading, writing and swimming. She also likes "hanging out with friends and driving around, watching movies, laughing and kidding around." Her piece about a first kiss was published in *Teen Ink* magazine last year.

Alissa Deschnow currently attends college and works part-time. In her spare time she enjoys babysitting and volunteering for her church. She says, "My life isn't that exciting, but it's mine," and she thanks Shelly "for making my life as wonderful as it is now." Alissa wrote her essay as a high-school sophomore.

Robert Dixter wrote his emotion-filled piece as a high school senior. After graduating from college with a degree in English, he realized he wasn't going to change the world single-handedly, so instead he took a job at MTV, hoping that through music television programming, he could help create a utopian society! Robert continues to write, sometimes for television, and his hobbies include watching films from the 1980s and playing hockey.

Nicole M. Docteur finally got her driver's license last year (after failing the first time!) and is now happily driving her grandmother's 1985 Oldsmobile Cutlass. A college sophomore, she is studying anthropology and is secretary of the anthropology club and a member of an honor society. This past year she organized a community-service program to benefit local migrant farmers and rural families, and plans to spend a semester abroad next year. In her free time she enjoys reading and writing. Having written her piece as a high school junior, she gives special thanks to her mom and dad for their support.

Erica Doughty enjoys "singing, reading, writing and sleeping (hee, hee)." She currently works and attends a technical college, and she believes "insignificance is so underrated." While in high school she volunteered on the AIDS Quilt Project and was honored for her creative writing. Erica's hysterical depiction of her prom was originally published in *Teen Ink* magazine last year when she was a senior.

Jennifer A. Eisenberg is a junior in college studying elementary education and history. She is a member of a sorority and chairs the philanthropy club. Jen wrote about her roots while a senior in high school. She has since discovered her original birth certificate which includes her birthparents' names and birthplace. After graduation, she plans to visit Mexico to investigate further. She dedicates her piece to her parents, grandmother and Pamela Rico, who brought her back to health. She writes, "Without them I would not be here, and I want them to know how very much I love them."

Kerri Erskine wrote about becoming a teen mother as a junior in high school. She is now married to her high-school sweetheart and is the mother of four. When she's not working part-time as a pharmacy technician, she spends every minute with her family. Even though she's older now and has a family of her own, Kerri still strongly believes it's better to wait until adulthood to become a parent. She dedicates her piece to her parents—"If it wasn't for them, I wouldn't have been able to go through everything"—her husband, Chris, and her children, Corey, Justin, Ashly and their new baby.

Crystal Lynn Evans is a college freshman studying music education. Her dream is to teach children the art of putting words to music. In her free time she enjoys being with her friends and family. She is active in her church and community music programs. Crystal wrote her poem as a junior in high school. She thanks her parents for "their love and encouragement and the little prayers they've said for me along the way."

Emily Evans took her photo during her junior year in high school where she was a member of both the swim and track teams. She is now a college freshman studying physical therapy and clinical science. She still swims with the college team and is involved with crew. She dedicates her photo to her friend, Rachel Farahbakhsh, for being "a willing subject."

Gulielma L. Fager is a college junior focusing on Latin American studies. She is a member of the campus Green Party and a volunteer with mentally-disabled adults. In her spare time she enjoys writing and traveling. She is working on starting a monthly feminist magazine and is planning to spend this summer in Costa Rica. Guli wrote her retrospective piece as a senior in high school. She dedicates it to Lea Morgenstern and gives special thanks to her parents.

Colleen Fitzgerald and her friend, Lindsey, were "just joking around at a beach near home" when she took her photograph last year. She is now a college freshman pursuing a career in nursing. She explains, "I love kids and people, and I like to take care of them." A member of the field hockey team in high school, she still enjoys skiing, swimming and taking pictures with Lindsey.

Barry Floyd wrote about his experience as a senior in high school. He is now a college sophomore majoring in film. He works as the cameraman for student events and hopes to become a scriptwriter and director. His favorite directors include Spike Lee, Quentin Tarantino and M. Night Shyamalan. Most of his free time is spent watching movies and hanging out with his friends. Barry dedicates his piece to his parents and gives special thanks to his eleventh-grade teacher, Dr. Walsh.

Devin Foxall still believes firmly in nap time (and probably takes too many naps). Now a sophomore in college studying English, he is news and managing editor for the newspaper and a contributor to the literary magazine. He also enjoys boxing and plans to start a monthly news, literary and arts magazine for his college campus and surrounding community. One of his most memorable moments was when he jumped into an icy river to save a small Shetland hound from drowning, performing CPR to save its life. Devin wrote his essay as a senior in high school and feels he was inspired by all his high-school English teachers.

Mike Friedman writes, "Something funny: Two sausages sit side-by-side in a frying pan and they're frying. The first sausage turns to the second and says, 'Boy, it's kinda hot in here, huh?' The second sausage looks at the first one and says, 'Aaah! A talking sausage!' That's my favorite joke." Mike wrote about his memorable experience as a senior in high school. Now a college senior studying psychology and French, he enjoys music and working in a French lab. He still reads and writes both for class and himself.

Jennifer Fusco is a senior in high school. She likes to make believe that she played the role of "The Wind" in Bette Midler's song, "Wind Beneath My Wings," and "won" three gold medals for miniature golf in the Olympics. She "starred" as a rockette at Radio City Music Hall and "tipped" the Leaning Tower of Pisa. She really enjoys creative writing (in case you hadn't figured that out). Jen dedicates her poignant story to her dad, whose real-life struggle inspired her to write her piece.

Caycie Galipeau is a college sophomore who enjoys art, photography and gardening. She also loves to sew and has recently taken up cooking. In high school she was active in the drama club and still returns to her school to help with plays. She proudly admits, "There is a lot of talent there!" One of Caycie's most memorable experiences was the European tour she took with her art class during junior year. Visiting Portugal and Spain was "a great experience." Her photos appeared in *Teen Ink* magazine and the *Teen Ink Poetry Journal.*

Megan Galipeau, in addition to photography, enjoys singing, writing and attending musicals. Someday she'd like to travel the world taking pictures and experiencing other cultures. Megan shot her photograph with a Pentax K-1000 and 400 film for her first photography class. Now a college freshman studying art education and photography, she thanks her former photo teacher, Becky, for "all the encouragement and special lessons she gave me. To my mom, dad, sister Caycie, Mémère Noëlla and Mémère Teresa, my entire family and all the friends who supported me in my decision to attend art school, I haven't words enough to thank you."

Kristi Gentile wrote her touching poem during her junior year in high school. Now a college freshman studying elementary education, she is involved with the Irish Club, Habitat for Humanity and other community-service groups. She is also a member of the club lacrosse team. Kristi has received many awards for her writing and was featured in two other national publications. Her poem is written in memory of her good friend, Julie Dawson, who committed suicide three years ago.

Mai Goda admits her hair is back to its original color and says, "I have 'settled down' from those rebellious times in high school." Her insightful piece was originally published when she was a senior. Now a college junior majoring in philosophy, she works as a teaching assistant for the language department and is the flutist for a Latin band. She is also a mentor, helping first-year students adjust to college.

Olivia L. Godbee is a senior in high school. She enjoys art, photography and tribal belly dancing. She started her own business creating jewelry, and hopes to launch her own photography business. Her piece about finding love was published in *Teen Ink* magazine two years ago. Olivia thanks Mrs. Reinagle for her support and encouragement, and Mr. Hitchens for his ability to motivate her. Most of all, "I would like to thank Robert for all his love and the happiness he has brought me."

Bat-Sheva Guez wrote her realistic short story as a junior in high school. Now a college sophomore, she is studying film and mathematics. She is president of the TV club and is a technical trainee in the drama department. She also works at a local NPR radio show. In her free time Bat-Sheva relaxes by playing the piano and writing; she hopes to write a feature-length screenplay for her senior thesis.

Amber Delphine Hall created her self-portrait in charcoal during art class, using her reflection in a mirror as a guide. A sophomore in high school, she has liked drawing since she was little. She prefers drawing human faces in chalk and pastel. In her free time she enjoys being with her family and listening to music—"anything that catches my ear!" Amber dedicates her drawing to her Aunt Mary. She says, "I miss you, though I feel you've been here with me."

Megan Hayes is enjoying her last year in college where she rooms with her six best friends in a beach house. She is studying communications and art, and in her free time works in an art gallery. This summer she plans to travel to Europe with her mother and grandmother. Megan wrote her lovely portrait of her mother as a high-school senior. She dedicates it "to my mumma, the most important person in my life and the person I look up to the most."

Meghan Heckman wrote about her good friend as a freshman in high school. Now a college senior studying English and journalism, she is the news editor and police beat reporter for the school's paper and a member of the varsity sailing team. She is also an avid skier and has been an instructor since she was fourteen. In her free time she enjoys writing and running. Meg hopes to be a newspaper reporter and eventually a magazine writer. She thanks her high-school teachers, Ms. Brown and Ms. Phinney, "for giving me a voice," and Mr. Lesniewski, "who taught me to think on my feet and stand up for what I believe in."

Jodi B. Heller developed her photograph using a page she selected from a magazine. The resulting cool effect comes from the images on both sides of the page. A senior in high school, Jodi is a member of the show choir and Girl Scouts. (She's currently working toward her gold award.) In her free time she enjoys sleeping and hanging out with her friends and her boyfriend. She is also active in her church and hopes to study religion in college this fall. She lovingly thanks her family and Jason Brunson.

Meredith J. Hermance is a college senior studying journalism. She works at the campus newspaper and is busy writing her final honors thesis on the TV coverage of the Olympics. Her second passion is rugby; she has been part of the team all through college. Meredith wrote her poignant depiction of her teacher's death as a senior in high school. She writes, "Thanks to all my teachers, especially Mrs. Berman, who taught me as much about life as she did about writing. Mr. Svensen, I will always remember you. Thank you for teaching me to be strong and making me believe in myself."

Amy Hochsprung wrote about her beloved cat, Sassy, as a junior in high school. After graduating from college with a degree in history, she worked with AmeriCorps∗VISTA running a literacy-tutoring program. She is currently pursuing her master's in teaching and hopes to teach high-school history when she graduates. For fun, Amy enjoys her two passions: playing the violin and dancing.

Erica J. Hodgkinson was published in *Teen Ink* magazine many times while in high school. Now a sophomore in college, she enjoys skiing, reading nonfiction and hanging around with her friends. She enjoys photography of all kinds, but takes mostly black and white photographs. Erica shot her photo during her senior year in high school using a Canon EOS Rebel camera. She thanks her high-school photography teacher, Mr. Kelly, who served as the model for her photo, and to her mom she says, "Thank you and I love you."

Andrea Jalbert loves taking photographs, especially since, "I can't draw very well, so it allows me to show my art skills." Now a high-school senior, she is captain of the hockey cheerleading squad, a peer mentor and a teacher for a first-grade religion class. She also babysits and works at her family's store. Andrea's photograph appeared in *Teen Ink* magazine last year. She thanks her photography teacher, Bill Kelly, for encouraging her to work hard and do her best.

James T. Kalil II is a college senior studying business administration. In his free time he enjoys reading and writing, and he especially loves working on his favorite car, his Cobra Mustang. James wrote about his childhood memory as a senior in high school. Each year as a child he would devise a plan to capture Santa to prove to his friends that Santa really existed. Although he always failed, he wants to thank his parents who made Christmas so special and helped him see that all children need a Santa at certain times in their lives.

Marwan Kazimi took his photograph as a junior in high school. He has since graduated from college with a degree in chemical engineering and biology and is in medical school. Unfortunately, his studies allow little time to pursue literature and photography (as he used to in high school), but he still manages to visit museums in his free time. Marwan also plays basketball and skis whenever possible, and serves as a volunteer at a student-run medical clinic.

Melissa Thornton Keys graduated from college with a degree in English and religion, and is pursuing her master's to teach English as a second language. She also works as a newsroom clerk supervisor at a local newspaper. Her interests include travel, world cultures and linguistics, and she lives happily with her "wonderful husband, David." Melissa wrote her moving poem as a high-school sophomore.

Ellie Kreischer shot her photograph during her junior year in high school when she was confused about her life and where it was going. Currently a college sophomore studying art and environmental studies, Ellie now realizes that all her interests mean something and she can use them to impact her world on campus. She especially enjoys using her love of art to help educate others to the beauty and importance of nature.

Maya J. Krolikiewicz enjoys drawing, painting, making sculptures and taking photographs. She has taken college courses in photography which have inspired her to have "a different and more aware look at the world." She also enjoys traveling, hanging out with her friends, and "going to the mountains and lakes and spending time around nature." A senior in high school, Maya plans to major in art when she attends college this fall.

Richard Kuss is a sophomore in high school, where he is captain of both the JV football and basketball teams. In his free time he enjoys reading and writing poetry "because it doesn't really stop and continually flows." Richard's favorite band (the only one he listens to) is Metallica, and he shaves his head so he doesn't have to comb his hair in the morning. He writes, "Thank you, Mrs. Ihlefeld, for allowing me to write freely and smoothly."

Eliza Larson keeps busy as a senior in high school, dividing her time between school, family, church, music and other activities. As vice president of her church youth group, she helps with fundraisers and other projects. She also loves playing the cello, singing, reading, sewing and painting. Eliza acknowledges her family, especially her dad, for encouraging and supporting her. She also thanks Ms. Lamuth for being the first teacher to believe in her writing abilities. Eliza's incredible short story was first published in *Teen Ink* magazine last year.

Karen Lee was "just playing around with the film" when she took her photo as a junior in high school. She decided to take a whole roll of film and then reshoot the roll again, and felt that this was "one of the best." Now a college senior studying health and biology, she hopes to start medical school this fall and someday become a pediatrician. In her free time Karen enjoys tae kwon do, drawing and photography. She still takes pictures like crazy and hopes to have her own darkroom someday. She gives special thanks to her mom for always being there.

Marissa Nicole Lefland is a junior in high school. She is involved with model U.N., the French club, peer tutoring and her temple youth group. For relaxation she enjoys playing the guitar, violin and lacrosse. One of her most memorable experiences was visiting Israel last year and consequently, she is excited to participate in the Urban Mitzvah Corps this summer. Marissa's touching memory of her father originally appeared in *Teen Ink* magazine last year.

Jonathan Levine loves skiing, music, cars and the guitar. He is a member of the ski team as well as the math and English honor societies at his high school. A senior, Jon wrote his moving poem as a sophomore. He especially dedicates it to his father who was recently diagnosed with cancer, creating a difficult time for the family. He writes to his dad, "You're a trooper, hang in there. We all love you very much."

Kendra Lider-Johnson wrote about her experience as a junior in high school, where she was editor of the literary magazine. She has since graduated from college with a degree in English and works in publishing. She began her first "novel" to get attention in the fourth grade when she was the new kid in class. It worked and she's been writing ever since. Her greatest literary inspirations include *The Bluest Eye* by Toni Morrison and *To the Lighthouse* by Virginia Woolf.

Gretchen Loye loves taking photographs of "abstract things in different perspective." A high-school junior, she enjoys playing the xylophone and drums, and playing with her guinea pig, Carmella. She also loves to travel and spend summers at her family's cabin, "four-wheeling in the woods, swimming, fishing and picking berries." She recently visited China and Singapore, and she hopes to visit Europe this summer. Gretchen thanks "my photography teacher, Dalen Towne, for all the encouragement she's given me over the last two years, and my brother, Jonathan, for inspiring me."

Selena Lu enjoys reading and writing, "the greatest way to express my feelings and ideas." A junior in high school, she is a member of the computer, Spanish and Latin clubs, Science Olympia and math honor society. One of the most significant events was coming to America, where she learned "how to speak English and what it is like to be an American." She gives special thanks to her brother, Thomas, who always tells her she can do anything she puts her mind to. Selena's whimsical piece was published in *Teen Ink* magazine two years ago.

Doug Mahegan is a senior in high school. He enjoys sports and is a member of the varsity football, wrestling and lacrosse teams. He plans to major in physical and health education when he enters college this fall, and is considering a career as a high-school physical-education teacher. Doug took his photo while vacationing on Cape Cod during his junior year.

Jeanette René Mayer has enjoyed art since she was young. She especially loves drawing flowers and people as "a way to relax." She declares, "I love sharing my work with others who enjoy art as much as I do." In high school she assisted with the wrestling team and was a member of the national honor society. She was also active in volunteer work. Now a college freshman, Jeanette enjoys going to the movies, playing pool with her boyfriend, cooking and baking. Her artwork was featured in *Teen Ink* magazine last year.

Jessica Mazonson was at the beach with her best friend, Lexie, when she took her photograph "to get the texture of the sand." In high school, she played field hockey and was active in community service, including educating peers on racial issues, being trained to combat domestic violence and volunteering at a women's shelter. Now a college freshman interested in studying Spanish and anthropology, she is active in women's issues and is a peer counselor for victims of sexual assault. Jessica's photo appeared in *Teen Ink* magazine last year.

Kathleen McCarney is a college sophomore studying journalism. She likes watching movies and reading books, magazines or anything that sparks her interest. She loves writing, learning and trying new things. She is inspired by life in general, the good and the bad. Kathleen wrote her poem as a senior in high school. She explains, "I am grateful I found poetry and writing as an outlet, as the best listener ever. . . . I wish everyone could find such a meaningful way to vent, to cry, to live."

Carrie Meathrell wrote her poignant poem as a junior in high school. Now a college junior studying English and French, she enjoys reading, traveling, British history, writing and film. Last year she even spent the summer studying Shakespeare in England. At school she is a member of a sorority and works at the student union. After graduating Carrie hopes to pursue her Ph.D. in English or work in the film industry. She writes, "I just want to tell my boyfriend, Matt, that I love him!"

Marissa Meerbach graduated from college with a degree in wildlife biology and management, and is currently working at a university pathobiology department. Her favorite pastimes include photography, writing and spending time outdoors. She also loves to travel to foreign countries and recently visited Estonia, the birthplace of her parents. Marissa took her photo as a high-school senior for an assignment on portraiture. She used her dad's 1967 Nikon, which she called "The Beast." Marissa explains, "It weighed a lot and was a basic, early camera with a broken light meter." She thanks Gillian for being such a patient model and her former photography teacher, Mr. Allen.

Jessica A. Melillo is a college senior studying biology and Spanish and hopes to attend medical school or pursue a Ph.D. in neuro-genetic research. At college she worked in a research lab and was involved in volleyball, student government and many community-service activities. She especially loves reading, art and experiencing the history and diversity of cultures around her. Jessica wrote about her experience as a high-school sophomore.

Courtney Miller was on the front porch of her house when she noticed the pattern of the wood rails and thought it would be a neat picture. A senior in high school, she plans to study elementary education in college this fall. At school she is a class officer and member of the lacrosse team. She also enjoys photography, skiing, hanging out with friends and traveling all over the world with her family. One of her favorite places is Ireland, and she hopes to visit Australia. Courtney's photo appeared in *Teen Ink* magazine last year.

Kerry Elizabeth Miller wrote about her first work experience as a junior in high school. After her brief stint in the restaurant industry, she delved into the exciting world of retail as a stock person. She is currently a college freshman where she is a staff writer for the paper, an intern with the campus radio station, an ice-hockey player and a mentor for teenagers. She daydreams about spending a few years as a Pulitzer Prize-winning reporter, editing her own magazine, before saving our nation's public schools by implementing far-reaching reform.

Luis Steven Miranda is a freshman in college. He works part-time as a dental assistant and plans to become a dentist. He writes, "The honor I received was the look on my mother's face when she read my piece in your magazine. . . . I thank you for the opportunity to share my gratitude for the most important woman in my life." Luis also acknowledges his former teacher, Ms. Simon, for her "encouragement, support, patience and understanding in the development of a young mind."

Vanessa Montes created her drawing as a senior in high school, where she was vice president of the national honor society and a member of the basketball team. Now a college freshman studying art therapy, she also runs her own small perfume and gift shop. Vanessa spends most of her summers visiting her relatives in Mexico. In her free time she is active in volunteer work, and recently spent a week building houses in Tijuana, Mexico. She loves to draw "fairies, butterflies and all mystical stuff." She dedicates her drawing to her art teacher, Pat Scully, and in loving memory to her *abuelita* [grandmother].

Kerri Lynn Morrone wrote her insightful poem during her freshman year in high school. Now a college senior studying English and psychology, she loves to play with her calico kitten, Abby, who she's proud to say can sit and fetch. Kerri also enjoys creating both poetry and short stories; her favorite author is Roald Dahl. After obtaining her Ph.D. in English, she hopes to be an author and college professor.

Tess Morton had a photography assignment on light and dark when she took her "spur-of-the-moment" shot last year. She and her friends,

Megan and Amy, were playing around with props when she got the idea for her photograph. Now a freshman in college studying business, Tess is a member of a sorority. In her free time she loves to ski and hopes to take photography classes in the future.

Kirsten Murray wrote her piece about her friend during her junior year in high school. Now a senior in college, she plans to pursue her master's degree in health-care administration this fall. She is a nationally ranked athlete and captain of her college sports team. In her free time she enjoys volunteering in a children's hospital and teaching elementary school students during the summers. Kirsten is happy to say that she enjoys college much more than high school.

Lindsay Starr Muscato is a college junior studying journalism. She has interned at *Newsweek* and is interested in graphic design and geology. She believes "any emotional crisis can be solved with Ben & Jerry's Chocolate Fudge Brownie ice cream." Lindsay wrote her riveting short story as a senior in high school. She gives special thanks to her former teachers, Mrs. Ihlefeld and Mrs. Doerr, who always believed in her.

Beth Anne Nadeau wrote her thoughtful poem during her senior year in high school. Now a college senior studying creative writing and rhetoric, she is a member of the National English Honor Society. In 1999, her mother was in a car accident that left her in a coma for fifteen days. For her senior thesis, Beth and her mother are collaborating on a book recounting her mother's experiences while comatose and through her recovery.

Margaret Nolan still has moments of inspiration to write "poetry, weird ramblings and sometimes short stories." Currently a college sophomore, she crafted her realistic fiction piece as a senior in high school. She has been involved with the theater since middle school and currently does technical work with her school's theater department. One of her favorite productions was *Much Ado About Nothing*. Margaret enjoys "discussing the meaning of life and spending time with my friends," and she hopes to visit Europe.

Emily L. O'Brien wrote her hilarious tale as a junior in high school, and she still recalls this first experience whenever she shaves her legs! Emily graduated from college with a degree in medieval renaissance history and just recently received her Ph.D. in medieval history. She loves producing plays and reading fiction. Her favorite playwrights include Noël Coward and Shakespeare ("the old tried and true") and one of her current favorite authors is Stella Gibbons. She also enjoys the Harry Potter books and studying in England where she delved into the culture and history that surrounded her.

Laura Alison O'Donnell wrote her touching short story last year as a senior in high school. Now a college freshman studying psychology and English, she enjoys volunteering at the humane society and her church. She loves to read whenever she can and still wants to develop her writing skills; her goal is to be published and recognized some day. For Alison, being published in *Teen Ink* is "quite an honor." She thanks Mrs. Rutter and Mrs. Lueck, her high-school English teachers who gave her so much encouragement.

Laura Oberg is a senior in high school where she is president of her class, captain of the varsity cheerleading squad and secretary of the Spanish club. She loves going to the beach, working out and spending time with her friends. She hopes one day to fulfill her dream of traveling to Europe. Laura is happy to say that since her piece appeared in *Teen Ink* magazine last year, Jen and her family have moved back and so her best friend is (geographically!) close once again.

Rebecca Danielle Onie wrote her riveting piece as a sophomore in high school. After graduating from college with a degree in history and science, she served as founder and director of Project HEALTH whose goal is to ensure that every child grows up free of obstacles imposed by poor health. In October 1999, she received the Do Something Brick Award for Community Leadership as one of ten "dynamic young people under the age of thirty, with the passion and drive to improve their communities." Rebecca is currently in her first year of law school. She writes, "Thank you to my parents, who are my inspiration and my editors, then, now and always."

Mallie Allison Owsley was a senior in high school when she wrote her inspiring piece about her niece. After giving college a try, she decided to follow her dream of becoming a country-music star. She currently works in accounting but is still pursuing her goal to sing (a dream she's had since she was ten). Although moving away from her family to pursue her career was difficult, it was "a major step for me . . . and one of the best decisions of my life." Mallie thanks Lauren for "being an adult and having a strong will and heart. She is precious and very dear to my whole family. We love her and find it a blessing that she is in our lives."

Chris Parsons enjoys photography and reading. A senior in high school, he has received many state and school awards, as well as the scholastic gold key for his photography. He also has a mop-top haircut which he thinks is very funny. Chris thanks *Teen Ink* for publishing his work. He writes, "Being published in *Teen Ink* inspires me and gives me the confidence I need as an artist in the competitive art world of today."

Emily Kate Peloquin graduated from college last year with a degree in liberal arts, theater and psychology, and currently is an early-intervention specialist with infants. She also works part-time at an adolescent psychiatric unit where she utilizes writing, music, drama and dance skills as means of expressive therapy. Emily wrote her piece as a senior in high school. She thanks her teacher, Mr. McManus, and *Teen Ink* for giving her an opportunity to express herself when she needed it.

Amy Danielle Piedalue is a college sophomore studying South Asian studies and Classical Greek. She spends much of her free time reading and writing. She loves music and going to tons of live shows. Her favorite band is Pearl Jam and once she even attended four concerts in five days! Amy wrote her essay about visiting her sister as a senior in high school and dedicates it to her sister, Alicia, who has graduated and now lives in the same city as Amy. They remain close and see each other all the time.

Aimee K. Poulin wrote her poignant piece as a freshman in high school. Now a senior, she is involved with the French and Spanish clubs and the student senate. She is also vice-president of the leaders club and she plays flute in the band. In her free time she enjoys going to the movies with friends. Aimee's greatest passion, however, is dancing. She takes ballet every night and weekends, and spends summers dancing with a professional dance company. She hopes to become a professional dancer.

Caite Powers is a junior in high school. She enjoys reading, photography, dancing and swimming. She works at a candy store after school and during the summer, and she also studies kickboxing. Her favorite summer activity is swimming. Caite thanks Mr. Kelly, her photography teacher, for "teaching me good techniques when photographing. I always enjoyed his classes and useful tips!"

Matt Puralewski enjoys shooting pool with his friends and writing poetry. One of his greatest inspirations is Sir Thomas Wyatt, whose poems cover one wall of his bedroom. Matt believes "the figurative language is so great. Two lines can mean so much more." He also loves music and playing the guitar. His favorite artist is Dave Matthews and favorite guitarist is Stevie Ray Vaughan. Now a senior, Matt plans to study creative writing at college. He dedicates his poem to Mr. Dermody, "my creative-writing teacher who helped me get published the first time."

Benjamin P. Quigley was a senior in high school when he shot his photo for a class assignment on light and shadow. Now a college freshman studying business, he enjoys running and road biking. He is also an avid tennis player and has been teaching tennis since he was twelve. Ben dedicates his photo to his grandfather, who was "a real photo enthusiast." He will always remember him and his love of photography.

Stephanie Quinn took the photo of her young neighbor during her sophomore year of high school. It was an "ordinary" picture until she started playing around in the darkroom by putting developer solution on her hands. Now a college sophomore studying psychology, Stephanie enjoys living at school and having fun with her friends. She credits her photography teacher, Mr. Berube, and Caitlin, for being such a patient subject.

Ana Raba-Mickelson loves drawing, painting and writing; her favorite is drawing in oil pastels. Her collage of Andy Warhol (one of her favorite artists) was her first attempt at pure collage during her senior year in high school. Now a college freshman studying art history, she enjoys playing the guitar and piano in her free time. She also has fun singing with her band, which sometimes performs in a local coffee shop.

Lauren Ratchford wrote her piece as a high-school senior. Having graduated from college with a degree in international relations, she is pursing her master's in social work. She still loves to write and wants to write a novel some day. She also enjoys reading, playing tennis and running. Lauren dedicates her story to her family: "Now that my tumultuous adolescent years are behind me, I have grown to appreciate and depend upon my family who has always loved and supported me."

Ellie Roan is a college sophomore studying English and East Asian studies. She spends most of her time "looking for lost pencils, trying to start those fifteen-page English essays due yesterday, and walking the path to enlightenment with my Taoist kazoo orchestra." She enjoys crushed ice, punctuality, kung fu and translating popular songs into Chinese. She also has a strong belief in the Pythagorean Theorem and the letter "W." Ellie wrote her creative piece as a senior in high school. She dedicates it to Rita: "You rock!"

Jen Roman took her photo last year for a class assignment on shadows. She saw the chair in her backyard and thought it made interesting shadows on the grass and itself. A junior, she is involved with the yearbook and a literary magazine. Jen is also a member of Amnesty International and a local committee working to build a teen center. In her free time she enjoys reading, photography, art and theater.

Jonathan Roper shot his photograph by a pond near his house as a freshman in high school. He was "looking for an interesting angle" when he noticed the wooden bench. Now a senior, he is a member of both the varsity hockey and lacrosse teams. He also enjoys skateboarding and working at a yacht club during the summers. Jon plans to study liberal arts in college this fall, and he hopes to get back into photography in the future.

Laura Marie Rovner is completing her associate's degree in engineering science and hopes to pursue both a bachelor's degree in mechanical engineering and an MBA. Laura wrote about her perfect moment as a junior in high school, where she was active in student council and was class historian. In her free time she volunteers at a summer camp and the American Heart Association. She writes, "I would like to dedicate this to my mom for always being there. I love you."

Hart Sawyer has always loved art in all forms. At the age of three, she painted her arms and hands with peanut butter until her parents found her! Now in eighth grade, she has won a number of awards for her art and is currently in her third year of adult pottery classes. Her other favorite pastimes are photography and composing songs on the piano. Hart plans to be a great artist one day, and she also hopes to model and sing. She gives special thanks to *Teen Ink* and her teachers, Mr. Mormano and Mrs. Coy.

Sally Schonfeld wrote about her life-changing experience during her junior year of high school. Now a college junior studying biology and geology, she runs track and earned all-conference honors in cross-country. During the summers Sally has worked at a camp, leading canoe trips and as a sailing instructor. She loves the outdoors, music, her friends and family. Sally is very thankful that her mom is now healthy and she appreciates her family for their craziness and love.

Lisa Schottenfeld is a senior in high school, where she is editor of the newspaper and literary magazine and is involved with chorus and the debate group. She has performed in many school theatrical productions and volunteers as a director for her temple's drama club. Her greatest passion is Shakespeare. Lisa has been published many times in *Teen Ink* magazine, and wrote her reminiscent poem as a sophomore.

Julie Schultz wrote her insightful piece as an older teen while a junior in college. After graduating with a degree in religious studies, she received her master's in social policy and Jewish communal service with a concentration in fundraising. She works as a financial and human resource development consultant to nonprofit organizations. In her free time Julie teaches a comparative religion class for teens, is involved in community theater and participates in volunteer work with her boyfriend and friends.

Amy Scott is a college freshman studying psychology. She still loves to write, although she doesn't write creatively as much as she would like. She spends as much of her free time as she can dancing and traveling, although she admits, "the latter is hard since I'm a busy college student." Amy is active in her sorority and loves participating in her school's dance marathon, one of the largest student-run philanthropies in the country. She wrote her engaging story as a junior in high school.

Lee Ann Sechovicz wrote her piece about friendship in the sixth grade. After being published in *Teen Ink* magazine, she pursued athletic and academic interests but never forgot about writing. She has since graduated from college with a degree in international relations and works as a financial advisor. She is still an avid reader and plans to write a book about how to survive the financial Internet world. Lee Ann tips her hat to her English teacher, Mrs. Rogers, who "taught me how to express my feelings through writing. Her kind words, constructive criticism and enormous heart shaped me more than she will ever know."

Charlie Semine is a college sophomore majoring in theater with minors in English and Italian. Last summer he studied Shakespeare at the Royal Academy of Dramatic Arts in London, and he is a member of his college's only improv comedy troupe. In his free time he enjoys playing the sax, singing and traveling "to Europe or anywhere. But especially Italy—the Renaissance is cool." Charlie took his photo as a high-school sophomore for a photography class assignment entitled "shadows." (The shadow in the photo is his father's.)

Jessica Shaw was vacationing on Cape Cod when she took her photograph as a sophomore in high school. With a college degree in American Studies, she works in human resources for a local NPR news station (and hopes to write and produce for radio in the future). In her free time she is an avid runner and still enjoys photography as a hobby. Jessica thanks her ninth-grade English teacher, Ms. Burgoon, "who always encouraged us to submit written pieces, drawings and photographs to *Teen Ink*."

Melody Shaw is a sophomore in high school. Someday she hopes to find a career that involves everything she loves: painting, drawing, writing and communicating with many different people. For fun she is learning Hungarian sword-fighting, and hopes to join her school's fencing team. Melody thanks her local paper for her summer internship where they treated her like an equal (even though she was fresh out of eighth grade). She also thanks *Teen Ink*: "Not only has this magazine allowed me to touch the lives of others, it has created a window from which I can see and be touched by the hearts of people vastly different from me."

Robert Sickel wrote about his sister as a sophomore in high school. Now a college freshman, he enjoys political science and playing sports. He was on both the cross-country and baseball teams in high school, and is currently playing rugby. His other passions are playing Risk (which is "very entertaining; it's fun to take over the world") and writing. Rob was voted best creative writer as a senior. He explains, "I don't understand poetry, and novels are too ambitious." Rob gives special thanks to his former English teacher, Mr. Fischer, "the most intelligent man I'll ever meet."

Stephen Siperstein is a junior in high school and a musician "to the core." He has been playing the guitar and piano for years, and has taught children how to play. Photography is a fairly new avocation for Stephen, although he has already had an exhibition in his hometown. His photographs have been published many times in *Teen Ink* magazine.

Katherine Smith is a junior in high school. She founded a Christian fellowship club at her school and is active in volunteer work. She has been involved with her community's teen court program and each year she spends her birthday at a food bank. Katherine loves "being around people. Making a difference is the biggest thing." She enjoys photography, softball and children, and hopes to be an elementary school teacher. Katherine's personal piece about her friend Nick first appeared in *Teen Ink* magazine last year. She writes, "I'd like to thank God, for his grace in my life and the opportunities and talents he has afforded me, and my parents, who are truly very supportive. I get so much love from them. It's great to have them in my life."

Andrea Denise Starkey is a junior in high school, where she is a member of both the snowboarding and community service clubs. In her free time she likes to draw and paint, play guitar, and go snowboarding and wakeboarding with her friends. Andrea writes, "I enjoy making art because it gives me a chance to create with total freedom." She dedicates her artwork to Angie Flores, "the bravest girl I know."

Gwen Steel wrote her insightful piece as a high school junior. After her sophomore year in college, she is taking time off, and working as a receptionist and Webmaster for a banner manufacturer. At college she worked at the campus art museum and was active in the activist collective that tackled issues ranging from affordable housing to Mumia Abu-Jamal. She still interns at the college radio station and would like to pursue voice work. Gwen is interested in reading, writing and the arts.

Erin Temple was inspired to write her poem as a freshman in high school when her mom explained she was too young to vote in the presidential election. After high school Erin worked and traveled around the country. Now a college freshman, she loves animals and plans to be a zoologist researching reptile behavior. (She practices with her iguana, Goldberg.) She loves dancing, hanging out with friends and keeping a journal. Erin thanks her mom and dad for encouraging her writing.

Jessica Tenaglia wrote her poignant story as a high school sophomore, where she was active in student council, editor of the paper and captain of the swim team. Currently a college junior studying political science and Spanish, Jessica spent a semester in Mexico and is a peer leader and tutor. In her free time she enjoys being a news broadcaster on the campus radio, reading, writing e-mails to friends and having fun.

Jennifer Tepe is a freshman in college studying communications. Her two favorite pastimes are dancing and writing poetry. She has studied ballet, tap, jazz and modern dance, and her poetry has appeared in a number of publications. Jennifer took her photo during her senior year in high school. It was totally unplanned; her sister was "just being a goofball" when Jennifer took her picture. She gives special thanks to her mom, Lisa, Brian, Sarah and Hannah (and her chocolate lab, Zoe!), and she dedicates her photo in loving memory to her father, David Tepe.

Kymberly Anne Terribile enjoys going out with her friends and doing "normal, stupid teenage things" now that she is a senior in high school. She especially loves writing since it allows her to be herself in a way that no one else can judge. Although she loves her family more than anything, she is excited about going to college away from home. Kym wrote about her first love as a sophomore. She writes, "Thank you, Mommy, for always pushing me to do my best!"

Cara Tibbits studied elementary education and psychology in college and works as a police dispatcher. She has a wonderful husband and spends her free time with their two great daughters, Kelsey and Julia. She still enjoys watching football on television and attending high-school games. Cara wrote about playing football as a high-school sophomore. She thanks her coach, Mr. Auffant, for being open-minded and allowing her the chance to play when others wouldn't.

Justin Toohey is a senior in high school. He is a member of the cross-country team and he plays clarinet in the school band. He also works part-time in a hardware store. In his free time he enjoys reading and writing; one of his favorite authors is George Orwell. He also enjoys spending time with his family and friends. Justin plans to attend college this fall where he will major in materials engineering. He writes, "The race dramatized in my piece was real, but a fluke! To this day, I've only won two other races." He gives thanks to his brother, Mark, and, of course, Coach Steffy.

Olga Tsyganova loves to read and write, as well as play the saxophone and piano. She is a cross-country runner, which she finds "a very unique clear-minding sport." She also enjoys drama and writing an "Ask Olga" column for her school newspaper. Now a sophomore, Olga thanks her family and friends who give her a great deal of support, urging her to do well in school. She also thanks her English teacher, Mr. Hogue, for "making me work to better my writing." Her piece about a "kind stranger" was published in *Teen Ink* magazine last year.

Louise Turner's photograph of her bedroom windowsill was in the first roll of film she took as a junior in high school. After spending her junior and senior years in the United States, Louise and her family have moved back home to Sweden. She plans to start university in the fall and study "everything from medicine to media and TV." Louise enjoys snowboarding and photography "just for fun," and loves to dance and listen to all kinds of music. She gives special thanks to her parents and friends.

Lia Kristyn Underwood is pursuing her associate's degree and working full-time at a candy store, which she loves! In her free time she enjoys creative writing, and arts and crafts. Last summer she read her poem, that she wrote as a high school senior, and shared her personal experiences with adolescents at a rehabilitation center. Lia found this experience tremendously rewarding, believing that it's always better to try to help than do nothing. She writes, "Thank you to my family, my elementary art teacher, Mrs. Lefluer, my creative-writing teacher, Mrs. Kavanaugh, and all members of my town's Exchange Club for my scholarships. If I can do it, anyone can."

Matthew Virag is a sophomore in high school. He enjoys writing and working as an editor for his school newspaper. One of his pieces recently won a "Best of Round" award in a local writing competition. In his free time he likes to ski, travel and study archaeology. Matthew's poem was originally published in *Teen Ink* magazine last year.

Joanne Wang wrote her piece about her best friend as a senior in high school, where she was editor of the newspaper and president of the Hunger Task Force. Now a college freshman, she tutors at an after-school program and helps in the Christian Fellowship group. In her free time she loves to read and write fiction (her favorite novel is *Jane Eyre*). Joanne is happy to report that since their first comical experience, she and Stephanie have successfully skied black diamond trails. She also thanks Mrs. Krinsky for being "very challenging, inspiring and enthusiastic, and one of my best high-school teachers."

Cassie Warren has her green belt in karate, which she has studied for six years, and currently is working toward her black belt. She is interested in studying pharmacology at college this fall. Cassie wrote her honest piece during her sophomore year. She dedicates it to her brother, Brandon, who "has taught me about the true art of being unique and being true to yourself."

Michelle E. Watsky is a high-school junior. Her favorite hobbies include reading, acting, dancing and collecting anything related to James Dean. She loves going to theater and museums. Her inspirations include Ernest Hemingway, Sylvia Plath, Edgar Degas and Edouard Manet. She dedicates her piece to her English teacher, Mrs. Winkler—"without you, I could never have finished this piece"—and to her friends and family in thanks for their support.

Michael L. Wheaton wrote about his family's divorce as a junior in high school. He thanks his teacher, Mrs. O'Connor, whose "assignment gave me the reason to write this essay, which, in turn, gave me the strength to get past a tough point in my life." Michael has since graduated from college with a degree in English and psychology, and is working toward his master's in English. He works in the Special Education department and hopes to be an English teacher.

Julie White is a junior in high school, where she participates in drama and is on the varsity soccer and basketball teams. She has served as class secretary for three years and is a member of the National Honor Society. Julie is also active in community service, including SADD, a peer leaders program and the Special Olympics. In her free time she enjoys reading, writing, photography and art. She is especially looking forward to traveling to Israel this summer. Julie's poignant piece about her brother was published in *Teen Ink* magazine last year.

Cerys Wilson is enjoying life in the United States since moving here from England last summer. A junior in high school, she says, "I really like it here. I've made some nice friends and the photography is great." Cerys plans to join the soccer, cross-country and track teams. She also is "really into film, making my own videos and going to the movies with friends—especially small, independent films that are quirky and about strange people." An aspiring director, she plans to attend film school in the future. Cerys took her self-portrait using a tripod and Canon SLR camera. She was looking around her room when she came up with the idea of posing behind her bedroom window curtain.

Lisa Wojcik took her photo as a senior in high school. Now a college junior studying physical therapy, she enjoys cooking, hiking, exercising, photography, environmental issues clubs, reading and traveling. Her favorite food is vegetarian Indian, novelist is Milan Kundera, poet is Pablo Neruda, painter is Francis Picabia, and photographer is Eugene Richards. She thanks her former teacher, Ms. Kirdani, and her parents for always supporting her.

Jennifer Wood is a college senior studying television and video production. When she's not working as assistant house manager for a performance arts show, she loves to go to the movies. She hopes to create a children's T.V. program like "one I remember loving as a kid." She wants to sell her screenplay roughly based on her mom and brother. Jennifer wrote about her amazing experience as a senior in high school. Since then, her brother has learned to "find himself and find some good in the world. . . . He's taken all of that inward anger and learned to express himself in some beautiful ways." Jennifer thanks her mom and two younger brothers "for all the inspiration they give me. From the stories they have, I could write for the rest of my life."

Nurit Yastrow wrote her poignant short story as a senior in high school a year ago, where she was a member of the stage band and student council. She is now a freshman in college. One of her most memorable experiences was her bat mitzvah in Israel a few years ago. She has worked as a teacher's aide at her Sunday school, and in her free time she loves reading, swimming and playing the violin. She also enjoys writing; her work has been published in English and Hebrew.

Dan Zaslavsky took his photograph when he was visiting Bad Water in Death Valley, California, the lowest spot in the Western Hemisphere (282 feet below sea level). Now a junior in high school, his favorite pastimes include "eating, breathing, sleeping, skateboarding, music and my girl." He has been an avid skater for the last six years and is also interested in cinematography and video. He especially enjoys filming and editing skate videos with his friends. Dan thanks his family, his girlfriend and "anybody who appreciates skateboarding and art."

Permissions *(continued from page vi)*

"Still Handsome." Reprinted by permission of Julie White. ©2000 Julie White.

"I Grew Up at 14." Reprinted by permission of Jillian Balser. ©1998 Jillian Balser.

"My Mom and Me." Reprinted by permission of Megan Hayes. ©1996 Megan Hayes.

"Beach Shadow with Hat." Reprinted by permission of Charlie Semine. ©1997 Charlie Semine.

"The 'Stupidity' Choice." Reprinted by permission of Robert Sickel. ©1997 Robert Sickel.

"Another Chance." Reprinted by permission of Crystal Lynn Evans. ©1999 Crystal Lynn Evans.

"Locks." Reprinted by permission of Paul Constant. ©1994 Paul Constant.

"Apple Orchard." Reprinted by permission of Natascha Batchelor. ©1993 Natascha Batchelor.

"View Down Wooden Bench in Woods." Reprinted by permission of Jonathan Roper. ©2000 Jonathan Roper.

"The Gift in Disguise." Reprinted by permission of Mallie Allison Owsley. ©1998 Mallie Allison Owsley.

"We Go Together." Reprinted by permission of Amy Danielle Piedalue. ©1999 Amy Danielle Piedalue.

"I Love You, Uncle Kurt." Reprinted by permission of Lucy Coulthard. ©1998 Lucy Coulthard.

"Row of Bottles on Windowsill." Reprinted by permission of Louise Turner. ©2000 Louise Turner.

"My Inspiration." Reprinted by permission of Luis Steven Miranda. ©2000 Luis Steven Miranda.

"Somebody's Child." Reprinted by permission of Jennifer A. Eisenberg. ©1997 Jennifer A. Eisenberg.

"Grandma's Gift." Reprinted by permission of Andrew Briggs. ©1996 Andrew Briggs.

"Two Boys on Rock." Reprinted by permission of Teresa Bendokas. ©1995 Teresa Bendokas.

"Just Friends." Reprinted by permission of Kirsten Murray. ©1996 Kirsten Murray.

"Her Unforgettable Smile." Reprinted by permission of Lee Ann Sechovicz. ©1990 Lee Ann Sechovicz.

"Angel." Reprinted by permission of Lindsay Starr Muscato. ©1998 Lindsay Starr Muscato.

"Girl with Wings at End of Dock." Reprinted by permission of Jennifer Tepe. ©2000 Jennifer Tepe.

"No Mountain Too High." Reprinted by permission of Joanne Wang. ©2000 Joanne Wang.

"Lies and November Nights." Reprinted by permission of Rebecca Danielle Onie. ©1992 Rebecca Danielle Onie.

"Small Car at Roadside." Reprinted by permission of Dan Baldwin. ©1995 Dan Baldwin.

"Double Exposure with Faces." Reprinted by permission of Jodi B. Heller. ©2000 Jodi B. Heller.

"Railroad Blanket." Reprinted by permission of Matthew Virag. ©1999 Matthew Virag.

"View Down Railroad Tracks." Reprinted by permission of Gretchen Loye. ©2001 Gretchen Loye.

"Face Paint." Reprinted by permission of Katherine S. Assef. ©2000 Katherine S. Assef.

"Girl Painting Portrait of Girl." Reprinted by permission of Tess Morton. ©2000 Tess Morton.

"View Along Row of Lockers." Reprinted by permission of Megan Galipeau. ©1999 Megan Galipeau.

"Okay, I'm Up." Reprinted by permission of Talin Aprahamian. ©1996 Talin Aprahamian.

"Girl with Nose Ring at Locker." Reprinted by permission of Amy Annino. ©1994 Amy Annino.

"Prom Night." Reprinted by permission of Erica Doughty. ©2000 Erica Doughty.

"Senior Year." Reprinted by permission of Melinda Bruce. ©1997 Melinda Bruce.

"Wooden Bridge Reflected in Marsh." Reprinted by permission of Jessica Shaw. ©1993 Jessica Shaw.

"Mr. Svensen." Reprinted by permission of Meredith J. Hermance. ©1996 Meredith J. Hermance.

"Andy Warhol Face Collage." Reprinted by permission of Ana Raba-Mickelson. ©2000 Ana Raba-Mickelson.

"The Race." Reprinted by permission of Justin Toohey. ©2000 Justin Toohey.

"Obituary." Reprinted by permission of Kathleen McCarney. ©1999 Kathleen McCarney.

"The Great Goddess of Sleep." Reprinted by permission of Devin Foxall. ©1998 Devin Foxall.

"One of the Guys." Reprinted by permission of Cara LaRoche Tibbits. ©1992 Cara LaRoche Tibbits.

"Contemplation." Reprinted by permission of Beth Anne Nadeau. ©1995 Beth Anne Nadeau.

"The New Teacher." Reprinted by permission of Jennifer Beachley. ©1998 Jennifer Beachley.

"Balloon Guy." Reprinted by permission of Erica J. Hodgkinson. ©1999 Erica J. Hodgkinson.

"Who I Am." Reprinted by permission of Kristen R. Davis. ©1998 Kristen R. Davis.

"Girl Under Stairs." Reprinted by permission by Patrick Michael Baird. ©2000 Patrick Michael Baird.

"Still Me Inside." Reprinted by permission of Mai Goda. ©1998 Mai Goda.

"I Don't Understand." Reprinted by permission of Jessica A. Melillo. ©1995 Jessica A. Melillo.

"Temptation." Reprinted by permission of Eileen Carlos. ©1990 Eileen Carlos.